THE ARTIST
IN NINETEENTH CENTURY ENGLISH FICTION

THE ARTIST IN NINETEENTH CENTURY ENGLISH FICTION

Bo Jeffares

HUMANITIES PRESS
Atlantic Highlands, N.J.

Copyright © 1979 Bo Jeffares
First published in North America by Humanities Press Inc.
171 First Avenue, Atlantic Highlands,
N.J. 07716, U.S.A.

Published in Great Britain by Colin Smythe Ltd,
Gerrards Cross, Buckinghamshire

Library of Congress Cataloging in Publication Data

Jeffares, Bo
    The artist in nineteenth century English fiction
    Bibliography: p.
    Includes Index
    1.   English fiction – 19th century – History and
    criticism. 2. Artists in literature. I. Title
    PR868.A78J4   823′.8′09   79–685

ISBN 0–391–00976–1

Printed in Great Britain

For my friends

Contents

Preface		11
Acknowledgements		12
1	The Evolution of the Fictional Artist	13
2	The Artist's Appearance as Romantic Hero	29
3	The Artist Versus Society	51
4	The Vulnerable Artist and His Supernatural Attributes	75
5	The Artist's Tragic Temperament	103
6	The Declining Myth of the Artist	131
Notes		169
Bibliography		187
Index		193

Illustrations

page

'Ye Societie of our Ladie in the Fieldes'
  by George du Maurier   22

'The Two Apprentices' by George du Maurier   28

'The Happy Life – Barbizon' by George du Maurier   48

'The Fox and Crow' by George du Maurier   53

between pp. 92 and 93.

'The Artist in his Studio' by Gustave Courbet

'Curtius Leaping the Gulf' by Benjamin Robert Haydon

'Titian's First Essay in Colour' by William Dyce

'The Hand Refrains' by Edward Burne-Jones

'Astarte Syriaca' by Dante Gabriel Rossetti

'Cimabue's celebrated Madonna is carried in Procession
  through the streets of Florence' by Frederick Leighton

'Captive Adromache' by Frederick Leighton

The Arab Hall in Leighton House

'How They Met Themselves' by Dante Gabriel Rossetti   134

Sir Frederick Leighton's home in Holland Park   136

'Rossetti in his back garden' by Max Beerbohm   142

'A Footnote' by Aubrey Beardsley   148

'Self Portrait in Bed' by Aubrey Beardsley   166

Preface

This book sets out to prove that an artist, such as a painter or sculptor, was an extremely popular figure in nineteenth century fiction. Good and bad literature alike show that the fictional artist appealed to popular as well as intellectual imagination. Fictional artists embodied many elements of the romantic myth. In them, the student of romanticism finds, for example, a comprehensive symbol of the bohemian outcast and the suffering creator.

An examination of representative passages from fine writers, such as Henry James, when these are juxtaposed with the work of cruder novelists, such as Ouida, allows the reader to appreciate the subtleties in varying treatments of this romantic hero. And a certain ironic pleasure can be derived from casting an eye over some of the often amusing absurdities of the genre.

Acknowledgements

'Cimabue's Madonna carried in triumph' by Frederick Leighton is reproduced by gracious permission of Her Majesty the Queen, 'The Studio' by Gustave Courbet is reproduced by courtesy of the Louvre, 'Titian's First Essay in Colour' by William Ryce by courtesy of Aberdeen Art Galleries and Museums, 'Curtius Leaping the Gulf' by Benjamin Robert Haydon is reproduced by courtesy of The Royal Albert Memorial Museum, Exeter, 'The Hand Refrains' by Edward Burne-Jones is reproduced by courtesy of the City Museums and Art Gallery, Birmingham, 'Astarte Syrica' by Dante Gabriel Rossetti and 'Captive Andromache' by Frederick Leighton are reproduced by courtesy of the City Art Galleries, Manchester, the Arab Hall, Leighton House and drawing of Leighton House itself are reproduced by courtesy of the Royal Borough of Kensington and Chelsea Central Library, 'How They Met Themselves' by Dante Gabriel Rossetti is reproduced by courtesy of the Syndics of the Fitzwilliam Museum, Cambridge, and four drawings from *George Du Maurier* (1969) by Leonée Ormond are reproduced by courtesy of Routledge and Kegan Paul and the University of Pittsburgh Press.

The Evolution of the Fictional Artist

'Now, Mr. Longley,' said Miss Temple, 'I think you have a most enviable life. You can go where you like, see whom you like, and do what you like, and in no other profession is that the case.'[1]

The appreciative Miss Temple summed up a conception of the artist as a romantic hero frequently held in the nineteenth century. He was a popular subject with both good and bad authors. As a romantic hero, he also personified some of the century's romantic yearnings. There seemed to be an increasing need for emotional escapism of this kind as the harmonising effects of a predominantly agrarian society were destroyed in the increase of impersonal industrialisation.

Factory production was praised by T. A. Trollope, a now forgotten novelist, in *Lindisfarn Chase* (1864) for its speed, precision and practicality. However, the writer announced that such methods 'must not be expected to do the work of individually applied sympathy, heart and soul'. An increasingly neurotic cry for individualism was symbolised in the nineteenth century by the fictional artist. This creative figure who could be both exaggeratedly frivolous and morbidly spiritualistic reflected the era's inability to come to terms with a materialistic and utilitarian ethic.

For instance, Geraldine Jewsbury, in *The Half Sisters* (1848) illustrated how even those most ostensibly devoted to technical progress were touched by the artist's sensitivity and imagination, unconsciously recognising qualities which they themselves lacked.

Her Mr Bryant, a master miner, expressed himself in these terms:

> 'This is an industrial country . . . in our hearts we do not respect, love or honour fine art in any of its manifestations, as we do that which is scientific or practical . . . we naturally do not feel drawn to the society of artists; we have nothing in common with them – we do not admire them; neither do we feel disposed to introduce to the society of our wives and daughters a parcel of actors, artists, musicians, and so forth, who have no stake in society, who have little to lose, whose capital is all invested in themselves and their two hands, and who have, therefore, naturally cultivated themselves far beyond what we practical men have had a chance of doing, and are capable of throwing us into the shade in our own houses, whilst they show that they despise us. Let them keep their places, and let us keep ours! '[2]

This passage was cited by Philip Gilbert Hamerton, in what was probably the first essay about fictional artists,[3] as a fine example of how the rich trading classes combined 'prejudice' and a 'peculiar jealousy' when thinking of cultivated, and particularly artistic, people. Miss Jewsbury had managed to evoke very revealing transitions from cool, objective generalisations to less rational emotionalism. Mr Bryant – a master miner who thought that British civilization would be best worked out through railway development, a mechanistic medium suited to its national mentality – stated, quite impersonally, that the English people were, comparatively speaking, uninterested in the arts. Her speaker moved from an abstract discussion of art to observations on the artistic professions in a social context to a final overwrought fit on envisaging an artist penetrating his own home.

Elsewhere Miss Jewsbury provided a clue to Bryant's incongruous reactions. He damned artists as despicable because their only aim was to 'aspire to amuse'. Included in this tirade was a declaration that he would have nothing to do with artists unless in the 'peculiar exercise of their vocation' for which he was willing to pay. Bryant had slipped up. By selecting the word 'vocation', with all its religious and idealistic connotations, to express an artist's activities he gave the reader a telling glimpse of the reverential respect the bourgeois entertained, despite his better sense and material mores, for the kind of creativity he could buy, but not emulate.

In the eighteenth century the artist had frequently been dismissed as an inferior craftsman. This earlier equation between the artist's work and that of an unimportant tradesman had been amply illustrated in *The Vicar of Wakefield* (1766), where Goldsmith recorded how the Primrose family 'used' art. Wanting to impress their neighbours, they gave a limner, who 'took likenesses for fifteen shillings a head', a precise didactic and economical order – paying little heed to his imaginative impulses. Having decided on a large historical family-piece – 'This would be cheaper, since one frame would serve for all' – they then chose suitable subjects. Mrs Primrose was to be Venus, the painter being requested

> not to be too frugal of his diamonds in her stomacher and hair. Her two little ones were to be as Cupids by her side; while I, in my gown and band, was to present her with my books on the Whistonian controversy. Olivia would be drawn as an Amazon, sitting upon a bank of flowers, dressed in a green Joseph, richly laced with gold, and a whip in her hand. Sophia was to be a shepherdess, with as many sheep as the painter could put in for nothing. . . .[4]

The founding of the Royal Academy (1768), the knighting of Sir Joshua Reynolds, and similar developments began to add new kudos to the arts in Britain without tediously guaranteeing their respectability. This kind of ambiguity was frequently reflected in nineteenth century literature, which showed the artist making more successful bids for prestige but from a still precarious social position.

Thackeray reflected this ambiguous development in *The Newcomes* (1853-5). His eager artist hero, Clive, at one point gave Sir Joshua as an example of a gentleman artist of the standing of Rubens, Van Dyke, Titian, Raphael and Velasquez, while his conventional father, Colonel Newcome stated: 'An artist is any man's equal . . . I have no prejudice of that sort, and think Sir Joshua Reynolds and Dr Johnson were fit company for any person, of whatever rank.'[5] Thackeray, however, indicated that there were many mental qualifications to this categorical statement about artistic equality. Seen in context, Colonel Newcome's liberal remarks lost weight, for they were directly followed by a refusal to dine with a young artist whose father was in domestic service. Thackeray's implication was that while public honours, such as knighthoods, might make an artist acceptable, his talents alone could neither secure respectability nor negate the stigma attached to lowly birth. The very fact that the Colonel's son felt it necessary to defend his chosen profession, by listing its more illustrious names, indicated his awareness of the strong currents of disapproval still surrounding the arts.

Curiosity was provoked by situations of this kind. An ever-expanding reading public, which (unlike affluently civilized readers of the previous century) probably had little contact with artists, read fictional accounts of these developments – often enjoying their sagas in serial form. *Lippincotts' Monthly Magazine,* for example, published *Trilby, The Picture of Dorian Gray* and *The Light that Failed.* And although artists were a relatively alien force, unusual even when aligned with the establishment of the day, they had a distinct advantage over many other romantic heroes, for the average reader probably found stories about contemporary, identifiable artists more tangibly convincing than those about romantic figures in more remote geographical sites or misty historical periods. Readers who had had difficulty in escaping with assorted maidens from the Gothic strongholds of Scott or Keats, or languishing beside the sunny oceans of Byron or Tennyson, probably found it far easier to visualise themselves living a gay studio life.

Thackeray, advocating the advantages of a bohemian existence in *The Adventures of Philip* (1862), included a significant reference to lotos-eating. Where Tennyson's poem 'The Lotos-Eaters' had evoked all the sultry exoticism of a tropical paradise it had nevertheless been permeated by the atmosphere of tired negation first suggested in *Ulysses.* Thackeray, however, referred to lotos-eating in a way which helped to conjure up the lyrical idealism underlying his theme while skilfully avoiding this image's negative overtones. Tennyson had associated the lotos and the poppy, symbol of drowsy sleep, but Thackeray linked lotos and pepper – implying that the pleasures of artistic life were not just those of drugged oblivion but of heightened sensationalism. He not only described 'Bohemia' metaphorically as a mental kingdom without fences, guards or fuss, but as a 'land of lotos-eating (with lots of Cayenne pepper)'. This cheerful aside, reminding the reader of Keats's attempts to stimulate his palate with pepper, showed that he was not only praising a fraternity with a 'delightful capacity to be idle' but one enjoying the spice of life with a vigour lost by Tennyson's lotos-eaters. His wanderers were out of reach; left 'like Gods together, careless of mankind' reposing their weary limbs on beds of amaranth, moly and asphodel. Thackeray's convivial modern adventures must have seemed much more credible to nineteenth century readers seeking escapism, who could surely 'associate' with a tavern quicker than a bed of asphodel. Unlike Tennyson, Thackeray did not let nostalgia prevent him from projecting a picture of an immediate and hopeful paradise:

> What is now called Bohemia had no name in Philip's younger days, though many of us know the country very well. A pleasant land, not fenced with drab stucco, like Tyburnia or Belgravia; not guarded by a huge standing army of footmen; not echoing with noble chariots; not replete with polite chintz drawing-rooms, supper-rooms, oysters; a land of tin dish-covers from taverns, and frothing porter; a land of lotos-eating (with lots of Cayenne pepper), of pulls on the river, of delicious reading of novels, magazines, and saunterings in many studios; a land where men call each other by their Christian names; where most are poor, where almost all are young. . . .[6]

When nineteenth century authors did deviate from the freedoms of contemporary Bohemia – the land where 'almost all are young' – they showed a predilection for the Renaissance. Like Shakespeare, picking powerful historical prototypes to illustrate Elizabethan concepts of kingship, they grafted their own ideas about the artist's importance on to what they knew of his remarkable demands, and awards, in and around this particular period. Browning, for example, chose Andrea del Sarto as a sympathetic persona to represent his own conjectures about the nature of the artist's role. And Henry James made the sculptor hero of *Roderick Hudson* (1875) express his ambitions in terms of Renaissance daring: 'Excuse me if I brag a little; all those fellows in the Renaissance used to brag.'

Hudson went on to make a daring comparison between himself and Michaelangelo, explaining this master's inadequacies: ' "Oh, Michaelangelo was not me! " said Roderick with sublimity. There was a great laugh; but after all Roderick had done some fine things.'[7] James, by thus recording the other characters' response to Hudson's boast, indicated it should be taken seriously. The fictional sculptor wanted to create works which would fill the world with a kind of 'religious awe'.

A vital reason for the artist's popularity was that while many professions and other means of gaining a livelihood were concerned with repetitive tasks and bound to dull degrading sites, the lucky artist was unusually free not only in terms of time and place – living and working as the mood dictated – but also of method: he was a unique, imaginative creator, the complete antithesis of growing technology and drably standardised mass-production.[8] The artist's appeal depended on the idealism connected with his occupation, which, in an age more hierarchical than our own, could give him social prestige, irrespective of his birth, for the truth and beauty of his work seemed to show the workings of divine inspiration.[9]

Such an idealised view of the artist appears to have followed on from a changing concept of the significance of the writer. In a public lecture, 'The Hero as Poet' (1840), Thomas Carlyle discussed the poet as prophet. By the nineteenth century the poet had become, to many, a spiritual hero, because his instinctive gift prophetically revealed mystery to the masses. Many nineteenth century authors substantiated this view of the poet as a being who was, in the tradition of Gray's bard, glorified because of his creativity and perception – even if his passionate enthusiasm had begun to wane with the creation of misty mythical figures such as Macpherson's Ossian. Shelley, for example, in his *Defence of Poetry* (1840), stated that all improving systems of thought have their ultimate origin in poetic vision. He defined poetry as 'divine inspiration', condemning compositions produced on demand, as the result of rational toil, as being to poetry what mosaic is to painting. Furthermore, he argued, the instinct and intuition of the poetical faculty is 'still more' easily observed in the plastic and pictorial arts where a great statue or picture grows under the artist's power like a child in its mother's womb, while the very mind which directs the hands in its formation is 'incapable of accounting to itself for the origin, the gradations, or the media of the process'.[10]

The prophetic poet, as a type, was often unable to fathom his own Aeolian powers and was, therefore, very vulnerable.[11] In 'Adonais' Keats's untimely death was lamented, like Chatterton's, as a kind of martyrdom.[12] Shelley's own temperamental inadequacies were mythologised as those of a 'sensitive plant' whose thoughts 'Pursued, like raging hounds, their father and their prey.'[13] Similarly, whatever the ambiguities of 'Kubla Khan', Coleridge indicated that his artist-surrogate had divine aspects commending wondering respect and holy dread:

> For he on honey-dew hath fed,
> And drunk the milk of Paradise.[14]

The concept of the poet as a man apart obviously appealed to Byron, master as he was of the cult of personality. His individuality was at odds with the world, and its crowds:

> They could not deem me one of such – I stood
> Among them, but not of them . . .[15]

Although none of Byron's great heroes was an artist, he nevertheless used the word 'paint' as a significant verb to describe the writer's creative process, as, for example, in

> 'The slow, sad stanza will correctly paint'
> ('Hints from Horace', 1.258)
> 'One word alone can paint to thee'
> ('The Bridge of Abydos', 1.332)
> 'I felt . . . but cannot paint, his rage'
> ('Mazeppa', 1.410)
> 'Of something which you poets cannot paint'
> ('Werner, or The Inheritance', 1.710)
> 'Scott, who can paint your Christian knight or saracen'
> ('Don Juan' V, 1.75)

The character of the romantic literary hero, such as Childe Harold, often grew into the literary portrait of the artist. The evolution was gradual. The artist's growing psychological importance in the nineteenth century *zeitgeist* was sometimes mirrored in flattering romantic biographies. Lady Morgan's preface to her *Life of Salvator Rosa* (1824) shows this approach. She was influenced, she wrote, more by the peculiar character of the man than the extraordinary merits of the artist:

> For, admiring the works of the great Neapolitan master, with an enthusiasm unknown perhaps to the sobriety of professed *virtù,* I estimated still more highly the qualities of the Italian patriot, who, stepping boldly in advance of a degraded age, stood in the foreground of his times, like one of his own spirited and graceful figures, when all around him was timid mannerism and grovelling subserviency!
> Struck, as I have always been, with the philosophical force and poetical conception of Salvator's greater pictures, even to the feeling of a degree of personal interest in favour of their creator, I took the opportunity of my residence in Italy to make some verbal inquiries as to the private character and

story of a man, whose powerful intellect and deep feeling, no less than his wild and gloomy imagination, came forth even in his most petulant sketches and careless designs.[16]

This passage indicates how Lady Morgan, herself an Irish governess turned antiquarian and romantic novelist, was immediately attracted by the personality of the artist. Moved by a spirit of emotional verve rather than intellectual analysis, she eschewed the drier problems – Salvator's aims, production and working methods – to concentrate on his 'private character and story'.[17] She was determined to use all her emotive power to secure appropriate admiration for this artist. Her gushing if unobjective praise of his extraordinary merit, spirited grace, powerful intellect and deep emotion suggested the standard romantic hero. So, too, did her reverent view of him as a superior being isolated amongst a crowd of gibbering idiots – 'Among them, but not of them'. Byronic influence may be felt in her references to Salvator's energetic stand for freedom (Byron died at Missolonghi in the year she published this book about her Italian patriot), and also to his peculiar, imaginative character. The adjectives she chose in the passage quoted above – 'wild', 'gloomy', 'petulant' and 'careless' – indicate her interest in fashionably untamed melancholy.

In a manner similar to that of Lady Morgan French authors also helped to invest the artist with glamour. Some French writers took a greater interest than their English brethren in the fictional artist's work, as a means of describing and even anticipating what was going on in contemporary aesthetics, but there is evidence that the emotional tensions with which they imbued their artist heroes infected later English counterparts. Charles Nodier, who wrote *Le Peintre de Saltzbourg* (1803), was the first of a stream of French writers to create romantic artists.[18]

There are similarities between individual French and English authors (as, for example, when Henry James in his own story the *Madonna of the Future* (1873), drew attention to one of Balzac's tales about a fictional artist) but the French novel which most influenced novels about artists was Henri Mürger's *Scènes de la vie de Bohème* (1851). This slight novel epitomised youthful freedom and popularised the idea of the comic bohemian living from hand to mouth. At the end of his first chapter Mürger explained that his book:

n'a d'autre prétention que celle indiquée par son titre, car des scènes de la vie de Bohème ne sont en effet que des études de moeurs dont les héros appartiennent a une classe mal jugée jusqu' ici, et dont le plus grand défaut est le désordre, et encore peuvent-ils donner pour excuse que la désordre même est une nécessité que leur fait la vie.

He showed how the disorder, which he defended as a harmless and necessary facet of artistic life, permeated it at all levels. Disorder reigned over his hero's haphazard choice of clothes and furnishings as much as in his mental and emotional states. The novel opened with a description of a typical bohemian lodging where a single all-purpose piece of furniture was draped with various odd romantic mementos. The bohemians' quaint and picturesque garb, which usually comprised dingy ill-fitting remnants set off by a startlingly coloured velvet cap or waistcoat, not only distinguished them from the rest of society but served as a passport to mutual acceptance.

The autobiographical hero, Rodolphe, questioned as to his profession, confessed 'for his clothes betrayed him, to his relations with the Muses'. Both his appearance and profession secured him instant friendship from the local fraternity of impoverished painters, poets, sculptors, musicians, journalists and models. These people were impractical but charming.

After reading Mürger's anecdotes, the American artist James McNeill Whistler came hotfoot to the French capital in search of true bohemian bliss. While painting in Paris he met the young Du Maurier who later immortalised him in his own highly popular version of the bohemian myth, *Trilby* (1894). Du Maurier's descriptions of English art students working in Parisian studios provide many parallels with Mürger's *Scènes de la vie de Bohème*. English authors often tried to make their artists seem more exciting by depicting them in Paris and using Mürger's classic escapist work as a ready-made guide to avante-garde behaviour.[19] Basically, Du Maurier used the same kind of loosely-knit group sharing the same kind of generous, impractical impulses that Mürger caught in *Scènes de la vie de Bohème,* but there is a difference in tone. Mürger played on his reader's sentiments, but not cloyingly. His wit was flippant, his descriptions of pain brief and touching. He had an underlying irony which enabled him, at the end of a book glorifying the life of the impoverished bohemian, to dismiss it as foolishly unrealistic. The nostalgic Du Maurier, on the other hand, while obviously trying to evoke a bitter-sweet atmosphere of song and sadness, alternated laboured practical jokes with passages of priggish pathos.

'Ye Societie of Our Ladie in the Fields' (1857)

Here, Du Maurier captures incidents from his own youth in Paris where he studied as an art student with Lamont (seen lying in bed), Armstrong (seen walking with a stick), Whistler (seen with his feet against a mantelpiece) and others – many of whom later inspired characters in *Trilby* (1894).

Saturated in sentiment, he missed the earlier author's lighter touch.

Authors often created phantasies based on their own experiences, projecting personal elements into the exaggerated artists they created. Writers depicting artists appeared to envy the mode of life that such people led. It was as though the artist combined a subtler imagination with a more stimulating and exciting *oeuvre*. Authors made full use of the contemporary focus on realism: the equation of the female body with idealised beauty made nude models an essential element in the fictional artist's working life. Writers were attracted not only by the erotic but also the practical aspects of the artist's work. Hazlitt, for example, in his effusive essay 'On the Pleasure of Painting' (1820) favourably compared the painter's creative prowess with the writer's dull and colourless method of suppressing his inner mental processes. He lamented that he had

> not much pleasure in writing these *Essays,* or in reading them afterwards, . . . After I begin them I am only anxious to get to the end of them, . . . I sometimes have to write them twice over: often it is necessary to read the *proof,* to prevent mistakes by the printer; so that by the time they appear in a tangible shape, . . . they have lost their gloss and relish, and become 'more tedious than a twice told tale'.
>
> But I cannot say, from my own experience, that the same process takes place in transferring our ideas to canvas; they gain more than they lose in the mechanical transformation. . . . With every stroke of the brush a new field of enquiry is laid open. . . .[20]

Just as the infinitely tedious labour of writing and correcting pages which went towards the compiling of a literary masterpiece paled in comparison with the artist's creative process, so too did that of composing musical manuscripts, even though, once a piece of music had been composed, authors could derive some drama from the sight as well as the sound of it being performed. This is seen, for example, in *Daniel Deronda* (1874-76) where George Eliot made the most of Klessmer's volatile performances on the piano. This character's musical talent accounted for his personal peculiarities, rather as a fictional artist's eccentricities were often closely bound up with his creative abilities. A minor parallel occurs in Browning's poem 'Abt Vogler' where the musician's theorising could be compared with Andrea del Sarto's musings. Fictional musicians, however, although frequently members of mixed bohemian groups were – with exceptions of the kind in Shaw's *Love Among the Artists* (1887-8) – infrequently chosen as romantic heroes in their own right.[21] This was doubtless because music is so hard to evoke in words. It was often used, though, as a blanket source of inspiration, like 'Nature', not interesting in itself so much as a means of revealing an artist's sensibility, as when Thackeray described young J. J. Ridley's intense and ecstatic reactions to music in *The Newcomes* (1853-5). This sensitive listener's wet eyes, pounding heart and over-wrought imagination were a sure indication of his genius.

The artist was no longer considered simply as a mere craftsman. Hazlitt's rapturous early praise of painting – 'There is a pleasure in painting which none but painters know' – proved beyond doubt that it need no longer be considered in an inferior light. Painting was lauded as a medium for expressing ideas: a delightful occupation *per se* enriched by the element of 'mechanical transformation' previously linked with despised physical labour. The artist's creative fulfilment derived, Hazlitt explained, from his total absorption in his work: his mind was fully occupied while his hand and eye were 'equally employed'. Indeed, his practical application aided his critical judgment. Training himself to perceive form he learnt to distinguish character, reading men and books with an 'intuitive glance'.

Some authors cast envious aspersions on the popularity of the visual arts. Wordsworth's poem 'Illustrated Books and Newspapers' (published in 1850) concluded:

> Now prose and verse sunk into disrepute
> Must lacquey a dumb Art that best can suit
> The taste of this once-intellectual Land.
> A backward movement surely have we here,
> From manhood – back to childhood; for the age –
> Back towards caverned life's first rude career.
> Avaunt this vile abuse of pictured page!
> Must eyes be all in all, the tongue and ear
> Nothing? Heaven keep us from a lower stage![22]

Similarly, Matthew Arnold in his 'Epilogue to Lessing's Laocoön' (1867) found it necessary to defend poetry against what Wordsworth enviously derided as a 'dumb Art'. However, the exciting power of painting was summed up by Arnold's evocative phrase 'the canvas glow'd/With triumphs! '[23]

The practical techniques of the artist's profession frequently fascinated nineteenth century authors and their characters. Even someone who evinced no interest in art, such as the heroine of Charles Lever's *The Martins of Cro' Martin* (1847), could succumb to the artist's spell: 'Many drew near to observe him, and insensibly felt attracted by that fascination which the progress of a picture invariably possesses.'[24] There were detailed accounts of the artist's tools and materials; of paints, palettes, crayons, and oils as when Mrs Ritchie, praising the charms of the 'practice' in *Miss Angel* (1875), described the 'pleasures of actual manipulation' or the 'friendly mesmerism' of the brush travelling across the canvas. There were also many descriptions of the artist at work.[25] Taut sculptors were shown hacking away at mountains of marble or deftly manipulating clay statuettes, and sensitive artists were pictured standing entranced before huge canvases, now stepping back, now pausing meditatively, now lunging forward to make a spectacular dash of crimson, green or gold.

In *Immortal Youth* (1896) Morley Roberts paid a characteristic tribute to the colourful aspects of artistic life. The author was ostensibly writing a story about the development of a lily-livered young writer but obviously found this basic material so flat and uninspiring that he borrowed from the art world to add spice to his otherwise unenterprising novel. Roberts introduced Lacy, his puritanical seventeen year old hero, to the kind of bohemian society which a Salvation Army officer described as a Gomorrah.

The fast-learning lad, who had been shattered to see a bed in an artist's workroom, and then to find himself alone with a woman for the first time while in an arist's *atelier,* was seduced by a promiscuous 'daughter of the studio'. Roberts, mustering all his romantic clichés, described how Sara, a nymphomaniac figure-model, gently locked him inside a studio where he became increasingly conscious of the darkening night sky seen through the skylight, and the heat of a red hot stove: 'The atmosphere in the studio was full of strange odours, full of shadows, enticements.' Sara pointedly set a study of the nude on the easel and began comparing it with her own superior charms, which the hero had already glimpsed, semi-draped:

> 'Did you really think I had a pretty figure?'
> 'Yes, yes', said St Antony.

'Perhaps you couldn't really see it', said Sara regretfully.
George shivered.
'Oh yes, I think I did'.
'I'm sure you couldn't properly. I had very thick drapery on.
Perhaps –'
And she sighed.
'Oh George! And I'm sure you didn't; I'm sure. If you'll
kiss me again, George – '

*   *   *

And George's weekly letter to [his mother in] Ullswater was
three days late.[26]

Roberts's coy suggestions, complete with stars and dashes, were
characteristic of the innuendoes associated with artists' models
and studio behaviour. Roberts described Sara, who surprised the
hero by winking at him the first time he found her modelling in
scanty garments, as a lesser Venus of the Chelsea Venusberg, a
Lilith of the studios, a serpent from a Battersea Eden.
While Lacy's personal experiences with this nubile daughter of
the studios provided him with the realistic material he needed to
put in a novel, Roberts showed how the artistic processes which
he witnessed in the studios provided an ideal creative stimulant:

> . . . It was a good training for him, this studio training. The
> sketches, the little talks, showed him men even in the work-
> shop. Had he plunged into so-called literary society, he would
> have seen only results, painful products. What he learnt now
> he learnt unconsciously, and saw things in the making. Literary
> criticism he might have shied at – did shy at. . . . But here
> everything he heard or saw was a criticism, and he felt it with-
> out being conscious. It was a drama. . . .[27]

This dismissal of the writer's profession – as one which could
reveal only hard-won finite results – in favour of the artist's
creative process was elaborated as the novel continued. It provided a typically sentimentalised and idealised view of the artist.
Many authors used the persona of the artist as a useful mask.
The artist provided both a safe shield and an extravagant banner,
behind which the writer could divulge the problems of his own
creative art, thus satisfying his instincts for both vanity and dis-
cretion. This close association with the entity of the artist

resulted in many authors producing characters who were all the richer for being partly autobiographical, rather than merely studied or invented.

Many authors and art critics, such as William Hazlitt, wrote about art with great sympathy and knowledge, having begun their careers as bad painters. Although James, one of the most prolific creators of fictional artists, failed to become an artist he nevertheless retained what John La Farge, the painter under whom he studied when young, termed his 'painter's eye'. Authors writing apprentice novels partly inspired by their own 'éducation sentimentale', often chose an artist hero, as in the case of Du Maurier, an ex-art student, or Kipling, who had strong artistic connections.[28] This made their use of the artist as a literary mask even more involved. Moore, who had attempted to become an artist, summed up his own predicament in a sonnet, interesting because of its plaintive theme, which he entitled 'To a Lost Art':

> Gone from me, dead, O child of my weak heart!
> Child, yet a mistress, wooed most lover-wise,
> Wooed long, – but never won, – with weary sighs,
> With toil and many tears; but tho' we part
> For e'er I love thee still, I now must start
> Upon another path, with other eyes
> And hands to beckon me. Will they despise
> No as thou didst? my sweet, my own lost Art.
>
> Tho' I have wed thy sister, thou, my sweet
> Will keep thy place in my most hidden sense;
> My dreams and secret thoughts will ever pour,
> Not gifts of tribute shells around thy feet,
> But love's sad offering of my impotence,
> A fruitless wave that can but kiss thy shore.[29]

'The Two Apprentices'

In this illustration to *Trilby*, Du Maurier captures the essence of the jaunty bohemian, the other side of the tense coin illustrated by Haydon in 'Curtius Leaping the Gulf'. The casual curls, clothes, and gestures of the figure on the left place him in the tradition of the eccentric artist. The fact that this frivolous figure was based on Whistler, by an author who drew on his own experiences in the art world, indicates the close links between art and literature, fact and fiction, in this period.

The Artist's Appearance as Romantic Hero

He is naturally what he is, and breaks out into costume as spontaneously as a bird sings or a bulb bears a tulip. And as Dick, under yonder terrific appearance of waving cloak, bristling beard, and shadowy sombrero, is a good, kindly simple creature, got up at a very cheap rate, so his life is consistent with his dress.[1]

The artist's visual impact was continually stressed, for his appearance constituted a major part of his romantic appeal. It also provided indirect characterization. His physique, clothing, dwelling, and the surroundings to which he gravitated all illustrated, and were emblematic of his way of life. The extraordinary characteristics which made individual artistic heroes appear unique in specific literary contexts were, paradoxically, so extreme that when they were viewed *en masse* they generally provided an almost self-caricaturing pattern.

The standard artist was attractive in the manner of most romantic heroes: a sensitive face, graceful body, and eccentric attire combined to produce a picturesque effect. He was usually distinguished by an intelligent forehead, fine bones, regular features, a 'sensitive' sensual mouth and luminous, magnetic, 'spiritual' eyes. His hair, which was long and distinctively coloured, was either remarkably glossy or interestingly tangled. His body was never gross, but almost always slim and elegant. The expressive quality of his face and grace of movement added to his charm.

Lewis Seymour in George Moore's *A Modern Lover* (1883), a typically handsome painter, was described as a dark, elegant youth, whose face 'had the rare charm of touching the imagination, it was as suggestive as a picture by Leonardo da Vinci'. . . .[2] Amongst his attractive features his creator gave special attention to his high forehead, shining hair, hypnotic eyes, long hands, and 'natural ability' to arrange himself in graceful poses. In the second edition of the story the attractions of the artist's physique were recorded still more emphatically.[3] Seymour recounted that he had once sat for his fellow students in a life class, when the usual model was ill, and his contemporaries, including one Lily Saunders, had liked his figure so much that they had asked him to sit through the following week. Encouraged by the thought that what Lily Saunders had admired would doubtless be equally attractive to others, he tested this with another woman, launching upon a successful seduction with a full display of his charms. Taking advantage of a moment when his prey had left the room to 'slip into a teagown', he quickly undressed. She was delayed, unclasping her stays, and when she returned he was aesthetically stationed on the drawing-room carpet in the pose of a dancing faun.

Similarly, the limbs and torso of Taffy, one of the artists in *Trilby,* delighted onlookers, who also marvelled at his long whiskers or 'Piccadilly weepers'. His delicate and indeed puny friend, Billee, whose soulful countenance easily compensated for a lack of vulgar muscle, reflected more 'sensitive' visual characteristics:

> Little Billee was small and slender, about twenty or twenty-one, and had a straight white forehead veined with blue, large dark blue eyes, delicate, regular features, and coal-black hair. He was also very graceful and well built, with very small hands and feet. . . .[4]

The artist's appearance was often all the more romantically intriguing because it exhibited not only various forms of extremism – to give an obvious example, an unusually extroverted coiffure – but also various contrasting elements which combined to form a curiously ambiguous whole. In Watts-Dunton's *Aylwin* (1898) both Cyril Aylwin and D'Arcy provided excellent examples of this kind of attractively puzzling synthesis.

In the fullest account of D'Arcy the contradictory sides of his nature were brought out in the description of his extraordinary face. His dominating features were his forehead and his eyes. The former, which showed up against his dark hair, was the 'tone of marble', and its 'form was so perfect that it seemed to shed its own beauty over all the other features'. The latter, despite spectacles and rather unexciting pigmentation, were remarkable for the wonderful lights shining in them which an entranced admirer described as moving and alive in the deeps of the pupils.

His 'perfect' pale sculptural forehead, and the 'indescribable lights' in his eyes combined to suggest a character of refined, almost spiritual, intellect, but this was qualified by the fact that the beauty of the face was entirely confined to the upper portion. It did not extend lower than the well-shaped cheek bones, and his mouth was decidedly unattractive. His lips were disparagingly described as 'loose and baggy', which suggested a sloppy sensuality, and his laughter created a similarly dubious effect; his mouth had a satiric twist, and his teeth were bared like those of an animal.

In an age when it was far easier to judge someone's occupation and success by his appearance, the artist's clothes and accessories automatically made him conspicuous because they were generally quite unlike those of other people. The motives behind his choice of strange attire were varied, but usually contained a blend of bravado and indifference. He seemed to dress oddly, partly because he enjoyed provoking the public, declaring his individuality, and attracting all the attention he could, and partly because his mind was on higher things, and therefore his appearance was of no consequence to him. This characteristic coexistence of two emotional extremes, bravado and apathy, was visually symbolised by that still traditional item from the bohemian wardrobe, the soiled velvet jacket. The superior sensitivity of the unselfconscious artist manifested itself in his ready and even covetous appreciation of anything exotic and colourful, such as velvet, and also in his ignoring anything tedious and mundane, such as dirt. Absent-minded Mr Theobold, the painter hero of Henry James's *The Madonna of the Future* (1873), wore a distinctive black velvet jacket and mediaeval biretta which 'revealed a rustiness which marked it as an original'.

Ouida provided a typical example of the way in which an artist's appearance could suggest a romantic personality in *Two Little Wooden Shoes* (1874). Ouida's adoring heroine, a Flemish girl, fell hopelessly in love with a painter who, to someone accustomed to broad, blunt peasant faces, seemed to belong to a different species. She felt he must have come from 'Rube's Land', referring to Ruben's rich images, which, for her, conjured up an exotic dream world, that of fine and elegant creatures who 'live

in the gold frames'. The graceful dark-eyed artist, an art historical cross-breed blessed with a 'Murillo head' and a 'face like one
of Jordaen's or Rembrandt's cavaliers', was clad in 'picture-like'
velvets. The glamour of the artist's sensual coverings was also
stressed in *Guenn* (1883). Here Blanche Willis Howard described
another innocent maiden whose passions were similarly stirred by
a painter's sophisticated tastes: 'While he painted her on his canvas, she engraved him on her heart'.[5] She was entranced by his
beautiful Christ-like looks, and watched the movements of his
firm, well-shaped hands with indescribable fascination. After
these talented fingers had gently turned her head and moved her
shoulders, she resented rougher handling from her rustic friends
– speaking irritably to an honest friend who did not deserve it,
even if his breath smelt of grog rather than cigarettes and his
jersey 'was not a painter's brown velveteen coat'.

Thackeray was particularly pleased by the flamboyance of the
artist: 'I love his honest moustache and jaunty velvet jacket, his
queer figure, his queer vanities, and his kind heart'. This avowal,
combined with his maxim that every 'Dick Tinto' gave his genius
a 'romantic envelope', breaking into costume as spontaneously
as a bird into song – or a bulb into bloom – forced the reader to
consider the peacock-like display of Clive Newcome, hero of *The
Newcomes,* as an integral part of his artistic temperament.
Thackeray was convincing in describing Clive's desire to enhance
his natural advantages with added ornamentation; it was his
natural instinct:

> 'Clive in his youth was of the ornamental clan of mankind –
> a customer to tailors, a wearer of handsome rings, shirt-studs,
> moustachios, long hair, and the like; nor could he help, in his
> splendid costume or his nature, being picturesque, and gener-
> ous, and splendid. . . .'[6]

The popularity of *The Newcomes* was shown by Charles Clark
in *Lord Falconberg's Heir* (1868). He echoed the links which
Thackeray had stressed between the artist's appearance and personality, restating Thackeray's association between the artist's
'queer figure' and 'queer vanities' in his own terms:

> Hundreds of artists and artists' homes have been described,
> from [Clive's master] Gandish and his pupils downwards. I say
> downwards, because modern literature finds itself incapable of

going upwards from Thackeray. There is among these writers a conventional pattern for these sorts of characters, pretty much alike with just a difference in type . . . German, Italian, English. All long-haired, bearded, moustachioed; one red, the other black, the third brown. All dirty, eccentric, prematurely solemn; or jovial, beer-drinking, pipe-smoking, unkempt; getting their meals in a curious family hog-tub-fashion.[7]

Trollope's artist in *Barchester Towers* (1857), Bertie Stanhope, whose magnetic eyes, long hair and untrimmed bohemian beard had made him an early example of Clark's 'conventional pattern', was also addicted to the spectacular. Trollope did not generally describe his apparel 'because it was so various; but it was always totally opposed in every principle of colour and construction to the dress of those with whom he for the time consorted'. He did, however, give a memorable example of this visual eccentricity when he recorded how his artist amazed discreetly clad clerics at a formal clerical reception by appearing as an incongruous vision in selected shades of sky blue.[8] The unusual cut of his garments, such as his wide trousers, was also conspicuous. Loose trousers were also worn by an artist in Edmund Hodgson Yates's novel *Land at Last* (1866). This character shared Bertie's love of colour and unconventionality – he wore red morocco slippers, without heels. But where Bertie had chastely fastened his blue scarf with a coral ring, this informal artist defied propriety to an even greater extent, daringly leaving his big turned-down collar 'open at the throat'.[9]

In *Roderick Hudson* (1876) Henry James created yet another artist whose unorthodox, decorative clothes indicated a taste for the dramatic, or melodramatic. His naturally 'delicate' countenance and graceful body were strangely set off by the shabby 'mock elegance' of his clothing. When first introduced by James he was

clad from head to foot in a white linen suit, which had never been remarkable for the felicity of its cut and which had now quite lost its vivifying and redeeming crispness. He wore a bright red cravat, passed through a ring altogether too splendid to be valuable; he pulled and twisted, as he sat, a pair of yellow kid gloves; he emphasised his conversation with great dashes and flourishes of a light silver-tipped walking-stick, and he kept constantly taking off and putting on one of those slouched sombreros which are the traditional property of the Virginian or Carolinian of romance. When his hat was on he was very picturesque. . . . He evidently had a natural relish for brilliant accessories and appropriated what came to hand.[10]

James indicated that the sculptor did not conform to normal rules. Not only was his white suit badly tailored, but it had lost its 'redeeming' crispness. The choice of the adjective suggested that a completely white suit could only be excused by pristine starching. Without this freshness it showed ungentlemanly pretension. This element of careless display was continued in Hudson's piratical scarlet scarf held, in an acute phrase, by a ring 'too splendid to be valuable'. James, who had already skilfully slipped from a description of the artist's physique to one of his choice of clothes, began, in this passage, to expand the reader's impression of the artist, subtly accumulating and building up further visual clues to his character. The colourful sculptor did not present a static but a dramatic picture. His yellow gloves girated, he used his silver-tipped cane, an attractive if superfluous accessory, as an extension of his personality in order to emphasise his remarks, flashing it with flamboyant eloquence. Further he indicated his abundant supplies of nervous energy by keeping his hat permanently on the move.

As a slouched sombrero was, as James stressed, the traditional property of the Virginian or Carolinian of romance, it added to the imaginative appeal of the dark, curly-haired artist. Indications of his extroverted vitality transformed a note of dubious incongruity into one of experimental charm. James's words 'natural relish' gave great buoyancy to his ambiguous statement that Hudson 'appropriated' whatever brilliant accessories came to hand. They suggested healthy appetite rather than vulgar theft, lending the artist the romantic immunity of youthful, theatrical virtuosity. Hudson, in James's phrase, spent money 'intellectually'.

George Moore emphasised Lewis Seymour's startling good looks by describing his similar selfconscious awareness of a need to match his looks by dressing the part. An astute writer, piqued by Lewis Seymour's personality, visited him at home and read the moral character of the artist in all the external appearance of his studio.

Between ourselves and our surroundings an analogy can always be traced; but in Lewis' case this likeness was singularly marked. For between the febrile forms of beauty he strove to explain, in his pictures, and his own feminine face and figure, the general arrangement and character of the furniture, down to the patchouli scented handkerchief, that cast a sharp odour through the room, there was a logical sequence. . . .[11]

This shrewd observer, inspecting the artist's habitat, immediately registered the obvious clues which helped to elucidate his temperament, in this case a preciously effeminate one. Similar, if undeclared, analogies were pointedly drawn between other artists and their decorations. Thus there was a similar, expanding 'logical sequence' from visual descriptions of other artists' physical presentation, to descriptions of their choice of clothing and accessories, and from them to their choice and arrangement of bulkier, more domestic items.

The pleasingly odd character of the fictional artist was suggested, again, by supposedly fascinating visual images and unexpected contrasts. A typical artistic hero, complete with luminous spiritual eyes and animalistic lips, sporting a rich, casually-soiled velvet jacket, gave the impression that he might well leave the remains of his lunch on his best furniture and then sit on it. The artist showed his rare, refined, sensitive, aesthetic vision by surrounding himself with peculiarly beautiful objects, but his treatment of them revealed his chaotic lack of logic. Picturesque effects, whether contrived or accidental, were always more obvious than practical organization.

Whatever the financial status of the fictional artist, his studio, whether ostentatiously lavish or ostentatiously sordid, generally showed the antithesis of ordered and matching domestic taste. Mary Anne Hardy, describing a studio at the beginning of *The Artist's Family* (1857) referred to a human skull, together with skeleton hands and feet upon the mantelpiece and to broken vials, worn-out brushes and other fragments of artistic material filling 'the rusty fire-grate, which, notwithstanding the piercing cold, had not had fuel in it for many a day'.[12] In an orthodox nineteenth century family the mantelpiece was considered the formal place of honour for decorative and treasured possessions. This writer's placing of a skull and bones in the place of, say, an inlaid clock and pair of china dogs, was obviously intended to provoke, just as her inclusion of an unpolished and littered fireplace was obviously intended to shock. At a time when a well-tended fire was the practical centre of any smoothly run household, a neglected hearth was a potent symbol. So, too, was the remark that the many objects filling the studio, which she described in some detail, lay about in 'inconceivable confusion'. The untidy studio became a cliché of this genre – a microcosm of the artist's erratic mind.

In *Romola* (1862-3) George Eliot described the dwelling of an artist who liked extremes, who seemed to 'love the blending of the terrible with the gay', and whose rooms indicated his versatile appreciative powers. His painting equipment was festooned with cobwebs, and beside a bank of ashes in the open hearth there was a prominent basket full of broken eggshells. In direct contrast to the artist's functional working materials, and the evidence of indefinitely postponed housekeeping, this accomplished author moved to a description of three pieces of obviously rare and extremely valuable furniture, as though beginning to indicate that this artist's love of beauty was unhampered by any vestige of worldliness.

Edmund Hodgson Yates and William Black are among minor nineteenth century authors who used similar descriptive techniques to conjure up an unorthodox atmosphere. Describing a studio in *Land at Last* (1886), the former included virtually forensic evidence of loose living. The atelier's filthy floor was enriched with spilt tobacco and trodden-in cigar ash, while the focal point of the room, a table, was crowded with litter amongst which a pewter pot 'raised itself conspicuously'. William Black, in the first volume of *Love or Marriage?* (1868), gave a comparable account of a ramshackle studio containing both torn and completed works. He mentioned a tray on a solitary table which contained, amongst other articles, envelopes, a catalogue, a tea-service, 'oily, sticky' colour tubes, 'smeared' brushes and a pot of marmalade. The unlooked-for presence of marmalade in an artist's equipment, and its close proximity with other equally messy, gummy materials indicated a totally unorganised, relaxed – indeed almost an organic – attitude to life.

George Eliot, in describing the artist's garden in *Romola,* had caught this perfectly. Her character not only kept a completely anachronistic garden – a tangled thicket or 'wilderness' of fig trees and vines trailed amongst nettles and hemlocks, and a tall, dark cypress emerged from a stifling mass of yellowed mulberry leaves – but also allowed it, along with its inhabitants, to invade his studio. There was no sharp delineation between logical civilization and natural chaos: the confusion of the artist's wild garden had begun to penetrate his house: the door was permanently wedged open, tufts of fennel sprang up in a confused heap of marble fragments and rusty armour, and a large stone vase, tilted on one side, seemed to be pouring out the ivy that streamed all round it: several speckled and white pigeons perched or strutted about, and 'three corpulent toads were crawling in an intimate and friendly way near the doorstone'.[13]

Gentlemanly amateurs, like more refined magpies, tended to create more *recherché* havoc:

> The front room was a studio and presented the usual untidy appearance of an artist's workshop, especially when the artist is a batchelor. There were odds and ends of all kinds thrown together in strange confusion, bits of gaudy drapery, tinselled tissues, and calico embroideries, which, when arranged with due attention to taste and tradition, formed the costume of a Grecian beauty, a Roman matron, or even a Belgravian belle. Plaster casts, some defaced and broken, were lying about; a hand here, a foot there, a beautifully moulded arm strung up with the head of a Satyr against the wall. In one corner, in a reclining posture, was a veritable skeleton, strung together with wires; looking as if it had just cast off humanity, and was lying down to rest.[14]

Despite her inclusion of an exhausted skeleton, presumably intended to awaken mild surprise, Mary Anne Hardy missed, in this passage from *Paul Wynter's Sacrifice* (1869), a splendid opportunity to enlarge on filthy floors, dirty brushes, empty grates, broken egg-shells and endless examples of primitive extemporisation. Although she refers blandly to the 'usual' untidiness of an artist's workshop, her description here of the amateur's studio is subtly bewilderised when compared with what she had written earlier in *The Artist's Family*. Not only were these casts picturesquely arranged and fractured, but the various colourfully embellished draperies, used 'with due attention to taste' to adorn female sitters, gave a pervasively decorative note.

Taste, or his interpretation of it, ruled George Moore's self-conscious artist hero in *A Modern Lover*. Lewis Seymour's aesthetic sense subjected everything to a conscientious fashionable scrutiny. The odd effects which could be obtained by unexpected juxtapositions of the absurd, the exotic and the revolting were therefore toned down, but Lewis remained a typical nineteenth century fictional artist in that his domestic arrangements revealed a romantic temperament at play. Both in his choice of domicile and in his choice of furnishings, he showed an overwhelming concern for what was emotionally exciting and visually attractive, rather than practically viable and soberly secure.

After much searching in London for a suitable studio he eventually discovered what really appealed to him. The artist had characteristically selected the only unusual and uniquely picturesque property in a district of tediously respectable houses. Whereas they conformed to a uniform pattern, the artist's chosen house represented 'the only bit of romance' in an otherwise altogether bourgeois area.

A delightful feature of the tree-shaded house was the soft, luminous effect made by the sunlight filtering through the interlacing leaves of the enormous verandah. When the artist first saw this he was thrilled, and immediately considered it subjectively, as a prop or adjunct to his personality. He imagined himself in the role of a captivating host giving charming parties beneath its atmospheric awning. Ignoring the possibility of structural improvements (although a prosaically honest, if inartistic, visitor had drawn his attention to its tumble-down condition and damp walls), he made his house more agreeable, or so he thought, with a series of ornamental rather than functional effects. He was busy camouflaging a hideous staircase with rose-coloured drapery and considering the taxing question of whether a Turkish or a Japanese lamp would look more artistic.

Moore had shared his character Lewis's concern to appear tastefully unusual in his autobiographical *The Confessions of a Young Man* (1888), where he recalled how, having decided to abandon art for literature, he had moved into a new apartment with his artist friend, Marshall, who had undertaken the task of furnishing and

> lavished on the rooms the fancies of an imagination that suggested the elaboration of a courtesan of high degree and a fifth-rate artist. . . . The drawing-room was in cardinal red, hung from the middle of the ceiling and looped up to give the appearance of a tent; a faun, in terracotta, laughed in the red gloom, and there were Turkish couches and lamps. In another room you faced an altar, a Buddhist temple, a statue of Apollo, and a bust of Shelley. The bedrooms were made unconventional with cushioned seats and rich canopies; and in picturesque corners there were censers, great church candlesticks, and palms; then the smell of burning incense and wax and you will have imagined the sentiment of our apartment in Rue de la Tour des Dames. I bought a Persian cat, and a python that

made a monthly meal of guinea pigs; Marshall, who did not care for pets, filled his room with flowers – he used to sleep beneath a tree of gardenias in full bloom.[15]

Green and gold vine leaves adorned the walls and furniture of their salon. If this description showed the influence of Pre-Raphaelite taste, and the kind of designs made by Morris and his friends, there were other descriptions which echoed it far more obviously, such as some of the visual images in *Aylwin*. Here Watts-Dunton's strange, 'aesthetic' artist, D'Arcy, created many romantic and Pre-Raphaelite effects reminiscent of Kelmscott House in his own dwelling: the old, odd structure and furnishings of 'Hurstecote Manor' – a grey stone, gabled building, with oak-beamed attics – suggestively indicated the cult for medievalism and handmade, hand-decorated objects, a fashion connected with the Pre-Raphaelite movement.

In complete contrast with the curious but certainly European objects and painting equipment which filled most of the house, the writer described how his fictional artist had placed a 'strange' and beautiful piece of furniture under a 'gorgeous awning ornamented with Chinese figures in ivory and precious stones'. His friend Cyril had a studio in Chelsea which also was filled with oriental pieces. It was the fashion to juxtapose European and oriental works, as Moore had, when he included a Japanese lamp and a Buddhist temple in the decorations of his ostensibly European studio. Cyril told a guest that 'nothing artistic is quite right now unless it has a savour of blue mould or Japan'.

It was in keeping that an avant-garde artist, such as Cyril, should have tastes well in advance of most people's, and that he should understand and appreciate what more ignorant philistines simply dismissed as 'monstrosities'. His sensitive aesthetic sense delighted in the exciting novelty of the then extremely weird and incomprehensible art-forms of the orient. He did not explain any of the technical attractions of Eastern art, such as the Japanese artist's linear fluency and startlingly asymetrical designs, but he did surprise his visitor with his grasp of the dead-pan, unsentimental humour inspiring many Japanese works.

'That', said he, pointing to a picture of a woman [who seemed to be drunk] who was amusing herself by chasing butterflies, while a number of broad-faced, mischievous-looking children were teasing her – 'that is the masterpiece of Hokusai. The legend in the corner is "Kiyó-jo chó ni tawamureru", which, according to the lying Japanese scholars, means nothing more than "A cracked woman chasing butterflies". It was left for me to discover that it represents Yoka, the goddess of Fun, sportively chasing the butterfly souls of men, while the urchins, the little Yokas, are crying, "Ma! you're screwed".'[16]

Thus the artist, whether surrounding himself with beautiful, romantic, medieval objects, or with curious, exotic, oriental ones, or with extravagant combinations of both, again proved, by creating such an unusual environment, that he was an altogether exceptional type.

The choice of where the artist was to live offered authors an opportunity to expand the impression created by his appearance and choice of décor. Pursuing his affinity with both the picturesque and the unorthodox, the artist naturally gravitated towards excessively and ostentatiously romantic environments; places which provided him with characteristically interesting backdrops. Many of those fictional artists who had the misfortune to be born in England were eager to leave their native land for more inspiring shores. Paris, magnetic and alluring, particularly enthralled their imagination. The ostensible reason for her attraction lay in her rich artistic heritage and contemporary schools of art, but her unique aura of decadence was equally, if not more, potent.

In *Trilby,* the romantic nature of Little Billee was stressed by his close and appreciative association with the picturesque landscape of Paris, whose 'very name had always been one to conjure with, whether he thought of it as a mere sound on the lips and in the ear, or as a magical written or printed word for the eye'. He was portrayed first in a studio – itself full of picturesque items such as a cheetah skin and a trapeze – from whose window he looked out 'over the roofs and chimney pots of Paris and all about with all his eyes'. Chewing a roll and a garlic sausage, he gazed

> with a sense of novelty, an interest and a pleasure for which he could not have found any expression in mere language.
> Paris! Paris!! Paris!!![17]

Lewis Seymour, in *A Modern Lover,* provided a perfect example of an artist who discovered that Paris offered him an idyllically harmonious setting. He came from London to Paris, initially to study. The change delighted him. He felt immediately at ease and found the informal Parisian atmosphere – an attractive blend of visual charm and moral flexibility – utterly *sympathique*. This city provided him with an authentic continuation of his own personality. He was temperamentally in tune with Parisian life, all the more seductive for being a little dangerous, and his creator used this to build up his image of the artist's lighthearted, unconventional charm and sensuality.

Moore established the sort of romantic climate Paris represented before he actually placed his hero in a Parisian setting. The painter decided he would go there partly because he had a vague notion that all he had to do to become a great artist was to go to Paris, but also because he wished to spite his beautiful hostess for her 'intense selfishness' – or refusal to sleep with him – by luring her to Paris, where he would surely be successful. How could she hold out against him there? In the second edition of the novel Moore was perfectly explicit about the artist's strategic use of a sojourn in this stimulating metropolis: 'People do things in Paris they would not do in London'.

This, indeed, was the first reaction of the doomed hostess and her companion – a pair of eminently respectable English ladies – when Lewis told them of his projected visit to the dreadful place. The old companion, shocked, dropped her knitting in the grate, and warned of the moral dangers of the French capital. The reflections of the younger woman, however, were of a rather different order. Paris stimulated a sequence of disturbingly racy images in her startled stream of consciousness. She connected Paris with memories of her honeymoon, and her villainous husband, a Parisian Englishman, a type with the virtues of neither country and the vices of both – 'Sometimes curious stories about him reached her ears, fantastic duels, in which actresses' names were mentioned.' E. F. Benson, in *Limitations* (1896), was another of the many English writers who played on the idea of French, and particularly Parisian, immorality as opposed to British morality of the kind symbolized by Victoria and her correct German spouse. Vice in Paris was certainly never boring.

Moore's respectable ladies followed Lewis to the wicked city – to keep an eye on him. Mrs Bentham's conscious distrust of both Paris and the artist was probably all the more paradoxical, even poignant, because it was obviously based on her subconscious fascination with them both. She had already fallen into 'reveries' about both before exercising her critical judgement, and so her intellect was virtually seduced in advance by her ideas of the place and its permissive possibilities. When she drove round Paris with the painter she succumbed to his advances far more readily than in England. Lazily she laughed and whispered with him, recalling the past and talking dreamily of the future: her former reserve had been subtly undermined by the irresistible combination of charming artist and romantic Parisian setting.

Later that evening Lewis suggested that all three of them should dine out in one of Paris's open-air restaurants. Moore contrasted the different attitudes of the adventurous young artist and Mrs Bentham's staid, elderly companion to this venture. Her astonishment and bewilderment provided a foil for the painter's instantaneous immersion in the scene: 'Lewis, who loved the fantastic, was enchanted. . . .' To the passionate painter the city seemed like 'a voluptuous siren, dreaming to the strains of amorous music, and following the simile out he longed to place his hand on hers and lay his head a while resting on the beautiful bosom she held to him'.[18]

Another close link was forged between the charms of both the artist and the city when Mrs Bentham, trying to get the painter out of her mind, stood looking out over the trees of the orangerie and the Champs-Elysées. Her convincing chain of thought, ranging from an appreciation of the 'persuasiveness' of the Parisian scene to amorous reflections about the artist, was interrupted by the entrance of the latter, not slow to avail himself of what he termed 'his chance'. Frightened at first by his tactically liberal views on fashionable liaisons and his suicidal threats, the lady 'grew more interested when she heard of the pleasant life they would have together in Paris'.

A second drive in the French capital cemented their affection: 'The beauty of the city acted on Mrs Bentham and Lewis like a narcotic'. George Moore's equation of Paris with a drug was effective. The idea of an artificially neutralised conscience and blissful lack of control was neatly echoed in Lewis's physical condition. He had to catch his breath with a sense of 'sweet suffocation', overcome by the enchantment which surrounded him. His sense of passive surrender and utter relaxation, at odds with his actual movement, suggested a drugged suspension, like the moral ambiguity surrounding the recumbent women who sped invitingly past:

At this hour the boulevard was full of carriages, crowded omnibuses, drawn by immense gray horses, often stopped the way. Now and again a victoria containing a gaudily-dressed woman, her tiny feet resting on an embroidered cushion, would speed past; the lady casting amiable glances to the right and left, until perhaps two young men would tell their coachmen to touch up the high stepping bay, and follow in the wake of the reclining beauty.[19]

Moore was successful in discreetly nourishing the carnival atmosphere suggested by the amiable lady and her followers – omitting any references to work as such. Instead he described the sensual holiday pursuits of tourists and idlers who, enjoying the evening air, gathered round kiosks, walked arm in arm, or sauntered into brilliantly illuminated cafés where they sat in the great squares of light thrown on to the pavements:

> drinking, talking, or watching the crowd as it surged past. Women, too, were not wanting, and a gleam of a white petticoat or the elegancy of a lace stocking relieved the monotonous regularity of trousers and men's boots. Out of this seething mass of life the tall houses, built in huge blocks of grey stone, arose and faded into darkness, whilst the boulevard with its immense *trottoirs,* and its two interminable lines of gas lamps running out and into a host of other lights, extended until lost in what appeared to be a piece of starry sky.[20]

Moore adds to the artist's romantic charisma by skilfully suggesting that he moves in an element of endless pleasure: Paris – brimming with visual and hedonistic delights – is boundless. By giving no precise definition of its size he also avoided a sense of finite limits and boundaries. The essence of Paris was a turbulent, fluctuating, Baudelairean crowd. Movement was confusingly amorphous: different kinds of beings and vehicles conglomerated, separated, paused and passed each other at unco-ordinated speeds. Just as individual details within this seething mass recalled details from Manet or Pissarro, so the overall method of linking these flickering effects was impressionistic. While creating a sense of loose cohesion (and also of size by using such words as tall, huge, immense and interminable) Moore was uninterested in tight architectural structure: not only did the boulevards evaporate in light, but solid stone Parisian houses hovered between the undulating crowd and the blurred shadows of the night sky. Lightly-sketched images were highlighted, almost at random, within the overall darkness. He described huge abstract patches of light reflected from glaring café windows, indiscriminate figures, the gleam of a white petticoat or outline of a lace stocking (another characteristic *soupçon* of happy voyeurism), the glow of gas lamps distantly mixed with still more lights themselves drawing the city into the infinite by mingling with the stars.

After the light, brilliantly fashionable aura of Paris, Rome (or Florence, which was awarded a very similar kind of treatment) was more discreetly decadent. Rome supplied artists with an equally romantic but slightly less frivolous background. The artistic profession regarded Italy, as Mrs Oliphant put it in *The Three Brothers* (1870), as the country of renovation, the fountain of strength. Rome provided a contrast to the more lively and exciting atmosphere of nineteenth century Paris mainly because of the archaeological flavour of the massed volume of her buildings, monuments, and unique art treasures.

These generated a more solemn atmosphere, captured by George Eliot in *Middlemarch* (1871-2). In this she gave a complex description of Rome, the city of visible history, where the past of a whole hemisphere seems moving in funeral procession with strange ancestral images gathered from afar. The young bride Dorothea's sensitive impressions of Rome, which provided a slightly puritanical norm between the exaggeratedly pedantic reactions of the scholarly Mr Casaubon, and the amorously romantic vision of the young 'art student', Will Ladislaw, were typical in suggesting the rather cloying fascination of

> Ruins and basilicas, palaces and colossi, set in the midst of a sordid present, where all that was living and warmblooded seemed sunk in the deep degeneracy of superstition divorced from reverence; the dimmer but yet eager Titanic life gazing and struggling on walls and ceilings; the long vistas of white forms whose marbled eyes seemed to hold the monotonous light of an alien world: all this vast wreck of ambitions, ideals, sensuous and spiritual, mixed confusedly with the signs of breathing forgetfulness and degradation.[21]

In describing the impact of Rome on Dorothea, George Eliot also wrote that its various images at first jarred her as with an electric shock, and then urged themselves on her. If the richness of Italy's artistic heritage could be almost too impressive to the tourist, then its scale and prestige could be equally challenging to the artist, who, in such surroundings, automatically invited comparison with past creators.

The humbling effect of past perfection was suggested in Henry James's pathetic story, *The Madonna of the Future*. The narrator arrived in Florence late at night, but before going to bed decided to walk through the city. Seeing the Palazzo Vecchio he was vastly impressed by the statues of David and Perseus, which gleamed magnificently in the moonlight. As he stood gazing at those awe-inspiring works, a man emerged from the shadows, and interrupted him, thus providing his first glimpse of the painter hero Mr Theobald, who struck him as 'picturesque, fantastic, slightly unreal'. The divine power of the enormous David, and the sinuous energy of the metallic Perseus, whose very names evoked connotations of great achievement, were so impressive as to dwarf this feeble artist.

Roderick Hudson, another Jamesian hero, but one with intense vitality and energy, managed to hold his own in a Roman setting, and thus was able to profit from, and absorb, elements of its grandeur. The artist, fresh from provincial America, gained status imperceptibly when placed in the romantic context of majestic Rome. Hudson who had been unable to decide, in Paris, whether Titian or Mademoiselle Delaporte was the greater artist, became much more seriously impressed with the general atmosphere of the ancient imperial, and papal, city. It was the 'natural home' for people of his temperament – those with a deep relish for the artificial elements in life and the infinite superimpositions of history. Unlike his puritan ancestors, he revelled in Rome's baroque ceremonies, her 'most extreme sights and customs'.

The artist, who was delighted by the melancholy sublimity of his studio and its environs, seemed equally in his element among the stately remains of the Colosseum. Here, James staged a dramatic scene in which the sculptor was about to risk his life by climbing these perilous ruins to satisfy a lady's whim for a high-growing flower. In that impressive site, traditionally associated with courageous sacrifice, James made a potentially pig-headed gesture assume a 'sort of masculine eloquence'.

Although artists generally lolled about in the more picturesque and squalid parts of famous cities, they sometimes made excursions into the countryside. It could provide a safe refuge, with almost the standing of a retreat into the respectability of a man's club in London. Little Dorrit, in Dickens's novel, concluded her description of the life of the second-rate, wife-neglecting painter, Henry Gowan, with the remark: 'Then he goes into the country to think about making sketches'.

A scene which could easily have sounded petulant or pretentious in, say, the conditions of kitchen sink drama, could take on an element of heroic pathos when delivered in the unearthly calm of a perfect vista. Conducting his artist around Como, James compared this idyllic Alpine scenery with the imaginative glamour of the scenes found on the vignettes of music sheets or on the painted drop-curtains of theatres. These comparisons were telling, for they not only suggested charming romantic views in a visual sense but scenery used as a deliberate prop to enhance and intensify emotional scenes – in this case lending distinction to one of the sculptor's desperate outbursts.

When Roderick Hudson died in the Alps, James again employed natural effects with great strategic power. He set the first intimations of Hudson's disappearance against vivid images of the foreboding felt by the artist's already anguished friends, and of the gathering gloom of a violent black storm. This menacing display, demonstrating the threatening power of the elements, contributed to the growing tension surrounding the artist's fate, and romantically stressed his isolation.[22]

The full fury of the storm, with its portentous thunderpeals, flashes of lightning, and torrential downpour was succeeded by quiet and the promise of cloudless calm:

> the snow peaks reared themselves against the near horizon in shining blocks and incisive peaks. . . . The silence everywhere was horrible; it seemed to mock . . . impatience, and to be a conscious symbol of calamity.[23]

The author's emphasis on the disconnecting, grave stillness pervading the air after the storm, on the literally and cathartically purified atmosphere and the abstract beauty of the scene lent an epic quality to the subsequent search for the artist. James continued to build up his dramatic effects, continually impressing the reader with the idea of the terrifying scale and abrupt contours of these bright, empty mountains. This area of natural avalanches transformed the possibility of a slight slip into something more finite. The discovery of the sculptor's body at the bottom of a rocky ravine produced an appropriate sense of awe.

Despite signs of the storm which he had faced alone – the rain had spent its torrents upon him and his clothes and hair were as wet as if the 'billows of the ocean had flung him upon the strand' – Hudson's body had a perfect beauty. The artist who had lately lived such a tormented, negative existence had now attained 'a strangely serene expression of life', lying in the brilliant sunshine under the blank and stony cliff face from which he had fallen. The impersonal splendour of this momentous setting was of great significance in James's final scheme, that of establishing his romantic sculptor as a tragic hero.

The Welsh mountains were employed to a lesser extent by Watts-Dunton in *Aylwin* as a background for romantic artists. An amateur artist called Hal Aylwin sojourned in them for some time. Enlarging on his own 'nature-ecstasy', he said that one did not appreciate the scenic qualities of a particular spot merely because one had been born in it. A real concern for nature depended on the individual's inherited capacity for feeling. The romantic sensitivity of his own sensations showed the influence of a gypsy grandmother, who had used music to summon up the 'strange spirits of Snowdon'. This area, as the chapter heading 'The Magic of Snowdon' indicated, was associated with rarified, Celtic mysticism: his preference for this particular kind of landscape indicated that he was a superior being.

On one occasion he walked, with a friend, through the lovely glades between Capel Curig and Bettws-y-Coed, where the light playing on the cascades gave the impression of molten jewels. Here they suddenly came upon two sketchers. One called out to the other: 'You have an eye for composition; what do you think of this tree?' Instead of drawing the reader's notice to the significant features in the landscape which the artist had chosen to study, the author focussed attention directly on the artist himself, and the unusual visual impression which he created. Hal reacted immediately: 'The speaker's remarkable appearance attracted my attention'. His appearance was described, as was that of his companion, who, 'sitting upright on his campstool, was busy with his brush'. What he was actually doing with his brush was left to the reader's imagination.[24]

Again, it might be observed that even an undistinguished writer of minimal powers of romantic invention could utilise both urban and rural settings, not to discuss a fictional artist's work so much as to suggest idealised qualities in his personality. In Joseph Hatton's *The Tallants of Barton* (1867) Arthur Phillips, one of the nineteenth century's less dramatic fictional heroes, who defied romance by working hard and marrying happily, gained a convincing modicum of unworldly prestige through Hatton's method of presenting his environment. This author, after dressing his big-eyed hero in a characteristically casual 'loose blouse', described him in the context of his picturesque treasures: items such as sketches, the inevitable lay-figure, and a guitar were strewn, with clichéd abandon, about his curious old room in a cathedral close whose mullioned windows looked out over graceful scenery.

'The Happy Life – Barbizon'

Here, Du Maurier shows his 'three musketeers of the brush' coming on another artist painting in the forest: it is significant that while this illustrator chooses to depict these figures in some detail, he doesn't give any indication of the kind of image on the canvas. He is obviously more interested in personalities than painting.

Hatton engineered a telling conversation between Arthur and a connoisseur friend, leaving the reader in no doubt about the underlying significance of these disordered 'treasures'. The artist's appreciative visitor, although used to the finest luxury at home, said that he had his happiest hours in the painter's 'den', asking his host what made it

so free and easy, and yet so *distingué*?'
'One gets out of the world, and a little nearer the better land, in a room consecrated to art, even if the prophet be but a dotard, perhaps,' said Arthur.
'And its perfect freedom – the absence of conventionality – the Bohemian character of the class called artists – their opposition to the forms and ceremonies, eh?'
'The artist only worships one goddess, I suppose; and she permits smoking, loose garments, unwashed hands, and slippers. Light your cigar,' Arthur went on, carelessly, offering his friend a fusée.[25]

Hatton thus manipulated his hero into clearly expressing the well-known equation between material laziness and mental liberty. This was indicated by the way in which he connected the artist's final speech and gesture, for the painter's (apparently unwashed) hand casually offering his companion a cigar provided an apt, if unoriginal, gesture of bohemian relaxation. In a later passage, subtitled 'Arthur Phillips at work', the author linked the painter's hand and eye to suggest not freedom from mundane cares, but superiority to them.

Whereas, in the former quotation, Hatton made a fictional commentator present the painter's studio in terms of a pleasant absence of formality, ceremony or conventionality, in the subsequent example he used observers' glimpses of the painter in the countryside to help to build up still more decided effects. Phillip's studio had represented a limited escape from the world, taking one – in his own words – a 'little nearer a better land'. Transported into the vistas previously defined by his studio window, he became an integral part of that idealized existence.[26]

The author described the artist sitting under an oak by a stream. He used rustic props, as he had earlier used more sophisticated ones, to create a romantic aura. Hatton's strict avoidance of any natural phenomena with crude or unpleasant connotations – such as dung, nettles, midges, cadavers and the like – and his interest in contrasting visual effects of rough and smooth textures suggested by the juxtaposition of knotted roots and flowing water, placed him in the picturesque tradition.

Hatton, with customary crudity, brashly informed the reader that the 'artist and his spectators' would have made a 'pretty picture', thus blatantly revealing the romantic desire to focus attention on the creator rather than his creations. This writer obviously wanted to lead the reader into further admiration for the artist by showing the varied watchers drawn by his presence. The uninspiring nature of a wandering tramp, a slovenly woman and some schoolboys was obviously designed to concentrate undivided attention on the artist's intensely rapturous absorption – which was noticeably too 'earnest' for the schoolboys' powers of concentration. But while Hatton indicated that this absorption of the painter could isolate him from fellow humans, he also implied that it did not disturb the natural fauna and flora (although a moth got stuck in his paint). Remembering that Phillips had described an artist's environment as a consecrated place even if its 'prophet' was a dotard, the reader feels the full force of the author's suggestion achieved by making him the nucleus of such a harmonious pastoral.

This painter-prophet, then, was placed in visual conditions suggesting the peak of fulfilment: sitting amongst strands of fruitful amber foliage, he was flanked on one side by a vista adorned with rich autumnal colouring and on the other by harvesters. Hatton seated him beneath an oak, whose benign strength was increased by full summer sunshine. The artist's pantheistic power was symbolically confirmed when the blazing sun was momentarily masked, revealing that the visionary artist had created a secondary light source; his painted leaves were 'illuminated as if gleams of sunshine had gone through them'. Hatton, as usual unable to resist spelling out his strategies, left the reader with no doubt that this peaceful landscape had been tailor-made to show off the artist's refined emotional sensitivity. Phillips, leaning back on his camp stool, reflected with congratulatory self-interest on the scene before him: 'his heart was grateful for the running brook, the whispering trees, the broad expanse of distant hills and meadows, and above all, for the sympathy which he possessed in his own nature for the beautiful and sublime'.[27]

The Artist Versus Society

'I don't want to be respectable, and I hate
commercial pursuits.'[1]

Characteristic descriptions of the artist's physique, his dress, his
habitat, and finally his visual environment, all combined to project a general impression of an unusual romantic. This impression was strengthened by the artist's human environment. Intriguing juxtapositions in the artist's own personality, displayed
microcosmically in the strangely combined items of his clothing
and décor, were emphasized macrocosmically in the infinite
variety of the bohemian society to which he naturally gravitated.
The young artist, tending to surround himself with odd, colourful
friends, found that unorthodox bohemian cliques provided him
with both a sympathetic milieu and a picturesque entourage.

In *Trilby* the artist hero and his two closest friends – 'our three
musketeers of the brush' – were intimately associated with varied
bohemians. The author's obvious intention was to study the central characters in terms of their involvement with their companions, so that while they compared favourably, as individuals,
with more lightly-sketched and often caricatured bohemians, they
also gained romantic prestige from their close association with an
unorthodox group. Du Maurier's achievement was only partly
successful since his innate snobbery and pathetic sentimentality
prevented his ever achieving any romantic gusto; they led him to
describe foolishly naïve situations, and to create tepid characterisation with often ludicrous hyperbole. Yet his vignettes of

bohemian life curiously enough, gained great popularity and influence for the book, and this perhaps paradoxically, because of its literary failings. His work provided a perfect example of the kind of emotional, indulgently melodramatic writing frequently used to convey the idea of an artist in nineteenth century English literature, a subject which lent itself to pretentious effusion.

Du Maurier obviously attempted to make the artist's bohemian acquaintances as interesting as possible. Apart from describing obvious differences in age, appearance and temperament, he gave them a mixture of nationalities, including English, French, Swiss, Austrian, Hungarian, Greek and American. Their social origins, too, were decidedly mixed. The fact that they had varied occupations again added to the general motley impression: one was a sculptor, another a medical student, yet another a Jewish musician and hypnotist. Dodor and Zou Zou, aspiring soldiers, were several times raised to the rank of corporal or brigadier, but degraded next day, for general misconduct resulting from their too exuberant delight at being promoted. Neither of them ever said an ill-natured thing or

> ever even thought one; ever had an enemy but himself. Both had the best or the worst manners going, according to their company, whose manners they reflected; they were true chameleons.[2]

Their chameleon-like ability to adapt themselves, to fit in with present circumstances rather than to govern their behaviour by fixed principles was very much in the bohemian tradition. At the Fête of St Cloud they demonstrated this dexterous adaptability by dancing a riotous cancan swiftly modified on the approach of the authorities. They would generously offer anyone a friend's cigar, or invite anyone to dine with him, and were prepared at a moment's notice to fight 'either with you or for you'. Such characteristic bohemians, unhampered by legal or religious sanctions, came and went, using human resources as the spirit moved them. This friendly use of floating funds had been emphasised by earlier authors. Frederick Charles Wraxall in *Wild Oats* (1858) described a typically varied community, the 'Camden Town Bohemia', in which students receiving parental aid found themselves supporting other, lazier dependents: authors, artists, vets and medical students 'all join in firm fellowship and are ready to help each other to the last shilling'.

'The Fox and the Crow'
    Du Maurier, drawing on his own recollections of initiation ceremonies at Gleyre's studio in Paris, suggests an energetic student ritual in a bare-boarded room with a background of nude sketches and graffiti. This is a symbolic image where an ecstatic artist hero is seen encircled by bohemian companions.

Many facets of bohemian life were governed by the principle of adaptability, which made morality relative and pleasure easy. Pleasure was stimulated also by participation: bohemians were usually so wholeheartedly and energetically absorbed in the activities around them, undistracted by sad memories of epic projects, that they gained great enjoyment from existence. Bohemians seemed to lend themselves to exploiting humorously melodramatic situations. As a group, they naturally abhorred the faintest suggestion of pretension, which was one of their excuses for constant teasing and practical joking. When the cloyingly perfect romantic hero, Little Billee, first went to a studio in Paris, he was initiated into the kind of irrepressible frivolity which characterised his fellow art-students, whom Du Maurier called 'little lords of mis-rule', describing them all as animated by a pervasive *esprit de corps*.

The studio party was a recurring feature in descriptions of life among the artists. Du Maurier's splendid Christmas feast in *Trilby* brought out the casual incompetence of the three hosts, the total lack of order and method displayed by everybody and the resultant chaos, and also 'the noisiest, busiest and cheerfullest animation' by which the banquet that was to begin at six was made ready by ten. The communal cooking, it was felt, was almost better fun than the eating; for these Bohemians hugely enjoyed the whole process of improvisation, with all its ludicrous and imaginative overtones. They were very ready to adapt themselves to any opportunity for enjoyment offered by the unexpected and the absurd.

Songs, for example, were followed by a variety of amusements including human dumb-bell exercises and cockfighting with broomsticks. The last was voted 'a very good game'. Du Maurier's earlier use of the words 'better fun' and then this reference to a 'very good game' indicate the naïve quality of much of his writing. His escapism, although popular, was often puerile. Shouts of laughter could be heard on the other side of the river. A policeman who arrived to deal with the 'rassemblement' in the street and to quell the fearful racket, was given drinks, and, with two colleagues who later came to look for him, threw himself into the game with such abandon that the police made more noise than the original revellers, until all three fell into a drunken stupor and were pushed out of sight behind the stove. So law and order, sent for to protect the interests of a respectable community, were won over and – literally – intoxicated by the charm of the feckless and lawless.

Earlier, in *Hide and Seek* (1854), Wilkie Collins had touched on the bohemian's careless disregard for the police. The sprightly young artist hero, Zachary Thorpe, had been in revolt against authority from the age of six, when he shocked his orthodox parents by rebelling against their rigid Sunday disciplines, and later displayed a premature taste for drinking, smoking and adventurous outings. Efforts to incarcerate him in a Tea Broker's office in the City, a career with good safe, steady prospects, had provoked strong reactions: 'I don't want to be respectable, and I hate commercial pursuits.' This lively and enterprising lad thought automatically of art as his natural outlet. Feeling that his life would be far pleasanter if he became a painter, he apprenticed himself despite parental disapproval to a kind-hearted artist called Valentine Blyth, whose régime was less rigorous than that in the Tea Broker's office: they often played leap-frog together.

Collins gave his boundless energy and agile gallantry another outlet in the 'Snuggery' – a popular place where 'vice was wholly undisguised'. After setting a scene in which a number of drunks began to bait a man in a skull cap, a tall, hatless young gentleman distinguished by masses of curly hair leapt on to a bench waving his fists like windmills. This, of course, was our hero:

> 'Damn you all, you cowardly counter-jumping scoundrels!' roared Zack, his eyes aflame with valour, generosity, and gin-and-water. 'What do you mean by setting on one man in that way? Hit out, sir – hit out right and left! I saw you insulted; and I'm coming to help you!'[3]

The young champion and his companion were greeted with roars of applause. As they ran through the streets to escape the police, Collins gave a convincing account of the way in which a beautiful friendship blossomed between the two bohemian fugitives. Zach was soon clapping his new acquaintance on the back and asking why he wore a cap. . . .

> 'I come from America last,' replied Mat, as grave and deliberate as ever. 'And I wear this cap because I haven't got no scalp on my head. . . . Me and my scalp parted company years ago. I'm here, on a bridge in London, talking to a young chap of the name of Zack. My scalp's on the top of a high pole in some Indian village, anywhere you like about the Amazon country. If there's any puffs of wind going there, like there is here, it's rattling just now, like a bit of dry parchment;

and my hair's a flip-flapping about like a horse's tail, when the flies is in season. I don't know nothing more about my scalp or my hair than that.'[4]

This scalpless layabout, who had tried to find an overland road to the North Pole and driven cattle in Mexico, subsequently turned out, as chance would have it, to be the young artist's natural uncle. This vagabond had arrived in England to avenge his sister, who had died in the poor house after giving birth to an illegitimate child. The child's father, coincidence being a fine thing, was no other than Zach's own, as Mr Thorpe Senior – although now a respectably married man – had concealed his passionate past. In addition to this, Zach's natural sister, a deaf and dumb mute of surpassing beauty had – by the purest fluke – been rescued from a circus by his tutor, Valentine Blyth. Collins's characters were well and truly intertwined. The close links established when Zack and scalpless Mat first fled from the police together held good to the end when Mat gave the young painter valuable buffalo-hunting experience in the new world.

Clive Holland described another bohemian encounter with the forces of law and order in *Marcelle of the Latin Quarter* (1900). Holland recounted a fracas in a packed bohemian restaurant where newcomers reeled in the smoke-filled atmosphere, and the waiter kept places for his customers at the end of a carving knife. Holland, in describing how the grisettes in the café quickly settled down as soon as the riot had subsided, successfully suggested the bohemian's natural buoyancy. Enjoyment of the present was all-important. His grisettes simply ripped the torn lace off their garments, patched up their faces in the café mirrors and, like cats after a fight, relaxed on the scene of battle.

Holland enlivened his novel with many slight vignettes of bohemian behaviour. He mentioned a beautiful model who would forget her commitments and stay in bed if the weather displeased her, and reported a fragment of conversation overheard in a bohemian restaurant revealing a refreshing lack of formality, or social restriction. A young man, having thoughtlessly informed his robust girl-friend that her magnificent proportions would be unsuitable for a religious study, received a characteristically uninhibited response. Holland's handsome English painter hero, George Brand, smiled and shook his head whenever people suggested that he should leave the distinctive district in which he lived, for he loved the Quartier too well – where else would he have found such romance (including his own eventual marriage to a girl whom he had brought up as his daughter), such good companionship and 'such freedom from conventional ideals'?

Bohemians, such as the much-publicised colony in the Latin Quarter, enjoyed all the escapist appeal associated with strange separatist groups. Thackeray expressed this idea when he introduced the word 'Bohemian' into the English language, and defined it as 'a gypsy of society, especially an artist, literary man, or actor, who leads a free, vagabond or irregular life and despises conventionalities'.[5] Other authors made similar comparisons, using the traditionally romantic picture of the nomadic gypsy as an attractively unrestricted adventurer to suggest similar qualities amongst artistic bohemians.

Watts-Dunton, fascinated by both unusual categories, closely connected bohemians and gypsies in his novel *Aylwin*. The swarthy hero was convinced that his unconventional artistic sensibilities were directly inherited from his gypsy grandmother. The imaginative appeal of the hero's childhood sweetheart was strengthened by her intimate knowledge of gypsy-lore, and when she disappeared Aylwin joined the gypsies to find her. While masquerading as a gypsy he accidentally stumbled on a relative whom he had never met before. The encounter between the two seeming strangers was significant. The hero's painter relative first made telling equations between the gypsy and the artist: the former, a member of 'a very limited aristocracy', was very like the artist who was similarly distinguished by orthodox talents and eccentricities. Watts-Dunton then showed that both types were equally beyond the pale. This painter 'of bohemian proclivities', the black sheep of his genteel clan, subsequently exploded with mirth on discovering he was being challenged to fight by none other than the heir-presumptive of his richly respectable clan – himself in the guise of a gypsy.

The artist, neither exhausted by monotonous drudgery, nor restricted by moral conservatism, seemed attractively free of conventional restraints and able to live a delightfully irregular, often nomadic, life. One such artist, who openly referred to himself as both a 'bohemian' and a 'vagabond' – and seemed to inherit the dashing charm traditionally linked with romantic non-conformist heroes such as gypsies, pirates and outlaws – was Felix Young, hero of Henry James's *The Europeans* (1878). His very name suggested his youthful, effervescent gaiety, brought out most successfully by James in a series of subtle Austen-like contrasts between him and other characters.

While his cynical sister considered that his 'capacity for taking rose-coloured views was such as to vulgarize the prettiest of tints',[6] she also realised that his sunny disposition was their greatest asset. When these two Europeans first landed in America, Felix's calculating sister sent him on ahead to captivate their unknown relatives with his ready charm. This particularly affected his newly-discover cousin Gertrude, whose reserved temperament provided a perfect foil for Felix's irrepressible *joie de vivre* from the moment she caught sight of him. James convinced the reader of Gertrude's boredom in preparation for the instant when, 'looking up, she beheld, as it seemed to her, the Prince Camaralazaman standing before her'.[7] Felix, dropped from the clouds like 'a king of dream', was a figure to satisfy any girl's romantic yearnings. James, by appearing to treat this provincial heroine with some degree of irony, was also able to caricature the attractions of the cosmopolitan painter. Felix seemed, in Gertrude's familiar world, to be a creature of fable.

James, after thus investing an artist with the glamour of *The Arabian Nights* – an association which Thackeray had already made in *The Newcomes* and Watts-Dunton was to make in *Aylwin* – continued to stress the imaginative appeal of this contemporary artist. His tales had the exciting unreality of fiction. Hearing him recount his escapades, Gertrude was reminded of the delight she gained from following the fortunes of *Nicholas Nickleby*. This visionary apparition – who, she had at first feared, might melt away as unexpectedly as he had come – was able to transport her from her restricted and monotonous existence to a 'fantastic world; she seemed to herself to be reading a romance that came out in daily numbers'.[8] The key to this romantic attraction lay, obviously, in the fact that he was an artist. His besotted cousin made it clear to anyone who would listen:

> She offered it to herself, as it were, by way of admonition and reminder; she repeated to herself at odd moments, in lonely places, that Felix was invested with this sacred character. Gertrude had never seen an artist before; she had only read about such people. They seemed to her a romantic and mysterious class, whose life was made up of those agreeable incidents that never happened to other persons.[9]

The other, ordinary, people in her circle also helped to emphasize the painter's attractions. When Mr Brand, a pompous young preacher, proposed to Gertrude she was unimpressed: 'It was supposed to be delightful for a woman to listen to such words, but these seemed to her flat and mechanical.' James deliberately stressed the contrast between this mechanical puritan and the spontaneous creator by a direct confrontation. Brand was walking in a joyless, meditative way when the artist called out to him on a 'sudden impulse'. Brand seemed static in comparison with the energetic painter, whose power was felt at the close of their interview when Brand, who had begun by loathing his rival, mellowed. He now appeared, against his better nature, to regard Felix with 'something akin to an acknowledgement of fascination', departing in a state of 'relaxed rigidity'.

Gertrude's father, like Brand, provided yet another foil to the romantic hero. Indeed, Felix was so accustomed to a threadbare and piratical life that he found Mr Wentworth's secure domestic routines a novelty. James used Mr Wentworth, and the rest of his combined family group, to provide Felix with an unpretentious, homely setting of the kind guaranteed to show up the artist's brilliant personality to the best advantage. Their comparatively undemonstrative, introverted characters eliminated serious rivalry, and made them doubly appreciative of the hero's gifts. They thought Felix 'remarkable'. Indeed the family provided the charming painter with an ideally attentive, lionizing audience; they were like a large sheet of clean, fine grained paper 'All ready to be washed over with effective splashes of water colour'.[11] The vivaciously colourful bohemian artist thus became the 'pivot and the centre' of this rustic circle, whose general limitations seemed only to enhance his own charm.

This element of lovable impudence which James created in Felix Young had also occurred earlier in Browning's poem 'Fra Lippo Lippi' which centred on a painter's fecklessness. Browning's friar, stopped by the night watch, revealed that he had let himself out of his room by a ladder made out of his bedding. His explanations, his knowing talk of the Prior's 'niece' and his half-apologetic, half-boasting masculine asides – 'I'm grown a man no doubt, I've broken bounds'[12] – were interspersed with serious remarks about his art and with snatches of song suggesting the essential innocence of his virile *joie de vivre*:

> *Flower o' the broom,*
> *Take away love and our life is a tomb!*
> *Flower o' the quince,*
> *I let Lisa go, and what good is life since?*
> *Flower o' the thyme. . . .*[13]

Another author fascinated by this artist's adventurous reputation was Margaret Vere Farrington whose history of the painter *Fra Lippo Lippi* (1890) was significantly entitled 'A Romance'. Like Browning, she tried to exploit his carefree nature, but with different results. Her limitations are interesting in this context because they are not only those of a minor talent but a specifically nineteenth century one. The age's general fascination with the bohemian artist, which had been alchemically refined by Browning's professional skill and detachment, was in this case simply reproduced in a cruder and popular form. Margaret Vere Farrington gushingly rehashed the century's uncritically sentimental desire for romantic escapism, without the aid of superior wit, irony or psychological understanding.

Browning had given his artist a wistful and rumbustious monologue which also created a convincingly realistic and likeable personality. He had made the most of his material by building his hero around a dramatic incident which both suggested the *risqué* nature of the 'monk's' secret adventures and revealed his bonhomie in his apt way of talking himself out of it. In contrast Margaret Vere Farrington was altogether less dexterous, although her message was clear enough:

> Life was no mere existence with Lippi. He loved light and air and mirth. To be in the great, real world, to feel its sunshine, its joy, its freedom, to chafe under the conventional, to break away and know the fascination of recklessness – this to him was life.[14]

She recorded how, as a cheeky urchin, he had been caught stealing the monks' cherries, and how he had later escaped from his monastery to sketch harvesters or revel in the chaos of the carnival, enjoying 'the mystery of masks, the flashing smiles, the tumult and confusion, the mirth, the mischief, the wild, the fantastic, the laughter, the whole exuberance of Italian city life'. This kind of impersonal reporting was bland in comparison with the immediacy of Browning's direct speech. It failed to catch the natural impression of irresponsible merriment Browning evoked by making his artist break into spontaneous song within the context of his interrogation.

Equally uninspiring were the large portions of the novel which were seen through appreciative female eyes, as, for example, when the reader is given Leucretzia Buti's admiring reactions to Lippi: 'She had never forgotten the acquiline outline of that artist's face – the dark eyes and the dreaming lids, the smile as frank as sunlight.' The high spot of the novel is Lippi's abduction of this tender novice. As one can judge from the sweet, infatuated sincerity of her tone, their nocturnal exchanges lacked the more amusingly worldly innuendoes inherent in Browning's confrontation between his painter-monk and the town guards, even though both these authors were trying, in their very different ways, to adapt historical sources to create a charismatic bohemian figure who would appeal to contemporary audiences.

In D'Arcy, too, one of the outstanding artists in *Aylwin,* charm was a dominant element; he was a superlatively romantic creation. Watts-Dunton described him in the usual extreme terms: everything about him pointed to an improbable, if magnetic personality. One infatuated admirer said that his musical voice seemed to delight and charm, not only her mind, but 'every nerve' in her body. D'Arcy's manner was unusual, to say the least. His spontaneous, if mercurial, spirits – which could reach unequalled heights of wit and poetic fancy – were reflected in his love of animals:

> The kind of amusement they can afford me is like none other. It is the self-consciousness of men and women that makes them, in a general way, intensely unamusing.[15]

Although D'Arcy spurned self-conscious society, he relished visits to the zoo. The unobjective, unscientific painter did not go there for any practical reasons connected with his art, but to watch, and to dramatise curious expressions and movements of the animals. His whimsical, irreverent nature delighted in Baptista Porta's theory that every human creature resembles one of the lower animals, and was perennially amused to find caricatures of his acquaintances in the animals he watched: with a fund of humour that was inexhaustible he went from cage to cage – giving each animal the name of some member of the Royal Academy.

As well as artists of superabundant energy, such as D'Arcy or the 'successful comedian' Felix Young, there were more soulful creators. Lewis Seymour, for example, speaking of his artistic aspirations in *A Modern Lover,* could utter words in a 'half-melancholy way, which gave them, above their meaning, that charm of youthful sadness so dear to youthful hearts'.[16] Moore made a former bohemian friend, who had been struck by the painter's potent attractions, describe him as one of those creatures who exercise a strange power over all with whom they come in contact, a contact that is purely physical yet acting equally on the more spirited as on the more gross natures, and leading us independently of our judgement. How can we blame the women for going mad after him.[17]

This artist's intoxicating personality was bolstered by a professional need for a continuous stream of attractively pliable models. He enjoyed a richly sensual life: his profession was a passport to pleasure. Moore exploited the tradition which made the study of the nude model an utter necessity for the artist. In a moralistic age it established a cover for otherwise *risqué* subject matter, and provided the fictional artist with an excuse for a series of titillating adventures.

Amongst Seymour's varied conquests was a pretty young servant girl. He explained to her that his only commission, his only chance of fending off destitution, called for a Venus, and 'No painter ever painted a nude figure without a model'. Gwynnie was torn between her sense of 'duty' – that of saving the artist's life 'as Lady Godiva had saved Coventry' – and her concept of chastity, which made her baulk at the idea of thus appearing naked before a man. After lengthy soul-searching she finally decided to sit for the painting of Venus:

> Bravely she threw the shawl away, and showed her arms and bosom. Then there was a pause. She held her skirts irresolutely about her, until at last, with a supreme effort, she threw them aside.
>
> If she could have stood as she was the worst would have been over, but Lewis had to tell her how to stand, to place her arms, her legs. . . .[18]

Moore was obviously more interested in indicating a sexually provocative situation than in discussing the artist professionally. Whereas he made the point that Lewis, after luring this desperately shy and extremely pretty girl into his studio, 'had' to tell her exactly how to arrange her body, Moore – in his time an enlightened champion of Degas – did not think it relevant to expand on the objective nature of her pose. The reader learnt nothing of its origins or originality, its structural relation to the composition as a whole, nor of the aesthetic challenges the artist saw in it; Moore made no use of opportunities to discuss how an artist could stylise linear arabesques, or portray arrested movement realistically, or use linear effects to induce sculptural qualities. Gwynnie's intense inner debate may well have been introduced as moral camouflage to make the episode more acceptable to contemporary pundits. In Moore's later twentieth century version of the story her reactions were less artifically and spiritually melodramatic. In a pre-Lawrentian, bowdlerising century, when love was synonymous with affection, physical descriptions were guarded to the point of nonexistence.[19] Nineteenth century authors contented themselves with the discreet mention of rarely glimpsed parts of the anatomy or avoided direct description, by relaying the usually shocked reaction of one character to the sight of another's naked body. For the most part, the then current climate of impractical restraint has made these manoeuvres, as in the example from Moore, seem as ludicrously coy to contemporary taste, as the unimaginatively explicit works of the present day would have appeared vulgarly dull to nineteenth century readers.

The amorous adventures of the hero of Kipling's *The Light that Failed* were less coy than most. This painter not only travelled beyond the normal European circuit but found particularly exotic company *en route*. Kipling, making fairly blatant sexual innuendoes, naïvely implied that the more foreign a woman seemed the more earthy and immoral her actions would be. He linked this artist hero with

> a sort of Negroid-Jewess-Cuban; with morals to match. She couldn't read or write, and she didn't want to, but she used to come down and watch me paint, and the skipper didn't like it, because he was paying her passage and had to be on the bridge occasionally.[20]

Hearing someone singing 'Annabel Lee', Dick Haldar was again reminded of his early working methods: 'the rough words that beat like the blows of the waves on the bows of the rickety boat from Lima in the days when Dick was mixing paints, making love, drawing devils and angels on the half deck, and wondering whether the next minute would bring the captain's knife between his shoulder blades'.[21]

Hardy in *The Well-Beloved* (1892) made a virtual caricature of the artistic libertine: he described the affections of his sculptor hero, Jocelyn Pierston, as 'migratory'. Pierston welcomed fascinated women from all social levels, from the lowest to the Countess of Chanelcliffe, and all physical types, from the frailest to a most sturdily Junoesque Miss Bencomb. He showed neither prejudice nor partiality:

> To his Well-Beloved he had always been faithful; but she had many different embodiments. Each individuality known as Lucy, Jane, Flora, Evangeline or what-not, had been merely a transient condition of her. He did not recognise this as an excuse or as a defence, but as a fact simply.[22]

The bacchanalian practices and personal eccentricities distinguishing the artist as an exceptional being also brought him into disrepute. Abundant appreciation of a romantic artist was usually matched by equally intense disapproval. One of the earliest examples of this occurs in *St. Ronan's Well* (1823) where Sir Walter Scott made a rare excursion into contemporary life, intending to imitate the manners of his time and show contemporary foibles.[23] The ladies and gentlemen of St Ronan's Well, most of whom were on the lookout for scandal and amusement, illustrated Scott's maxim that no intimacy can be supposed more close for the time, and more transient in its endurance, than 'that which is attached to a watering place acquaintance'.

One of Scott's opening gambits was to exploit the hypocrisy of this community by recounting their altering attitudes to his artistic hero Francis Tyrrel. Lady Penelope Penfeather led the hunt for Tyrrel, after accidentally discovering, and admiring, one of his sketches. He was invited to take 'Nectar and Ambrosia' with her and her entourage and was stalked, while out walking, by excited ladies referring to him as the Unknown and the Misanthrope. The tension which had been built up around this mysterious figure was dashed, however, when they actually met him. Instead of the eccentric genius they had fondly imagined, they were shocked to discover a suave character as well-dressed and as well-spoken as any gentleman. The writer exposed the absurdity of their romantic delusions about the hero as the company quickly tried to adapt their behaviour to suit an equal. Playing, cynically, with their prejudices Scott then showed a second change of face: they insulted Tyrrel, whom they no longer considered a gentleman, on learning that he used his skill in drawing to earn his living. Vain Lady Penelope, no longer an avid hostess or coy flirt, symbolized this general reaction. Embarrassed, she felt she must retreat from the 'easy footing on which he had contrived to place himself' to one which might express patronage on her part and dependence on Tyrrel's. Her subsequent condescension proved that the handsome and talented hero had been rejected on snobbish, economic grounds.

Throughout this story, Scott made Tyrrel a paragon of polite and dignified behaviour, always treating him with serious sympathy, while reserving his satire for the complacent fools who surrounded his unlucky hero. He satirised Lady Penelope's dilemma. Attracted by Tyrrel's appearance and piqued by his indifference, she felt obliged to disown the man she had so recently lionised. She now formally announced to the assembled ladies that Tyrrel was, in short, ordinary, and unsuited for their society. Scott, playing deftly with female jealousy, left her open to attack. Her rival, Lady Binks, commented bitchily that her ladyship's swan had proved a poor goose:

'My swan, dearest Lady Binks! I really do not know how I have deserved the appropriation.'

'Do not be angry, my dear Lady Penelope; I only mean, that for a fortnight and more you have spoken constantly of this Mr Tyrrel, and all dinner time you spoke *to* him.'

The fair company began to collect around, at hearing the word 'dear' so often repeated in the same brief dialogue, which induced them to expect sport, and, like the vulgar on a similar occasion, to form a ring for the expected combatants.[24]

Dickens, like Scott, showed that the artist's social position was a tenuous one. Gowan, the unpleasant painter in *Little Dorrit* (1855-7), chose his profession to spite some rich relatives from whom he had expected to benefit. His mother, an arrogant snob, tried to mollify the implicit disgrace of his becoming an artist by explaining apologetically to a friend that their family had never yet 'gone beyond an amateur'. This sort of antagonism helped to establish the artist as a vulnerable romantic hero, misunderstood by the more mundane masses. Such criticism prevented the escapist fantasies connected with the artist from seeming too unbearably idyllic, as in *Aylwin,* where in his impressionable youth Hal Aylwin found the gypsies and a gypsy-like artist unusual and romantic, a rosy view which was quite sternly countered by his middle-aged, middle-class mother's conviction that such bohemians were untrustworthy citizens.

The unreliably bohemian associations of artists and artistic life were also recorded in *Vanity Fair* (1847-8), where Becky Sharp climbed vivaciously from virtual obscurity to dubious and transitory social honours. Her immorality was hereditary. Her father had been an artist.

When she first attempted to trap a husband, to gain some security, the man's parents reacted with typical misgiving. His mother thought that her son would demean himself by a marriage with an artist's daughter, until she was forcibly reminded that she herself had married as a grocer's daughter, and her now prosperous middle-class husband had then been only an impoverished stockbrokers' clerk. Her more tolerant spouse praised Becky's good humour and cleverness, and condoned the idea of a marriage, for his stupid son seemed such easy game that it would be safer if he were legally bound before returning to India. Even an artist's daughter would be preferable to a 'black Mrs Sedley, and a dozen of mahogany grand-children'.[25] Despite his good will, Becky's suitor was scared off by an officious young snob who, thinking he would marry into the same family, shunned the embarrassment of such a socially suspect sister-in-law. Fulfilling such fears she later degenerated into a recognisably seedy adventuress, living for a time in an unsavoury hotel frequented by vagabonds.

Through disregard for conventional norms, the individualistic artist upset polite society, particularly its male members who often seemed jealous of his freedom and sexual successes. He had a flamboyant urge to shock. He looked odd, wore eccentric clothes, and behaved in an extremely unconventional manner. The antithesis of Uriah Heep, he completely lacked an ' 'umble', ingratiating manner which the more tedious members of the establishment had grown to expect. The artist was either naturally oblivious of social norms and conventions, or else he remarked them mainly in order to mock them.

A typical example of an artist who could combine tactlessness and frivolity so as to antagonise the more staid members of society occurred in Anthony Trollope's *Barchester Towers* (1857). Trollope had first shown how closely Ethelbert Stanhope adhered to the general artistic pattern. He had startling eyes, flowing hair, a voice of peculiar sweetness and wore extraordinary costumes. He was psychologically as well as visually rooted in the bohemian tradition: his career to date, both professional and amorous, had been decidedly experimental. He had essayed a variety of creeds, professions and admirers. His attitude to society at large was easy going. 'With a bishop indeed who thought much of his own dignity it was possible that he might fail, but hardly with a young and pretty woman.'[26]

Trollope's famed encounter between the bishop of Barchester

and his wife, Dr and Mrs Proudie, and this precocious young artist showed how the latter's aimiable approaches could surprise the pompous. The artist's antics were particularly disastrous because they disrupted the Proudies' first public reception. Hospitality was to be gauged in accordance with rank, curates and country vicars receiving cheaper alcohol than the dignitaries of the close: 'Marsala at 20s. a dozen did very well for the exterior supplementary tables in the corner'.[27] Bertie, however, did not perceive the need for any such gradations.

The august bishop, who had originally mistaken the artist's outlandish appearance for that of an extraordinary Italian servant or aristocrat, was increasingly mortified by the young man's democratic manner. The artist's informal *sangfroid* – which prompted him to inquire if Dr Proudie knew anything about the Jews – struck the bishop as presumptuous insolence. His fellow clergy were equally dismayed: 'Dignified clergymen of sixty years of age could not condescend to discuss such a matter with a young man with such clothes and such a beard.'[28] Trollope, in emphasising the way in which they reacted to Bertie, accepting his unorthodox appearance as an indistinguishable part of his unorthodox approach, indicated that the close links between the artist's visual and mental characteristics were just as strong in a negative situation as they had been in a positive one. Just as, to an admiring eye, the picturesque impression an artist created spelled instant romance, so, to a more critical observer, identical trappings produced immediate rancour. Similarly, in *Maud Skillicorne's Penance* (1858) Mary Jackson showed how bohemian locks and unusual clothes could be condemned as a kind of inverted snobbery in those whose extraordinary garments and beastly behaviour were both manifestations of the same saucy attitudes:

> Take them as a class – the young ones, I mean, – – are they refined? Are they elegant, spiritualised persons? No – but the very reverse: they're gross in their habits and tastes, snobbish in their appearance aping foreigners in wearing dirty moustaches and antediluvian cloaks, instead of keeping their faces clean and wearing well-cut coats; they smoke till their brains are dry, and drink till they are moist again, when they see tipsy visions of houris. . . .[29]

The full effects of artistic licence were carefully developed as Trollope continued his account of the Proudies' party. In an atmosphere of mutual incomprehension, increasing familiarity bred growing contempt: the initial bewilderment he had caused on entering the palace, culminated in a dramatic encounter with his hostess at the very centre of the reception. Trollope convincingly distilled the mounting irritation generated by Ethelbert's unorthodox behaviour into pure hatred.

While the bishop's wife practiced graceful condescension in the main salon, Bertie thoughtfully moved a sofa to provide comfort for his sister – a paralysed nymphomaniac. The artist, like a novice in a dodgem car, accidentally encountered his hostess as he pushed the sofa across the floor. It continued on its way accompanied by her more spectacular finery: 'As Juno may have looked at Paris in Mount Ida; so did Mrs Proudie look on Ethelbert Stanhope when he pushed the leg of the sofa into her lace train.'[30] Rushing to the disaster area, and throwing himself on one knee in front of the wrathful lady, he seemed to try to extricate her from the furniture. Trollope created a ludicrously histrionic scene, as though Ethelbert was melodramatically 'imploring pardon from a goddess'. The pompous matron, proudly attempting stoicism, dramatically demanded that he unhand her ruined garment. To which the kneeling painter replied: 'I'll fly to the looms of the fairies to repair the damage, if you'll only forgive me.' Mrs. Proudie was furious, thinking this allusion to the fairies was a 'direct mockery, and intended to turn her into ridicule'.[31] The frivolous artist had utterly antagonized this paragon of polite behaviour, now on the edge of a violent screaming fit.

Nick Dormer, the painter hero of Henry James's *The Tragic Muse* (1890), realized that the creative bohemian was socially suspect; for he was neither 'fish nor fowl'. Charles Lee, author of *Cynthia in the West* (1900), put his hero in a similar vacuum. Forester, an obscure genius who had been discovered behind a provincial counter, spent a time in a Cornish coastal village. Although the poor and hardworking villagers were charmed by his personality, artists were generally considered foolish creatures, and the painterly process a lazy game:

> Ah! Well, for doing nothing in p'tickler, if that's your trade, you couldn't have pitched on a better place. Artists! And they call it working! I've seed them at it. One dab, two dabs, jump back a yard, head on shoulder and eyes scriffed up. Jump for'ard agin, rub out what you've done. Off hat, set down, light your pipe, puff, puff, for ten minutes. Up agin, stick your

thumb in the hole av the machine, dab, dab, twiggle, splash.'[32]

Art, to such people, was an impractical indulgence. Similarly, the villagers who were forced to risk their lives at sea trying to get enough to eat, could not accept Forester as one of themselves: the kind of man who went out in a boat simply for pleasure was a mystery to them. The same point had been made in *Guenn* (1884), where Blanche Willis Howard described an artists' colony based on a fishing village, showing how a conservative rural community could consider artists alien beings. To practically-minded Breton sailors the activities of the able-bodied painter hero were simply incomprehensible. He was either a madman or a fool 'with perhaps a strong inclination towards the latter'.[33]

Lee, however, stressed that his hero was alienated from both rich and poor alike. Forester's respect for the brave, hardworking local people, and his sympathetic links with them, partial though they were, helped to distance him from his more snobbish companions. A significant incident occurred when Lee described an encounter between some of the hero's friends, whose interest in painting was certainly less consuming than his own, and Tregurda's fishing folk. The latter were engaged in the serious business of heaving in their boats, while the former, with detached interest, stood discussing the pictorial possibilities of the scene. Lee, who later stirred up class feeling with some success – 'Yah! Artisses, is ut? Yah! Let wan av 'ee come outside, and I'll make a woodcut on his face!' – stressed that the very different occupations of the two groups illustrated their social differences. After the artist helped the fishermen, he returned to his elegant if impractical friends. The marks of tar on his shirt resulting from his helping to haul in the boat struck his hostess as ostentatiously vulgar: it was a 'whiff of fried fish in her rose-perfumed atmosphere'.[34]

The disapproval which orthodox people, such as Lee's Mrs Wilmington, felt for the artist – a mixture of jealousy and alienation – was immediately intensified when the artist actually sought a bride from within the ranks of the establishment. Society took far greater exception to a permanent alliance with an outsider than to a mere acquaintanceship with him. It was all very well to come across a romantic artist now and again, but that was a far cry from actually welcoming the same careless, egotistical, bohemian spendthrift to your own hearth, and gladly handing him your precious daughter, especially if she had been lovingly reared to further, rather than diminish the family fortunes.

This theme was developed at length in Thackeray's *The New-comes,* where Clive Newcome, the artist hero, found that social hostility increased when he tried to marry a banker's daughter. Thackeray indicated that this hostility was both unfair and unfounded by firmly indicating that Clive was a paragon of good behaviour. His follies were simply those of youth. He was securely established, at this stage of his career, in the jovial bohemian pattern of a blithe, spirited, carefree young adventurer. As a young art student he easily learnt the ways of artists who 'open oysters with their yataghans, toast muffins on their rapiers, and fill their venice glasses with half and half. . . .'

In a chapter which he entitled, significantly, 'Youth and Sunshine', Thackeray took care to show the complete lack of calculation in Clive's nature. The writer made this ardent and impulsive character devote his youth to an innocent delight in living. All the sensual beauties of art and nature, 'animate or inanimate (the former especially), were welcomed with a gusto, and delight whereof colder temperaments are incapable'.[35] The idyllically happy young man 'as yet went through the world harmless: no giant waylaid him as yet'.[36] However, Thackeray's repetition of 'as yet' produced a warning effect: just as the hero of a fairytale would inevitably bump into some menacing giant, so Clive's carefree existence was bound to be jeopardised.

At first Thackeray made his criticism of Clive's chosen career amusing: it revealed the ignorance of the speaker without hindering the painter. Major Pendennis, for example, an essentially good-natured old bore who had no power to affect Clive's future, registered surprise in bold military language, reflecting that in his time a man would as soon have thought of making his son a pastrycook as an artist, by gad. In monitoring the reactions of Clive's closest friends, however, Thackeray employed a more lethal irony. The young man's father – although happily prepared to tolerate, and pay for, a passing interest in the arts – could not fathom Clive's desire to become a painter. This was a situation which the writer explained in general terms: 'The Muse of Painting is a lady whose social station is not altogether recognised with us as yet. The polite world permits a gentleman to amuse himself with her; but to take her for better or worse. . . ." Thoughts of marriage aroused the interference of Clive's cousin Ethel, who began to exert her influence on the misguided young man, as in a coy letter to his father, in which she hoped Clive would not be allowed to sell his pictures: 'An artist, an organist, a pianist, all

these are very good people, but, you know, not *de notre monde.'*
The vulgar world inhabited by artists and their disreputable associates also included writers, for Ethel, on becoming increasingly
virulent, jibed at Clive's 'low radical literary' friends. This was a
telling jab. Thackeray (who, after all, lived by selling his own
work, and made an unworldly author both a close friend of the
hero and occasional narrator of his novel) may well have been
drawing sympathy for Clive's stigmatised position from his own
personal experience.[39]

Thackeray's passages describing the amorous artist's dejection
when he was repeatedly refused admittance to visit Ethel while a
stupid young Marquis continually received welcoming invitations
always stressed the material reasons for the latter's popularity.
Lady Kew, Ethel's grandmother, was determined to marry her to
the 'best' man: if a richer suitor presented himself it would be
Farintosh's turn to find that Lady Kew was 'not at home'. As it
turned out, Lady Kew's own death prompted Ethel to jilt Lord
Farintosh. The dowager left her fortune to her grand-daughter,
as a congratulatory prize for securing the Marquis's ample means,
but as she suddenly died before the happy event had actually
taken place Ethel no longer needed to marry money. She had it
already. The final chapter implied, with Thackeray's customary
irony that, touchingly, she did marry the now wearied and
widowed painter, but he did suggest that this would never have
been possible if she had not first secured a fortune.

In *The Tragic Muse* (1890) James also used marriage as the
focus for the antagonism levelled against his artist hero, and as
the supreme test of his social viability. Nicholas Dormer, a versatile young man equally adept at painting and public speaking, was
frequently berated by more serious friends and relatives for dally-
ing with the arts.

Throughout this novel James contrasts two kinds of career. His
hero's desire to paint is constantly disturbed by others' efforts to
push him into parliament. His father's old friend, for example,
promised Nick vast wealth on condition he married Julia Dallow,
whose estates conveniently dominated the local constituency, and
who would be sure to wean him from the pencil and the brush –
which were 'not the weapons of a gentleman'. As a natural
politician (without a sense of humour) she, too, felt that a
gentleman could do no more than 'aspire to serve the state'. She
was sure that, in selecting him as the means to making herself a
Prime Minister's wife, she could pay him no greater tribute.
James used the unsteady relationship between Julia and Nick, as

Thackeray had used that between Clive and Ethel, to explore their different attatudes – showing that as they grew closer emotionally their antagonistic ideals became sharper and their distaste for the other's philosophy less controlled. Nick, gaining the reader's approbation by examining his beliefs with greater honesty, argued that the arts provided an equally if not more valuably idealistic career, which would allow him to develop his personal talents. James made him a mouthpiece for liberal albeit cynical views. The activities of the public man were, for Nick, based on a cultivation of the crowd, a misappropriation of power, and a shallow appetite for fame.

Ironically, although Nick had originally been steered towards a conventional marriage, by the time he came to accept the idea, showing he was even willing to take up public life as a sop to his future wife, she began to rebel. The more this conventional woman recognised his innate love of art the more she instinctively distrusted him. James showed this very effectively by crystallising her emotions in a single scene: she unexpectedly discovered Nick, now her official Member of Parliament, absorbedly painting a tempestuous actress in an informal bohemian atmosphere. To her shocked disapproval was added the clear realization that here, as nowhere else, he was completely in his element. Her veneer of superficial toleration cracked. Subsequently repulsing him, her bitterly resentful remarks illustrated the depth of her abhorrence for the inglorious subject which bigoted personal experience had turned to loathing:

> 'You're an artist: you are, you are!' Julia cried, accusing him passionately. . . . 'It's all right for you, but it won't do for me. . . . I was drenched with it before.' These last words, as they broke forth, were attended with a quick blush; so that Nick could as quickly discern in them the uncalculated betrayal of an old irritation, an old shame almost – her late husband's flat inglorious taste for pretty things, his indifference to every chance to play a public part. This had been the humiliation of her youth, and it was indeed a perversity of fate that a new alliance should contain for her even an oblique demand for the same spirit of accommodation, impose on her the same secret bitterness of the same concessions.[40]

Despite her passion for Dormer, the serious implications of accepting him as a permanent partner forced her to consider her own ultimate values, and, having done so, to realize that he was unsuitable, almost polluted, matrimonial material. The establishment – which she represented so forcefully – was indeed constitutionally allergic to the artist.

Similarly, Du Maurier brought his artist hero, Little Billee, to the verge of marriage and on each occasion brought him into direct conflict with the fixed views of polite society in ways which proved his incompatible unorthodoxy. The first time, when he wanted to marry the kind and beautiful model Trilby – a variation on the usual theme of an artist trying to marry a social superior – he showed that contemporary standards, both moral and material, meant nothing to him. When his limited middle class relatives succeeded in ruthlessly getting rid of Trilby, because of her low parentage and sexual experiences, he was filled with resentment. He pronounced himself immune to social stigma, especially as he had planned to live with Trilby in the Barbizon forest where there was a colony of isolated artists: 'Who cares for *their* social position, I should like to know . . . or that of their wives.'[41] Like Clive Newcome and Nicholas Dormer before him, this fictional artist was sickened by what he considered society's unnatural stranglehold over the more democratically idealistic standards which he felt were represented by beauty, art and love.

The second time Little Billee considered matrimony Du Maurier again brought him up against similarly inflexible and complacent attitudes, and again made him react against the morals of the establishment. He went home to sit with an 'old friend' (a dog), looking wistfully out over the sea, and considering the possibility of marrying 'Sweet Alice', the sugary daughter of the local parson.

Her parentage posed another problem of conformity for the independent artist, who found it hard to stomach church dogma, and considered her father a biased reactionary:

> he must willy-nilly go on believing, or affecting to believe, just as he is told, *word for word* or else goodbye to his wife and children's bread and butter, his own preferment, perhaps even his own gentility – that gentility of which his Master thought so little, and he and his are apt to think so much – with possibly the Archbishopric of Canterbury at the end of it, the *bâton de maréchal* that lies in every clerical knapsack.[42]

This spiritual guide (whose flair for business was later proved by a lucky speculation in stout) thought far more of sporting country squires than 'of all the painters in Christendom'. His disagreement with Little Billee over the significance of Darwin's *The Origin of Species* proved that the romantic artist and his previously projected father-in-law, the conservative parson, were utterly opposed on all fundamental questions.

Du Maurier's novel was a classic statement of artistic attitudes not only because of the way in which he manipulated his descriptions of bohemian life to include a carefree disregard for convention but also because he expressed an idealistic stance against materialism. In summing up a typically bohemian hero, like Little Billee, depictions of his abandoned gaiety should be balanced by accounts of the ways in which the painter tried to dismiss mediocrity. Du Maurier, who, in a festive passage like those quoted at the beginning of the chapter, made this painter laugh until he cried as unsober guests straddled their chairs to gallop round him, also directed his expressive emotionalism to more serious channels, as when, emitting sensitive little shrieks and yells, he took a stand against social hypocrisy, declaring:

An artist's life should be *away* from the world – over and above all that meanness and paltriness . . . all in his work.[43]

The Vulnerable Artist and His
Supernatural Attributes

... 'the effeminate brute; how I should like to kick him'.[1]

The kind of antagonism the artist encountered socially he also encountered in the sphere of his work. He found that the people he met in professional contexts, with the exception of certain connoisseurs and friends, were unsympathetic to his aims and ambitions. Characteristically ignorant attitudes of this nature appear in *Magdalen Wynard*: or, *The Provocations of a Pre-Raphaelite* (1871) by Averil Beaumont, who produced a tame version of the painter hero in Bernard Longley. Longley has no particularly odd or unusual associates, no deep-seated antipathy to work, and no grave problems when he thinks of marrying a rich girl. Yet, as the title indicates, he still is, or manages to feel, provoked. His other troubles are so minor that, by a process of elimination, his annoyances are necessarily professional.

They are essentially those of exasperation against unjustified interferences. For example, when a collector bought one of his works and then decided that it should be altered to suit his own taste, Longley's creative pride was hurt to the quick: 'He does not surely suppose that paying money for it makes it his!' Insensitive buyers occurred in *The Three Brothers,* where Mrs Oliphant created the archetypal bourgeois patron in Mr Rich, and in *Miss Brown* (1884), where Vernon Lee satirized a presumptuous collector whose cultural largesse reflected her husband's success 'in the currant trade'. A similar source of annoyance was provided by a northern dealer, from Sheffield, whose precise demands included a request for a series of studies which would be greener than those he had in stock. Longley was equally resentful of his conservative uncle's interference over his sales. Marmaduke Wynard sternly disapproved of the publicity Longley won in reviews, for it was 'most indecent' to receive such attention and advertisement unless one was something really low, like a chiropodist. Apart from the press Longley sought publicity through the Royal Academy. Like Mallard, Gissing's painter hero in *The Emancipated* (1890), whose mill-owning patron had taught him two things of importance, a belief that great work could only be done in landscape and a 'limitless contempt for the Royal Academy', Longley complained bitterly of unfair treatment from people without any true understanding of his particular problems. When the landscapist's laborious processes were combined to create a picture it was inevitably 'declined without thanks' by a jury of conservative figure painters or some man who had dipped his brush in bitumen all his life and cared nothing for the delicacy of colour.

Averil Beaumont's straightforward presentation of Longley's moody complaints is characteristic in itself, for nineteenth century authors took it for granted that every artist was open to provocation. Her extraordinary lack of irony, let alone cynicism, is part and parcel of an overall trend. Writers, perhaps dramatizing their own creative struggles, ignored countless opportunities to poke fun at their self-indulgent heroes, and concentrated on painstakingly portraying more serious artists as ill-used victims. Equally characteristic were her references to a Royal Academician as someone whose actual powers had no relation to his boorishly condescending mentality. The Royal Academy was introduced as an emotive symbol of the kind of dominating prejudice enveloping artists.

Young bohemian apprentices whose antics had so often revolved around ingenious ways of making good scanty funds and material needs by borrowing a friend's money or stealing his trousers, grew grimmer as they became older and the attractions of this student survival-system began to pall. Artists tired of wondering frivolously where the next meal was coming from and railed against the system with increasing force. Robert Barnabus Brough, in *Marston Lynch* (1860), gave an account of the embittering effects of poverty and alcohol on artistic aspiration in 'backslum' bohemia:

The Bohemian is improvident because he is poor. . . . He only receives money fitfully and uncertainly – often at long intervals; and your starving man is always intemperate. . . . If he has a nominal home to go to, the door is frequently guarded by a griffin in the shape of an unpaid landlady; or, still worse, it is the abode of beings who will close his harassed day by a repetition (if silent, all the less bearable) of the reproaches that the world is ever casting in his teeth for opportunities wasted and successes not achieved. . . .[2]

Margaret Roberts, in *The Atelier du Lys; or, An Art Student in the Reign of Terror* (1876), significantly equated artistic individualism with the aims of the French Revolution: art having, to a certain extent, shared the birth of new ideas in France, sharing in the struggles of these troubled times while 'shaking off traditional chains, and animated with fresh vigour'. The French desire for liberty and a just appreciation of merit was demonstrated in microcosm within the Louvre itself, which had formerly been a formal bastion of inherited power but now became a rowdy creative centre. Margaret Roberts summed up this transformation by saying that the 'Louvre had gone through its own special revolution since the days when a Court inhabited it; an aristocracy still dwelt there, but it was an aristocracy of talent, often as pitilessly exclusive and overbearing as that of birth'.[3] A former aristocrat, who was one of those to use the 'Atelier du Lys' found that the Revolution had indirectly liberated him, for he had learnt to be an artist while in exile – studying in England – an occupation which would have been considered impossible for one of his birth under the old régime. The principal artist, a temperate republican called Balmat, studied under the talented painter David, now seen, significantly, as the new monarch of the Louvre. It would have been as unthinkable for an agonised, revolutionary artist to have come to terms with the Royal Academy as for Hamlet to have settled down to happy domesticity in Elsinore. Just as nineteenth century authors were interested in the fictional artist as a romantic hero rather than as a means of exploring contemporary aesthetics, so they used the Royal Academy as a contrasting symbol of obtuse officialdom and reactionary thought, rather than explaining its professional aims. Where the romantic artist was seen as an isolated and essentially idealistic being the Academy was scorned as an organized branch of what would now be called a branch of the Establishment. The romantic artist generally resented the Academy for its two-fold power as a teaching and exhibiting body. Such controlling activities ran contrary to romantic concepts of creative genius. Where, for example, the sensitive artist was praised for his imaginative vision, the Academy might in passing be abused for presuming to lay down rules about how art could be taught. Romantic ideas about inspiration, as in Keats's theory of 'Negative Capability', were opposed to theories of authoritarian instruction. Talent was not accrued in ordered stages according to the principles which Dickens gave Gradgrind in Coketown where nature was as strongly bricked out as gasses were bricked in, in a school which considered 'taste' synonymous with 'fact'. It was significant that Kipling who seemed, like many of his contemporaries, attracted by the relative freedom of the French atelier system, praised a teacher in *The Light that Failed* for possessing encouraging rather than didactic qualities: Kami, who spent most of his time simply saying 'Continuez mes enfants,' taught by what Kipling described as 'personal magnetism'.

This romantic attitude to inspiration is illustrated in *Limitations,* where E. F. Benson described his sculptor hero at work on an impromptu piece:

The figure was charmingly fresh, and had a certain masterly look about it which showed through all its defects. Tom lost his temper with it twenty times a day, and twice crushed the whole thing into a shapeless mass, was sorry he had ever done so, and set to work again. He had never had any teaching, but there was no doubt that he had got artist's fingers, which are of more importance than many lessons. Lessons you can obtain in exchange for varying sums of money, and artist's fingers are a free gift, but they are given to the few.[4]

It was particularly apt that this untaught youth should have been making a wax figure inspired by a recent view of a cricketer – a freshly spontaneous subject on which the Academy would have frowned, because it kept its younger students on a strict, anachronistic régime, characterised by repetitive drawing from dusty Greek casts. Whereas Tom, who equated genius with the startling progress of a shooting star, spurned such dry, orderly methods – as can be surmised from the amount of emotional energy he expended on his work in terms of fury and regret. But the most revealing remark in this passage is about the origins of Tom's ability, the intuitive skill of his fingers, a 'free gift', not something to be acquired by following a doctrinaire academic formula.

The Academy indirectly caused much hardship by advocating the supremacy of history painting, since the production of large finished canvases of this kind could be arduous, expensive and often depressing for those who, after marathon efforts, found themselves left with unsaleable white elephants. Gandish's 'Boadicea' in *The Newcomes* was a case in point. Similarly, Mrs Oliphant in *The Three Brothers,* emphasised the dangers associated with 'Edith finding the body of Harold': artists attempting this particular subject had gone down like flies.

Two lucky breaks with 'The Finding of Moses' and 'The Abdication of Charles V' soon decided Simpson Crow, a painter whom Charles Lever included in *The Martins of Cro' Martin* (1847), that nothing else could be 'the subject of high art'. Yet Lever showed that, even for the adept, 'The Abdication of Charles V' was still a considerable challenge. The stresses and strains connected with this complex undertaking told on the distraught and dissipated painter – described by his kinder critics as a 'weak-brained enthusiast . . . born to failure' – who not only had to plan his painting but to find props and arrange sittings while contending with a large and unruly cast. An old Irish servant, when questioned as to his exact role, displayed a typically unco-operative attitude:

'Arrah, who knows?' said he, querulously. 'At first I was to be somebody's mother that was always cryin'; but they weren't pleased with the way I done it; and then they made me a monk, and after that they put two hundred weight of armour on me, and made me lean my head on my arm as if I was overcome; and faith, so I was, for I dropped off to sleep, and fell into a pot of varnish, and I'm in disgrace now, glory be to God! and I only hope it may last.'[5]

The underlying frustrations of history painting were similarly betrayed by his patroness's dog, a savage bloodhound which, objecting to the way he was marshalled during a particular sitting, bit the painter in the rump.

Individualism was similarly enraged by the Academy's presumption in judging and censoring those works admitted for their annual Exhibition, the contemporary artist's best opportunity for display and sales.[6] Fictional artists frequently vented deep despair at lack of public recognition and blamed the Academy, which was variously attacked for mediocre, fashionable taste, for a conservative lack of enterprise, for practising a 'closed-shop' attitude in favour of its own members. Thus Gissing made an erudite woman in *The Emancipated* (1890) automatically link genuine artistic integrity with a lack of success at the Academy. Speaking of the hero, she said: 'His pictures are neglected . . . but people who understand them say they have great value. If he has anything accepted by the Academy, it is sure to be hung out of sight.'[7]

The crowds who flocked to these much publicised exhibitions revealed their ignorance at every turn – as Moore explained in *A Modern Lover*. A fashionable lady, obviously attracted to an exhibition because it was a social event, expressed her approbation for Lewis Seymour's skill: 'how beautifully he paints satin'. Mr Seymour's pretty paintings, attuned to the pseudo classical style approved by the Academy, not only showed great taste in the arrangement of dresses but observed the principal art of portraiture – that of flattering his subjects. As one of his erudite viewers observed, 'what's the use of having an ugly picture?' Parts of the arena were given over to ritual blood-letting: a daringly unorthodox painting was 'not difficult to find; it was surrounded by a jeering crowd; ladies, critics and artists pressed forward smiling and curious to see, and then retired shaking with laughter'.[8] One critic in particular, appropriately named Ripple, reiterated all the latest aesthetic jargon. Such critics seemed to Frazer, the man whose painting was ridiculed, to be purely negative. He regarded them as fools and time-servers. His vulnerability to criticism, or rather the bitterness he felt, even when his work had been hung in the Royal Academy, recalled a passage in *The Tallants of Barton* where Joseph Hatton made another talented painter reflect on similar suffering. He remembered his years of patient industry and toil: 'the pictures returned from the Academy unhung; the adverse criticism when at last they were hung.'[9]

Moore, in providing unsympathetic images of the crowd and its spokesmen as they thronged through the precincts of the Academy buildings, had shown that there was no real distinction between the taste and attitudes represented by the Academy and the views and behaviour of the public. The Academicians by isolating vulnerably original works, or placing them in obviously inferior positions, encouraged intellectual philistinism.

Margaret Oliphant stated in *The Three Brothers* (1870) that she was not attempting to describe those successful artists 'against whom the Academy has no power' but the unfortunate younger brotherhood who lived 'in a state of chronic resistance to the powers that be, and profoundly conscious of all the opposing forces that beset their path'.[10] It was symptomatic of the barbed atmosphere surrounding the fictional artist's professional life that this author was able to introduce Welby, an unusually successful painter, as a convincing prophet of doom. This old Royal Academician sadly warned Laurence, one of the young heroes, that art was an uncertain siren, twice speaking of the 'shipwrecks' she caused. Mrs Oliphant made much of the symbolism underlying young Laurence's choice of an elegant but untrustworthy pleasureboat, subsequently referring to the way in which he and his brothers faced the rocks and perils of the sea of life. This kind of hackneyed imagery let the reader in no doubt about her fatalistic attitude towards the young painter.

Kipling made a much more dramatic portrait of the artist at risk in *The Light that Failed*. He first built up a picture of Dick Haldar, his romantic hero, as one of the most adventurous of all the fictional bohemians. When Haldar first heard that he had become popular in England he proved his worth by organizing an orgy in a walled compound where a woman whose silk garment kept slipping off her shoulders produced the 'tin-pot music of a Western waltz' as naked Zanzibar girls danced furiously by the light of kerosene lamps. But his bohemian gusto and studio merry-making were soon followed by a more ominous mood; indeed, Haldar's reactions were virtually paranoiac. He regarded society with a venomous distrust. He despised the sheeplike public, and felt there could not be more than twelve hundred people in the world who understood pictures; he obviously felt no sympathy whatsoever for the signs of civilization which greeted him on his return to Britain:

> 'Oh, you rabbit-hutches!' said he, addressing a row of highly-respectable semi-detached residences. 'You have to supply me with men-servants and maid servants' – here he smacked his lips, – 'and the peculiar treasure of kings. Meanwhile I'll get clothes and boots, and presently I will return and trample on you.'[11]

As the irate artist stopped to examine a burst shoe he was jostled into the gutter by a passer-by, an action he crossly noted saying: 'All right. . . . That's another nick in the score. I'll jostle you later on.' Kipling went on to show how this painter's apparently unwarranted persecution-complex was in fact fully justified. The Central Southern Sydnicate, an anonymous organization which had been publishing and publicising his work while paying him a pittance, suddenly tried to retain his original studies, thus depriving him of his only assets. The ambitious young man, who had already pawned his clothes and lived on a starvation diet, was swift to recognize their cold-blooded manoeuvres to defraud him: 'The first thing a poor orphan meets is gang robbery, organized burglary'.

Where Haldar had rightly called his persecutors a lawless body, other fictional artists were themselves frequently suspected of, and accused of, devious practices. Leitch Ritchie provided a superb example of this kind of condemnatory attitude in *Wearyfoot Common* (1854), where one of the characters waxed eloquent on the villainous artists who made dishonest use of their talents in order to deceive the innocently rich and respectable.

Galsworthy took artistic rebelliousness to its logical conclusion in *Villa Rubein* (1900) where he literally made the artist hero of this particular story a wanted criminal. He first described how Harz, a sensitive egoist who 'poised his brush as though it were a spear', had had an unhappy childhood and then, as a starving youth, become involved in a revolutionary bomb plot. Galsworthy next began to manipulate Harz's political extremism to give added zest to what the reader will recognize as the traditional fracas caused when poor painter meets rich girl: the latter's daddy was in for a shock. The author emphasized this by making the tense, casually-dressed painter seem awkward and out of his depth on first meeting the spruce *bon-viveur,* Herr Paul von Morawitz. The latter, after trying to put his unusual and diffident guest at his ease, was suddenly surprised by the turn their conversation took. Herr Paul blithely condemned individuality as pointless eccentricity the moment it fell outside his prescribed rules: he connected it with tasteless clothes and unreliable habits, such as intermittent shaving, and saw no reason for contradicting the reliable customs established by his social 'superiors'. Harz, on the other hand, derided the men whose birth, position and reputation restricted their every action. The artist criticized them as colourless creatures who daren't even smell of india-rubber and devoted their lives to effacing themselves. His host politely tried, at this point, to placate his guest: 'Come, come! . . . we are not anarchists' . . . 'Are you sure?' said Harz.[12] From this moment Galsworthy showed a genial entertainer beginning to metamorphose into a reactionary persecutor. His growing mistrust of the man his daughter loved was seen in his subsequent actions. He precipitated the police into chasing the fleeing painter whom they already regarded as a condemned 'outlaw'.

There seems to be no clear-cut contemporary reason for the extent of the tragedy which overtook many fictional artists in the course of their careers and made them outcasts of one kind or another. They seemed curiously doomed. However two archetypal concepts connected with the artist do help to explain this peculiar fatalism. The first, referred to here as the magic portrait motif, depends on the fact that people can often confuse an image of an object with the object itself, thus confusing art and reality.

The simplest early examples of this kind of association are seen in cave paintings, as cave-dwellers safeguarded their supply of provender by drawing pictures of wounded game, and created fertility symbols as a means of stimulating genuine conditions of fertility.[13] The theme of the magic picture or portrait recurred in folkloric tradition, where such images changed colour, dropped from the skies and aroused various strong emotions. Specialists in folklore related episodes proving the images' power over the superstitious mind.[14] This antique theme was also included in more complex philosophical systems. The literature publicizing the teaching of the 'Egyptian Moses', Hermes Trismegistus, for example, showed a great preoccupation with miraculous images. According to Cornelius Agrippa, a Renaissance scholar concerned with magical power, Hermes Trismegistus had written that 'a demon immediately animates a figure or statue well composed of certain things that suit that demon'.[15]

This magical identification between portrait and person found its way into literature, where it developed in subtlety.[16] The old folkloric connection between appearance and reality provided a popular means of deception, as, for example, in *A Winter's Tale* (1608), where Shakespeare used a lifelike 'statue' to awaken Leontes's love for his 'dead' wife. Similarly, Webster in *The Duchess of Malfi* (c. 1644) showed a less appetizing reversal of this deception when he used a wax image to persuade the Duchess that her husband was dead. Both these authors evoked magic, Shakespeare using the phrase 'mocked with art' and Webster the phrase 'plagu'd in Art'.

With the later emergence of the excesses of Gothic literature – a reaction against cooler eighteenth century reason – the old folkloric confusion about the connection between the apparent and the real became extremely popular. Gothic novelists welcomed the often illogical and superstitious possibilities which it offered them: there were many accounts in romantic fiction of pictures with different kinds of vitality. Magic portraits were shown to have extensive magical powers which roughly matched those of a standard ghost. They tended to be more introverted than extroverted in both action and conversation. Their talents were essentially impractical: devoid of any complex strategical or administrative flair, they tended to rely on the shock provoked by their mere appearance.

The portrait motif was specifically included in Eino Railo's *The Haunted Castle* (1927), a study of the most characteristic elements of Gothic literature. He found miniature portraits typical romantic fodder. Valued as the only remaining pictures of deceased loved ones, they awoke sentimental memories and provided a convenient stimulus for 'beautiful and legitimate tears in the silent watches of the night'. Such portraits could reveal marvellous, terrible and fateful secrets in the 'heated brains of romanticists'.

One such was Horace Walpole, whose introduction to *The Castle of Otranto* (1764) claimed that the story had been translated from an Italian tale written between 1095, the era of the first crusade, and 1243, the date of the last, or not long afterwards', and encouraged the reader to relax his credulity: 'Miracles, visions, necromancy, dreams, and other events, are exploded now even from Romances. That was not the case when our author wrote. . . .'[17] The incidents involving portraits in *The Castle of Otranto* all generated a melodramatic atmosphere of supernatural suspense.

The shocked amazement which Walpole tried to stimulate by the unnatural antics of these art works exploited the old folkloric links between appearance and reality. The statue of the deceased Alfonso the Good, symbolising the forces of law and order, was particularly active – manifesting its presence in magnified portions. His enchanted helmet effectively prevented a marriage between Manfred's cowardly son and an unwilling princess by flattening the former beneath its great bulk. The absurd richochetting energy of Walpole's description, skirting over the squashed prince in a flow of breathless exclamation to consider the helmet's size and feather accessories, indicated a general lack of cohesive explanation surrounding this kind of magic portrait.

Shortly afterwards, when Manfred, the foul usurper, decided to pursue the captive princess himself, he was thwarted by a disconsolate painted grandfather. Walpole introduced this supernatural image as a means of offering the princess a temporary respite. Gathering courage, she cried:

'Look! My Lord! see, heaven itself declares against your pious intentions!' 'Heaven nor hell shall impede my designs,' said Manfred, advancing again to seize the princess. At that instant the portrait of his grandfather, which hung over the bench where they had been sitting, uttered a deep sigh and heaved its breast . . . he saw it quit its panel, and descend on the floor with a grave and melancholy air.[18]

With natural curiosity, Manfred bombarded it with questions. But, bored perhaps by his ebulliently rhetorical manner, it merely sighed again and beckoned to Manfred, who promptly screamed that he would follow it to the gulf of perdition. Here Walpole was adroitly using a simple device to keep the reader in utter suspense about the true nature of the peculiar portrait, which he was using as a miraculous agent or *deus ex machina*: as Manfred pursued the spectre's sedate march and was about to follow it into a room, an invisible hand slammed the door in his face.

In *The Mysteries of Udolpho* (1794), Mrs Radcliffe concocted a less peevish and altogether more horrific portrait, having equally little connection with the structure of her novel. People such as Emily, her heroine, who quickly glanced at it in its dark corner, must have assumed, in the old mimetic tradition, that the gruesome wax sculpture was a genuine corpse. Mrs Radcliffe explained the psychological advantage of introducing an emotionally charged, if unexplained, art object in the early stages of her novel. She used the mysteriously realistic image to evoke unnatural awe, thinking a 'terror' of this kind occupied and expanded the mind; she stated that a terror elevated the mind to high expectation, was purely sublime, and led us, by a kind of fascination, to seek even the object 'from which we appear to shrink'.

M. G. Lewis, another Gothic author who specialised in the power of uncanny fascination, selected the close folkloric connection between a picture and the person it represented as the central theme for his pornographic novel *The Monk. A Romance* (1796).[19] The central character, fearing his chastity at risk, studied a painting of the Holy Virgin – feeling morally safe in idolizing her sanctified features:

'What beauty in that countenance! . . . how softly her cheek reclines upon her hand! can the rose vie with the blush of that cheek? can the lily rival the whiteness of that hand! oh! if such a creature existed, and existed but for me! were I permitted to twine round my fingers those golden ringlets, and to press my lips to that hand of snow! gracious God, should I then resist the temptation! Should I not barter for a single embrace the reward of my sufferings for thirty years? Should I not abandon – '[20]

At this point he remembered his own righteousness and reversed the argument. He reassured himself still further; since no mortal was ever formed 'so perfectly' as the picture, he could hardly be tempted. He declared his interest to be purely abstract: he was not concerned with the attraction of a mere mortal woman, but with the painter's skill and the representation of an ideal and superior being. Ironically enough this soliloquy was interrupted by a charming young novice, his most devoted companion, who came to reveal his true identity: '. . . "Father! " continued he in faltering accents, "I am a woman! " '

The abbot's appetites were gradually awakened by a rather solemn form of monastical strip-poker culminating in a startling revelation. The entrancing face of his sexy companion was identical to the one he had learnt to adore as the Virgin's. The writer showed how the perplexed monk, unable to distinguish between what he had come to worship in the painting, and now saw repeated in reality, became hopelessly infatuated with the tempting novice. Lewis based the uncanny nature of Ambrosio's seduction and subsequent corruption by the mock-Madonna, Matilda de Villangeas, on a *pactum cum diabolo*. The devil had made his pawn, the beautiful Matilda, sit for the supposedly religious picture as a means of directly establishing her personal power over the monk through the bewitching qualities of her portrait.

The most sinister magical portrait connected with the devil was created by Charles Maturin in *Melmoth the Wanderer* (1812). Maturin described how a young man, fetching wine for a dying uncle, found his gaze riveted on a peculiar portrait 'as if by magic'. His normally prosaic uncle then explained that this portrait of a middle-aged man, which had been painted long, long ago, was making him die of fright. Maturin let the uncle link the idea of the painted portrait and the person it represented as though they were a single indivisible entity:

'That man', and he extended his meagre arm towards the

closet as if he were pointing towards a living being; 'That man, I have good reason to know, is still alive'.[21]

Examining the picture again, the youth saw its demonic eyes move and its lips seem to move. In addition to this, a mysterious figure resembling the image made the first of a series of strange appearances when the old uncle fell into a final convulsive fit. After reading his uncle's will, which urged the destruction of the sinister image of a being who declared himself 'independent of time and space', his heir tried to burn the portrait. In describing this symbolic annihilation of the presence of the Wanderer, Maturin implied that the portrait had a supernatural life which was an extension of its sitter's personality. It seemed to smile ghoulishly as it burnt. And later, the horrified heir's attempts to annihilate it were confused with the idea of murder: the person in the painting appeared and identified himself with his image, whispering 'You have burned me, then; but those are flames I can survive, – I am alive, – I am beside you'. A disturbing, and convincing, sequel to this apparition was the convincing discovery in the morning of a pain in his right wrist, which Maturin described as black and blue, 'as from the recent grip of a strong hand'.[22]

Such exaggerated use of the portrait motif to provoke and indulge the reader's irrational sensibility could lead to the ridiculous. In *Northanger Abbey* (1818),[23] for instance, Jane Austen produced a delightfully ironic comment on Mrs Radcliffe's contrivance of sublime terror when Isabella discovered the guileless Catherine's most appropriate reaction to the hidden image behind the 'black veil' in *Udolpho*.

A more boisterous caricature of the overworked theme of the magic portrait occurred in Gilbert and Sullivan's comic opera, *Ruddigore* (1887). The very fact that such subject matter should be parodied in such a popular context suggests that the device would have been familiar to large audiences. Gilbert's chorus of family portraits stepped down from their frames in Act III and began to sing a pseudo-medieval chant parodying the historical concoctions of the Gothic writers. Any suspense which could have been derived from their formal account of themselves as painted emblems of a race 'All accurst in days of yore 'quickly vanished when they then began to insult the hero in familiar terms, referring to him as a tadpole, maggot, weevil and the like. While conversing with their leader, the supernatural shop steward Sir Roderick Murgatroyd, the hero asked:

Rob.	Are you considered a good likeness?
Sir Rod.	Pretty well. Flattering.
Rob.	Because as a work of art you are poor.
Sir Rod.	I am crude in colour, but I have only been painted ten years. In a couple of centuries I shall be an Old Master, and then you will be sorry you spoke lightly of me.[24]

Gilbert, by concocting this bantering exchange where a picture flippantly discussed its own merits and ironically looked forward to fading into fame, surrounded his magic portraits with a mood of cheerful absurdity.

So far the portrait motif has been viewed in a series of extreme modifications easily warranting, indeed often meriting the satire or comic treatment given by Jane Austen and Gilbert, but the curious fact is that whenever this image occurred in more serious nineteenth century literature its weird supernatural properties remained virtually unchanged. To take examples from either early or late nineteenth century fiction, Sir Walter Scott, in *The Bride of Lammermoor* (1819), and Thomas Hardy in *Tess of the d'Urbervilles* (1891) both illustrate how firmly earlier Gothic novelists had established this particular device. Scott had used it to give mysterious intimations: the unexplained presence of a sinister old portrait was used by three knowledgeable local hags to signal death. Hardy made a more sophisticated use of this theme, describing how Angel Clare found his affections for Tess soured when he saw parallels between her and some particularly unpleasant portraits. A painted ancestor over Tess's door seemed, in the flickering candlelight, to express sinister designs, her painted features revealing a 'concentrated purpose of revenge on the other sex'. The evil lineaments of this image, and its twin once seen, could

> never be forgotten. The long narrow features, narrow eye and smirk of the one, so suggestive of merciless treachery, the billhook nose, large teeth, and bold eye of the other, suggesting arrogance to the point of ferocity, haunt the beholder afterwards in his dreams.[25]

A still more hauntingly horrible portrait appears in Hardy's 'Barbara of the House of Grebe',[26] where an unhappy marriage was almost wrecked by a beautiful statue of the wife's first husband, modelled before he had become disfigured in a fire. As

Hardy developed his theme he persuaded the reader that this statue became increasingly identified, in the woman's mind, with the personality of her former husband – the man she had rejected after his accident. Her present husband was powerless against this consuming passion for a dead man until he made another sculptor hack at its perfect features and successfully simulate the gruesome singed remains of the victim of the fire, the sight of which shocked his wife out of her obsession. The writer thus described how the second husband successfully, if sadistically, obliterated his earlier rival by mutilating his image.[27]

Probably the best-known example of a symbolic 'murder' of this kind occurs in that popular nineteenth century story about a magic portrait, *The Picture of Dorian Gray* (1891). When Gray first saw the painting he expressed a spontaneous wish to exchange his soul for immortal beauty, letting his picture grow old in his place – a wish which came true. Meditating on the possibility of sympathetic magic, he reasoned that if thought could influence a living organism it might well influence dead and inorganic things.[28] Indeed, external objects might well vibrate in unison with people's moods and passions, atom calling to atom in 'strange affinity'. Alterations in the expression, age and colouring of the painted work which would have been appropriate to the living person, seemed extraordinary when they occurred only to the portrait.

The first magical change, one of expression, occurred when the insensitive hero abruptly and cruelly discarded his fiancée, who committed suicide. Wilde described how Gray arrived at home on the night he had last seen the girl. While still unaware of her death, his eyes fell upon the portrait Hallward had painted of him:

> In the dim arrested light that struggled through the cream-coloured silk blinds, the face appeared to him to be a little changed – the expression looked different – One would have said that there was a touch of cruelty in the mouth. It was certainly strange.
>
> He turned round and, walking to the window, drew up the blind. The bright dawn flooded the room, and swept the fantastic shadows into dusky corners, where they lay shuddering. . . . But the strange expression that he had noticed in the face of the portrait seemed to linger there, to be more intensified even. The quivering ardent sunlight showed him the lines of cruelty round the mouth as clearly as if he had

been looking into a mirror after he had been doing some dreadful thing.

He winced and, taking up from the table an oval glass framed in ivory cupids, one of Lord Henry's many presents to him, glanced hurriedly into its polished depths. No line like that warped his red lips. What did it mean?[29]

Despite the exaggerated empathy of shuddering shadows and quivering light, Wilde skilfully engineered a belief in a living portrait which could change of its own accord. He did this by making Gray pass so smoothly from vague wonder to worried involvement that the reader is imperceptibly carried along by the hero's growing acceptance. Wilde's transitional stages were deftly managed. Starting innocuously with a picture which merely 'appeared' to have changed, he went on to say its expression 'looked' different, thus sliding from the realm of possibility to that of probability. Indirect curiosity, carefully caught by the tentative, impersonal remark 'One would have said,' and positive recognition of strangeness later became effectively fused in his phrase 'the strange expression' which suggested growing conviction. This development was aided by Wilde's play on light as a symbol of truth. After originally seeing the portrait in a dim light, Gray's instinctive move to draw the blind and let in the natural light seemed part and parcel of his desire to fathom the mystery. Wilde, by showing that in the atmosphere of guileless clarity evoked by the bright dawn and ardent sunlight the portrait's strange expression not only lingered but grew more intense, doubly proved its existence: the daylight made Gray see it as clearly as if he had been looking into a mirror. When he then consulted this standard gauge of reality and found it reflected a cupid-like innocence, at odds with what he had observed in the portrait, he showed his belief in the latter's ability to change by not dismissing it out of hand, but considering it most seriously. He must have been very taken with this impression to credit it despite the mirror's lack of confirmation. In Gray's mind, however, what he had at first thought a problematic touch of cruelty had developed into a definite warped line, referred to factually by Wilde, as 'a line like that'.

The canvas with an 'inner life' – consistently recording a murder by Gray – oozed blood. He saw 'loathsome red dew that gleamed, wet and glistening, on one of the hands, as though the canvas had been smeared with blood'. Thus Wilde made the portrait reflect Gray's behaviour like a visual conscience. Once entering the room containing his portrait, Gray shuddered at an unexplained current of cold air and a light which 'shot up for a moment in a flame of murky orange' – devices traditionally used in Gothic literature to create emotional tension, and to indicate the presence of a ghost of supernatural presence just as Wilde used it in this instance, to highlight the portrait's extraordinary vitality.[30]

Wilde further induced his reader to believe in the portrait's peculiar 'life' by referring to its destruction in terms of murder, hereby implying that it had an almost human existence. He had skilfully sowed this idea, in embryo, when the artist decided, after a quarrel, to rip up his new, controversial masterpiece. Gray tore the knife out of his hand, flinging it to the end of the studio: ' "Don't, Basil, don't ! " he cried. "It would be murder! " ' [31]

As Gray grew increasingly certain of the Jekyll and Hyde relationship between himself and his portrait, he finally decided to get rid of his *alter ego* – attacking the portrait with a gleaming knife as though it were a living person, rather than quietly painting over the image, or untacking the canvas, dismantling the frame and simply disposing of the pieces. The image of the knife as a murder weapon corresponded with the blade of lithe steel with which the artist had earlier been about to 'murder' the portrait. And since then Gray had himself knifed the painter to death. Wilde, by making Gray subsequently use the same knife to destroy his portrait, cleverly suggested a parallel situation. In Gray's mind his two actions with the one knife resembled a double murder:

> As it had killed the painter, so it would kill the painter's work, and all that that meant. It would kill the past, and when that was dead, he would be free. It would kill this monstrous soul-life, and without its hideous warnings he would be at peace. He seized the thing and stabbed the picture with it.[32]

In attempting to destroy his picture Gray mysteriously took on its vile appearance and killed himself into the bargain. This was Wilde's conclusive indication that the portrait, which Gray referred to as his 'soul-life', did indeed have extraordinary attributes. Wilde's use of the term 'soul-life' showed how Gothic stories about portraits proving their supernatural powers in such naïve ways as physically vacating their frames became increasingly refined: the magical life of an image grew to be equated with the more subtle spiritual vitality of the soul itself.

Still more sophisticated was Henry James's use of a portrait in *The Sacred Fount* (1901); for his particular picture symbolized, in microcosm, the whole archetypal ambiguity between appearance and reality which inspired so many tales of 'living' portraits. Throughout this novel he dwelt on the *Doppelganger* theme whereby the sacred fount of life is mysteriously transmuted from one source to another. His narrator, for example, explained that he thought of the discrepancy between a couple's actual and apparent vitality in terms of mental-vampirism: a seemingly desiccated husband was actually far younger than his apparently flourishing wife who was taxing his vital energy.

James also explored the ambivalent flux existing between superficial social relationships and genuine emotional currents. He encouraged his readers to speculate on the intriguing formal and suspected links between the characters he created in *The Sacred Fount*. The man whose marital affection had already been described in sacrificial terms might, for example, be open to the invigorating love of the lovely May Server, who, in her turn, secretly stimulated the narrator's own concern. James projected these enigmas on to a picture of a figure with a mask.[33] Different people 'recognized' different characters in the painted face and its disguise, and so revealed how they construed various relationships. The narrator, particularly anxious to probe May Server's unconscious identifications and responses, led her to it, saying pointedly: 'It's the picture, of all pictures, that most needs an interpreter. *Don't* we want,' I asked of Mrs Server, 'to know what that means?' James did not follow this intense enquiry with a straightforward answer, but cleverly provoked his reader's curiosity by directly enlarging on the puzzling pictorial allegory:

> The figure represented is a young man in black – a quaint, tight black dress, fashioned in years long past: with a pale, lean, livid face and a stare, from eyes without eyebrows, like that of some whitened old-world clown. In his hand he holds an object that strikes the spectator at first simply as some obscure, some ambiguous work of art, but that on a second view becomes a representation of a human face, modelled and coloured, in wax, in enamelled metal, in some substance not human. The object thus appears a complete mask, such as might have been fantastically fitted and worn.[34]

James described this image of a figure with a mask in such a way that distinctions between the living man and the impersonal arte-

'The Artist in his studio'

In an era when many real, and fictional, English artists studied in Paris, this French painting provides a telling comment on the contemporary cult of the inspired bohemian. In his 'Allégorie réelle' of 1855, Courbet paints a deliberately bare and shabby studio setting (see the background wall) in which various representatives of society pay homage to the painter who has proudly placed himself in the centre of his canvas, a wondering child and attentive muse following his visionary gaze.

'Curtius Leaping the Gulf'

This painting of 1842 shows an artist portraying himself in a glorified heroic role, and thus paralleling many of the fictional artists of the time. In this visual work, Haydon projects an image of himself dominating a dramatic background. His choice of 'persona' implies that he is willing to sacrifice himself for his fellow men, like a noble martyr. The psychological tension in this picture is brought about by the peculiar combination of horse and rider – for the horse is all frantic energy, depicted as it leaps into the gulf, with the compositional lines of rocks, spear and cloak all emphasising its diagonal descent, while the taut figure of Curtius, staring upwards, suggests cool control.

Dyce takes an established old master to make a point with contemporary relevance (as Browning did in 'Andrea del Sarto'). In this 'Essay on Colour' (1856-7) it is significant that the brightest colours, including red and yellow, are in the flowers at the boy's feet and at the base of the statue. But Dyce has directed the lad's eyes upwards: the young artist is learning his skill by meditating on the Virgin and Child framed by pale sky. Dyce makes the attentive curve of his body link the earthly with the divine, stressing a belief in the artist's priest-like role, and the spiritual nature of artistic genius.

'The Hand Refrains'
One of the poignant images from Burne-Jones's wistful
'Pygmalion' series (1869-79), where a sculptor falls in love with
the beautiful female statue he has created, which then miraculously becomes flesh. This theme exploits an archetypal link
between image and reality (see Chapter 4) as well as illustrating
the idea, found in much nineteenth century fiction, that the artist
could – or should – fall in love with his art.

'Astarte Syriaca'
This dark, mysterious figure – painted in 1877 – provides a record of Rossetti's feelings for Mrs Morris. Contemporary photographs show just how closely this woman's actual appearance inspired this, and similar, images of Venus. Her influence as a *femme fatale* proves that fact and fantasy were often as closely interwoven in real life as in contemporary fiction.

'Cimabue's celebrated Madonna is carried in procession through the streets of Florence'
Painted at the beginning of Leighton's career (see Ch. 2), this painting celebrates the artist's role in society, and was bought, significantly, by Queen Victoria. The white, central figure of the artist (and the higher vertical of his painting) dominate this long horizontal composition.

'Captive Andromache'
Exhibited in 1888, when the painter was enjoying great worldly success, this work nevertheless reflects deep personal pessimism (see Ch. 6) indicated by the isolated, funereal figure in the centre of this crowded stage – a symbol of utter desolation.

'The Arab Hall, Leighton House'
Leighton's richly decorated Arab Hall, dating from the eighteen
eighties, is a perfect example of the way in which many nineteenth
century artists, like the artistic jackdaws in contemporary fiction,
cultivated – dramatic rather than useful – effects in their private
rooms and furnishings. Leighton's collection of oriental tiles, for
example, and the atmospheric use he made of them, were an
extension of his own picturesque personality.

fact were curiously blurred and merged. The funereal person seemed artificial, his white skull-like face suggesting an old painted clown, while the object, the 'ambiguous work of art', became a contrastingly life-like moulded and coloured human face. It was not just a crude symbolic head, but much more an alternative personality which could be 'fantastically fitted and worn'. It was typical of the general uncertainty James exploited in this novel that Mrs Server reacted to the contents of the painting with yet another question:

> 'Yes, what in the world does it mean?' Mrs Server replied.
> 'One could call it – though that doesn't get one much further – the Mask of Death.'
> 'Why so?' I demanded, while we all looked again at the picture.
> 'Isn't it much rather the Mask of Life? It's the man's own face that's Death. The other one, blooming and beautiful – '
> 'Ah, but what an awful grimace!' Mrs Server broke in.
> 'The other one, blooming and beautiful,' I repeated, 'is Life, and he is going to put it on; unless indeed he has just taken it off.'[35]

This hesitant interpretation of the action portrayed – of whether the figure had just revealed his true identity or was on the point of concealing it – shows the author still deliberately provoking his reader as to the perplexing laws of appearance and reality in this symbolic parable where a supposedly living man could symbolize death and a supposedly inanimate image could be described as the 'blooming and beautiful' essence of life.

The wide ranging treatment – from naïve Gothic exploitation to refined Jamesian exploration – accorded to the concept of the living, or magically vital image, showed what a strong hold this theme took on the imagination of writers. Different kinds of portraits were often incorporated in stories about artists. Nineteenth century authors doubtless found that a portrait provided their readers with an easily acceptable mimetic test, and portrait sittings could provide unusually intimate social situations.[36] They also popularized the portrait even when they slighted professional portraitists,[37] and stated that their fictional artists were absorbed by quite different aesthetic problems, such as theoretic and technical innovations in landscape. This is because they were primarily interested in the fictional artist as a romantic hero, rather than as a means of discussing what was happening in contemporary art movements.

English writers often preferred to explore new ways of creating images in their own medium, as Moore did in *A Modern Lover*, where he used impressionistic literary devices to produce his own Parisian nightscape. Instead of pretending that his hero had painted an impressionistic night scene, and then laboriously recounting a series of painterly effects at second hand, Moore employed the same fragmentary principles directly, using his own literary skills to build up a more evocative and spontaneous effect.[38] When this novelist did include a few remarks about purple shadows and modern painting they were generally in association not so much with the hero's development as with that of an extremely peripheral figure. There were, however, no real equivalents for the kind of artist hero described in *Manette Salomon* (1867) by the Goncourts or Zola's *L'Oeuvre* (1886).

When the Goncourts created their painter hero, Naz de Coriolis, and Zola created Claude Lantier, they obviously combined an interest in literary form with a keen curiosity about what was happening in the visual arts. They equated success with the pursuit of realism. They documented their heroes' technical experiments and aesthetic development with a thoroughness which showed their knowledge of and interest in painting. Manet's influence was felt when Zola recalled his pioneering piece 'Le Déjeuner sur l'herbe' in a description of naked and contemporaneously dressed figures in a light outdoor scene – the theme of Lantier's promising early work 'Plein Air'. The focal point of his final work, a daring attempt to create a new style and to depict the Isle de la Cité as the centre of modern life, was feverishly, hallucinatorily coloured. And when Claude Lantier, Zola's scarcely veiled comment on his childhood friend Paul Cézanne, hanged himself in front of his original but unresolved modern masterpiece, the Frenchman seemed to stress the affinity between the artist's personal and professional failure – both expressed in the ambitious, but incohesive, style of this last picture.

Ignoring the independent advance of contemporary aesthetics, many English writers concentrated on conveying a wealth of moral, psychological and symbolical meaning – frequently manipulating a portrait to achieve their ends. Where elements of the old folkloric tradition of the magic portrait, previously used as an isolated device, and new tales about artists overlapped, artists seemed to take on an altogether deeper significance. The true artists as Leitch Ritchie let one of his characters explain in *Wearyfoot Common* (1854), painted the mind as well as the external body (capturing in colours what the sitter was unconscious of himself) to reveal, 'flaws or beauties of character hitherto unsuspected'. They naturally gained invaluable cultural prestige when credited with creating such awe-inspiring, supernaturally lifelike works for 'to put soul into a smeared bit of canvas is what no Lord Chancellor in the world could do'.[39] There were also frequent references to artists not only being able to see, but also miracoulously to recreate the spiritual life, indeed, the very souls of their sitters.

This theme inspired the plot of *The Story of a Masterpiece* (1886) in which Henry James dwelt convincingly on the artist's uncanny power to capture the very essence of a personality. The masterpiece in question was a portrait of a pretty young blonde ordered by her infatuated future husband. His reactions on first seeing the finished image of his beloved disturbed him, for it seemed that:

> . . . some strangely potent agency had won from his mistress the confession of her inmost soul and had written it there upon the canvas in firm yet passionate lines. Marion's person was lightness – her charm was lightness; could it be that her soul was levity too? These things were the less to be eluded because in so many respects the painter had been so profoundly just.[40]

Ironically this disconcerted lover, who never felt his old infatuation again, did not realise that the painter, too, had been intimate with Marion and understood her selfish callousness. This knowledge, however, especially when combined with praise of the artist's accurate realism, prejudiced the reader in favour of the startling claim that the artist had potently grasped and recorded the true nature of Marion's innermost soul. He had not worked as a simple painter but had painted with 'something more than knowledge – with imagination and feeling. He had almost *composed,* and his composition had embraced the truth.'[41]

While the tragic crux of *The Story of a Masterpiece* was convincing because the artist had been in love with Marion and knew her well, George Gissing, in *Thyrza* (1878) showed an artist could achieve just such a *tour de force* with no personal knowledge of his subject. Gissing described how a sensitive, talented artist was asked to make a final portrait of the heroine, Thyrza, after she had died. Although told nothing about her except the 'bare facts . . . without names, without details', he proved his extraordinary powers by examining the lifeless face of her corpse and then recreating her very soul:

> The work was of course masterly in execution; it was no less admirable as a portrait. In those few lines of chalk, Thyrza lived. He had devined the secret of the girl's soul, that gift of passionate imagination which in her early years had sunk her in hour-long reverie, and later burned her life away. The mood embodied was one so characteristic of Thyrza that one marvelled at the insight which had evoked it.[42]

George Eliot made more complex use of artistic insight in *Romola,* in which an artist with abnormally alert intuitive vision, like his counterpart in *Thyrza,* spontaneously created an imaginative composition revealing the hidden drama of the hero's life. Within the context of the novel this painting acted as an important microcosm: the artist produced an image which succinctly distilled the tragic effects of betrayal; the keynote of this gloomy, disillusioning saga.

The story hinged on a beautiful young Greek called Tito Melema selling jewels in Florence and using them, not to find his devoted adopted father, who had been shipwrecked with him, and actually owned the gems, but for his own ease and profit. These motives also led to a misleading mock-marriage with a gullibly affectionate young contadina. Tito's slick infiltration of Florentine society was marked by his public betrothal to a paragon of beauteous virtue called Romola. He celebrated this betrothal by commissioning a painting from an ingenious painter called, unoriginally, Piero di Cosimo. Tito ordered an image of Bacchus and Ariadne surrounded by cupids, flowers, and sportive animals inspired by Ovid.[43] The alert painter, intuitively understanding that these figures were to be modelled on Tito and his fiancée, was particularly helpful about Tito's own portrait. He had it already. Tito, faced with a sketch, which Piero considered his best bit of portraiture, saw himself:

> . . . with his right hand uplifted, holding a wine cup in an attitude of triumphant joy, but his face turned away from the cup with an expression of such intense fear in the dilated eyes and pallid lips, that he felt a cold stream through his veins, as if he were being thrown into sympathy with his imagined self.[44]

Piero, while knowing nothing of the ebullient gallant's false manoeuvres and the gnawing horror of exposure which accompanied them, had nevertheless accurately associated his subject with unwholesome terror. Although the rest of the portrait was only sketched the figure of Tito was thoroughly finished because Piero, after seeing a fleeting expression of fear on Tito's face, the very first time he had met him, had been so struck by it that he had reconstructed it from memory. It was significant also that, at the time di Cosimo had unconsciously cast Tito in the role of a traitor, he asked the naturally bright youth to sit for a picture of Simon deceiving old Priam, arguing that the perfect villain would have just such an innocent air.

George Eliot reasoned similarly when she decided to preface a description of Piero's portrait with Tito's ideas for one. Tito's theme was enchanting. He blithely commissioned a delightful image of the patron of sensual festival, crowned in grapes. The reader, after being easily lulled by this fabulous concoction, which implied that the lad was a charmed being, will be the more struck by Piero's portrait. This abruptly recalls Tito's warped character, simultaneously stressing both the enormity of his presumption and the depth of Piero's vision. In this way George Eliot deftly exposed the artificial nature of Tito's projections of vine-crowned bliss by continuing his bucolic imagery, but with a new detachment: Piero intuitively painted Tito in a pose, an 'attitude' of triumphant joy, his dominatingly tormented face significantly 'turned away' from his flourished wine cup.

George Eliot's interest in the creator of the portrait as well as the object itself was shown by her drawn-out account of its development. Rather than introducing it as a finite creation, she let the reader observe the artist brilliantly building it up:

> 'You are beginning to look like it already', said Piero with a short laugh, moving the picture away again. He's seeing a ghost – that fine young man. I shall finish it some day, when I've settled whether it should look solid, like a dead man come to life, or half transparent, like a mist.[45]

Having already clairvoyantly sensed Tito's underlying fear and corruption, di Cosimo went on to isolate its prime cause. Noticing that Tito became paranoid with fear while shaking off a ragged old man who approached him outside a church, the painter took pains to catch up with the latter and persuade him to sit for him, using his likeness in completing his portrait of Tito. Thus di

Cosimo had, still unconsciously, picked on the one relationship which obsessed Tito: the apparently rich and successful courtier had indeed seen a 'dead man come to life' for the battered slave was none other than his forgotten father. George Eliot gave a sign that di Cosimo felt that authentic potency of his newly filled canvas by making him particularly anxious to conceal it from Tito's adoring wife. He seemed to have interpreted its effect on her accurately; for the guilty fear in the painted face froze and clarified previously unacknowledged doubts. Piero had now, in completing the drama, created not only a painted record but a painted prophecy anticipating the father's revenge.

While not directly intent on fostering the artist's importance, George Eliot's involved, unquestioning use of a painter with such uncanny perception and the ability to reflect it so startlingly in his work, shows how easily and generally acceptable this concept had become. Writing in days before the widespread acceptance of extra-sensory perception, nineteenth century authors managed, by implying that the artist had unusual visionary powers, to create situations in which he could easily be awarded a superiority verging on omnipotence.[46]

After examples like those in *Thyrza* and *Romola* in which artists miraculously grasp the essence of a personality as though performing a divine conjuring trick, the plot of *Oke of Okehurst* (1890) by Vernon Lee seems amusingly amateurish. The artist in this story acts more like a detective than a visionary in seeking to understand a weird sitter called Mrs Oke. Feeling that painting a portrait is no abstract exercise but a means of reflecting identity, this artist pursued his sitter's 'psychological explanation', seeking clues to explain her odd attitudes. He began to capture her enigmatic beauty only on realizing that she confused herself with a dead ancestress, sharing the latter's obsession for the poet who had been her lover. Mrs Oke, referring to the kind of passion which had given her life its meaning, said it was very rare 'but it can exist. It becomes a person's whole existence, his whole soul'.[47]

These varied examples from different authors show how many artists in nineteenth century fiction came to be described as the makers of portraits which revealed the souls of their sitters. The fact that fictional artists were frequently depicted achieving the impossible in this way naturally added to their general prestige. Just as references to a monarch's miraculous ability to cure illness – the king's evil, for instance – reinforced sixteenth century religious belief in the Divine Right of Kings, so an artist's ability to produce supernatural pictures provided proof of the nineteenth century's romantic belief in the omnipotent creator. A modern reader can sense the way these factors contributed to the underlying importance of an artist hero, in a novel such as *Cynthia in the West* (1900).

The author, Charles Lee, described his particular artist as a man of truly remarkable talent. Throughout most of the course of this sentimental novel he was described as being at work on a study of a female figure. This hero and this single picture contribute to the overall context of this chapter because the qualities of soul in his painting seem, if only by a process of elimination, to have been intimately bound up with Lee's claim that his artist was no ordinary person, but a genius.

A discussion of the hero's ability to create a living, soul-like essence whose eventual destruction called for a 'funeral oration', was accompanied by some telling remarks on the artist's role. Although he himself had only a modicum of talent, a reflective minor artist recognized that the artistic faculty was something quite apart from the rest of one's personality – it was something 'strange and miraculous. People speak of it as a *gift* with good cause'. When Forester seemed willing to abandon his superior gift, the heroine attacked him: 'You mustn't do that,' she said quickly. 'It would be wrong. You have a duty to the world; you hold your power in trust.'[48] Thus showing a romantic preference for evocative suggestion as opposed to clinical statement, Lee closely connected ideas collectively implying that his genius's prestige was based on his supernatural powers.

A sonnet by Dante Gabriel Rossetti provides a fitting conclusion to these representative examples of nineteenth century works in which the magical or spiritual qualities in created objects contributed to an artist's fame, for Rossetti was not only a painter, but one addicted to using literature to evoke artistic achievements. 'The Portrait', narrated in the first person, told the reader of an artist's ambition to capture his sitter's soul on canvas, and of the pride his achievement gave him. In painting his lady's portrait, the speaker was not simply interested in suggesting her sensual charm, but in glowingly representing her inner self, which he defined, in no mean terms, as

The very sky and sea-line of her soul.

Lo! it is done. Above the enthroning throat
   The mouth's mould testifies of voice and kiss,
   The shadowed eyes remember and foresee:

> Her face is made her shrine. Let all men note
> That in all years (O Love, thy gift is this!)
> They that would look on her must come to me.[49]

Rossetti made a significant progression from the word 'soul' concluding the first verse, where he suggested the spiritual horizons of his picture, to the climax of the poem, ending with the word 'me', where he reflected on his efforts. Having successfully enshrined and immortalized this painted personality – which can both remember and foresee – the artist then gathered in the immortal credit.

An artist whose realistic skills were buoyed up by visionary powers so that he could recreate the eternal essence of life was obviously an exceptional being; one gifted with more than earthly abilities. He obviously belonged to a different category from ordinary men and, given this exceptional superiority, could not reasonably be compared with them. He could, however, be more easily compared with the semi-divine artists of mythology – an underlying tendency suggested by Wordsworth in 'Lines' referring to the painter's 'true Promethean craft',[50] or by Morley Roberts in *Immortal Youth*. This writer compared the artist who copied eternal beauty with Prometheus who 'stole fire and gave warmth to miserable mortals'. His character Bordon the bronze caster (whose effect on Lacy, the hero of the novel, has been discussed in Chapter I) was described as a 'child of Vulcan', the Nordic equivalent of the great craftsman Hephaestus. Roberts, following established mythical prototypes, made equations between casting and smelting processes, including the 'secret art' of *cire perdu,* and life itself. The reactions of Lacy who had come to see Bordon open a mould were highly revealing, for 'at first, when the head stood clear of the earth-fragments a sense of disappointment touched him'. This was the work of fire, 'yet it flamed not; the work of breathing bronze and yet it breathed not'.[51] The viewer, by thus expecting the newly created bronze to give signs of life, paid a back-handed compliment to its creator, and yet one in keeping with the author's mythical descriptions of this contemporary craftsman as the bronze magician and the fire's magician.

The Promethean legend and variations of it helped, in many cases, to elucidate the almost inevitable suffering of nineteenth century fictional artists – especially as they were well popularized through a classically-biased educational system. Prometheus was frequently mentioned in the nineteenth century, and the myth was re-adapted by such writers as Shelley in 'Phometheus Un-bound', and Mrs Browning in 'Prometheus Bound', and later by Robert Bridges in 'Prometheus the Firegiver'. The mythical Promethean hero, like his nineteenth century counterpart, was so uniquely gifted that he rose above his own kind and challenged the creative, life-giving power of the gods. This ironic archetypal pattern explains how the relentless destruction of fictional artists may well have been caused by deep-rooted envy of the visionary powers which seemed to give them such sublime advantages over ordinary mortals.[52]

According to legend, Prometheus was credited with having ingeniously defied Zeus, daringly bringing the essential element of fire to mankind. He was cruelly punished for this – being bound to a mountain crest and continually attacked by a monstrous eagle which devoured as much of his liver as had grown again during the previous night. An additional tradition established Prometheus, known as the father of art and science, as the creator of man: Prometheus fashioned the first man from clay and water, just as Hephaestus made Pandora.[53] Both Prometheus and Hephaestus, the divine blacksmith, were linked in a dramatic creative venture – that of bringing Athene into existence by splitting her father's head with an axe, while Hephaestus was renowned for his creative skills as, for example, when he constructed two beautiful girls, golden statues which hastened to help him walk. These were necessary, as well as ingenious devices, since their talented mythical creator had been maimed, and taunted in consequence, from birth.

This theme was recounted, or restated, in nineteenth century literature where the fictional artist, who also challenged the powers of the heavens, suffered in proportion to his talents. There were echoes of Hephaestus's much mocked physical defects in George Eliot's marking out Philip Wakem's lameness in *The Mill on the Floss* (1860), or in Thackeray's singling out the precocious J. J. Ridley in *The Newcomes* as a sickly and 'almost deformed' child, and there was an element of perversion in Watt-Dunton's speaking of the heroine's regret, in *Aylwin,* when the hero lost his crippling infirmities. Sickness, whether mental or physical, was far more likely to track down, rather than to leave, the fictional artist, whose mental torments, set out with differing degrees of romantic effusion, seemed as inevitable as Prometheus's own. Where classical drama had obtained cathartic results from punishing the individual, nineteenth century writers appeared to obtain similar satisfaction from punishing a genre. They gave rein to their envy, pessimism and resentment in destroying the idols they built up to represent their overwhelming desire for excitement, idealism and supernatural prowess.

The Artist's Tragic Temperament

Genius was priceless, inspired, divine; but it was also at its hours capricious, sinister, cruel; and men of genius accordingly were alternately very enviable and very helpless. It was not the first time he had had a sense of Roderick's standing passive in the clutch of his temperament.[1]

The Prometheus myth and its variants suggest a recurring tendency to see the artistic creator as semi-divine, reaping both fame and retribution in relation to his supernatural skills. The laisser-faire liberties and sexual licence enjoyed by the fictional artist in nineteenth century tales of picturesquely amoral behaviour in atelier and café could be regarded as part of this mythological tradition. Accounts of bohemian life certainly reflected the pictorial artist's freedoms and were generally described in a correspondingly light-hearted way. This emphasis changed as artists acquired outstanding abilities. Just as Prometheus's daring had verged on hubris and arrogance, and Zeus's revenge had smacked of envy and resentment, so nineteenth century writers, many of whom were failed artists, seem subconsciously to have punished their heroes for their superior talents. As the struggling, experimental apprentice became a serious practicing master he lost his capacity for idyllic joys.

Browning described this ironic situation in 'Youth and Art', which began by evoking the early careers of two bohemians – a singer and a sculptor. The levity of this poem – which told us that the youthful singer was careful to lace up her corset well away from the hole in the lattice – evaporated when the ambitious pair became maturer, and more successful:

> But you meet the Prince at the Board,
>   I'm queen myself at *bals-paré,*
> I've married a rich old lord,
>   And you're dubbed knight and R.A..
>
> Each life unfilled, you see;
>   It hangs still, patchy and scrappy:
> We have not sighed deep, laughed free,
>   Starved, feasted, despaired – been happy.
>
> And nobody calls you a dunce,
>   And people suppose me clever:
> This could but have happened once,
>   And we missed it, lost it for ever.[2]

Browning, as his title suggests, exploited the age factor to record how a previously blithe student lost happiness as he gained prestige. Other authors, too, stressed an artist's developing isolation from an indiscriminate group as they began to place him in more awkward and tragic circumstances. This can be seen in Thackeray's marked differentiation between Clive Newcome and J. J. Ridley, and their contemporaries. When writing of the two friends he employed moralistic and idealistic overtones lacking in his more jocular early accounts of the artistic fraternity considered *en masse*. The same difference was illustrated by Du Maurier's early depiction of Little Billee, first as one of a bohemian community and then later when he was singled out for more solemn consideration.

The easiest way of recognizing when a nineteenth century author is beginning to convey the impression that one of his characters is a tormented genius rather than a simple student, is not only to look for a relatively mature and isolated character but one provoking an influx of wild, woolly mysticism. These writers presented their readers with artist heroes who had remarkable, unchallenged supernatural affinities, but these were never specific, never overtly sectarian.[3] The artist's undefined spiritual experiences, nebulous powers, and imprecise beliefs contributed to his already attractive aura, and again gave him a central position in the romantic movement, which tended to select the suggestive rather than the factual, evoking cosmic mystery, not organized religion.[4]

A tale devoted to this kind of evocative mysticism was Dante Gabriel Rossetti's *Hand and Soul* published in *The Germ* (1850). This was mystical in the sense of being virtually unintelligible. The childish pranks in *Trilby,* which provide a perfect example of the kind of frivolous environment associated with the bohemian apprentice, are complemented by the metaphysical absurdities of *Hand and Soul* which illustrated the supernatural complications dogging the more intense artist.

Two of the most confusing passages in the story described the visions of a thirteenth century Italian painter, Chiaro di Messa Bello dell' Erma. The first vision, which was trance-like and inspired by prayer, led the ecstatic artist to

> behold that day when his mistress . . . his mystical lady (now in her ninth year, but whose solemn smile at meeting had already lighted on his soul like the dove of the trinity) . . . even she, his own gracious and holy Italian art . . . with her unfathomable eyes, and the thread of sunlight round her brows . . . should pass, through the sun that never sets, into the circle of the shadow of the tree of life, and be seen of God, and found good: and then it seemed to him, that he, with many who, since his coming had joined the band of whom he was one (for, in his dream, the body he had worn on earth had been dead an hundred years), were permitted to gather round the blessed maiden, and to worship with her through all ages and ages of ages, saying, Holy, holy, holy.[5]

The phraseology recording this experience introduced a general tone of idealistic uncertainty. Art, for example, was virtually deified, but in a puzzling way, for it was described as the painter's unfathomable spiritual mistress, his 'mystical lady', in a poetical manner suggesting a blend of Dante's Beatrice and the Virgin Mary, both of whom were suggested elsewhere in the story. The reference to the dove, continuing the religious imagery, significantly selected the most mysterious and ethereal aspect of the Trinity, that of the indefinable Holy Spirit. The inclusion of the number nine and a circle of darkness may also have had some unspecified esoteric significance. The idea of a band of artists perennially engaged in worship, tirelessly reiterating the words 'Holy, holy, holy', conjured up comparable Biblical images of angelic devotion, indirectly nourishing the literary artist's ego.

Another factor contributing to the overall impression of mystical confusion was the abysmal nature of the prose. The passage quoted above was only part of a single rambling sentence whose clumsy, involved style and syntax did little to elucidate the subject matter. The metaphors Rossetti used were of an allegorical rather than a powerful symbolic nature. Their meaning is not immediately and indeed never may be recognizable to an imaginative, responsive intellect, neither is the ambiguity stimulating, as in romantic works like 'Kubla Khan'. The awkward, obtuse quality of the writing is indicated by Rossetti's repeated use of 'sun'. A description of a 'thread of sunlight' round the mystical lady's brows was directly followed by an intimation that she would pass 'through the sun that never sets, into the circle of the shadow of the tree of life'. The first image is confusing, for a halo of light round the head is an archetypal symbol of supernatural power, but this description mentions a thread of sunlight round the brows suggesting strangely that the lady had luminous lines like spiritual eye-makeup around her eyebrows. The subsequent solar image referring to a never-setting sun is equally perplexing: it suggests that the afterlife is comparable with eternal light, and also negative shadow. Rather than producing a poignant paradox, as Wordsworth did by equating eternity with the 'light of setting suns', this description is inexplicably irrational. A competent writer of genuine creative powers would probably have connected ideas about such a powerfully evocative image in order to fuse and emphasize his overall meaning, or to produce telling contrasts, but these two unrelated references merely neutralized each other.

There was a significant reference to a painting by Chiaro dell' Erma (bearing the legend *Manus Animam pixit*) in *Aylwin,* Watts-Dunton's rambling, otherworldly novel subtitled 'The Renascence of Wonder'. This included a weird artist called Wilderspin who had 'visionary' stamped upon his every feature, who owed his greatest inspiration to supernatural phenomena which were every bit as confusing as those in *Hand and Soul.* Wilderspin favoured a particularly involved kind of spiritualism, apparently showing some affinities with Blake, called Aylwinianism in deference to the novel's hero, Philip Aylwin, a half-baked esoteric writer. The talented painter was also under the spiritual guidance of 'Mary Wilderspin in heaven', a valiant creature who had previously been his earthly mother.

The most revealing information which Watts-Dunton gave about the nature of this artist's beliefs came from descriptions of his major work 'Faith and Love'; a tribute to Philip Aylwin's treatise *The Veiled Queen*. The veiled and confusing allegories in Wilderspin's painting – which included a procession in Greece, elements of Ancient Egyptian mythology, and sleeping angels – showed that, quite apart from this author's naturally involved thinking, obscurity was the order of the day. Watts-Dunton, obviously trying to make Wilderspin appear an exotic genius, allowed his narrator to say that there were passages of 'burning eloquence' in the painter's 'mystical jargon'. The fact that an artist such as Wilderspin voluntarily dedicated himself to such occult themes, labouring with such fervour, placed him, and others like him, in a quasi-religious position, in a revelatory or prophetic role.[6] This was first suggested by memories of his developing career, which was akin to a religious ordination. 'In no way has the spirit neglected the apostle of spiritual beauty. But long before I could read or write my mother knew that I was set apart for great things . . . that, unless the great world pressed too heavily upon me, I should become a great painter. . . . Art became my religion: success in it my soul's goal.'[7] Success, when it came, was automatically linked with spiritual vision: Wilderspin was proudly convinced that the non-material world was giving him a strength of vision 'second only to the Master's own. . . .'

The fuller implications of the underlying comparison between priest and artist, suggested in so much nineteenth century fiction, probably accounted for the essentially serious, often unhealthy reverential treatment awarded the developing artist hero. Analogies with priests provided potentially rich romantic subject matter, allowing for extremes of idealized drama and emotional tension in the artist's supposedly maturing private life, and suggesting the stereotyped patterns governing such situations. If, in the grandest interpretations, the artist's work could be equated with the achievements of a spiritualistic visionary, then it followed that other important aspects of a prophetic life would be equally germane. A degree of personal isolation fostered complete absorption and profound involvement in holy concerns. St Paul and other religious thinkers had stressed the importance and necessity of celibacy for deep religious attainment. This led to the feeling that the artist/priest should not marry, or form a permanent, passionate and exclusive relationship, but should concentrate his chief energies on his work or mission.[8] An intense emotional commitment to a specific woman, as opposed to mass philandering in an adolescent atmosphere of light-hearted bohemian revelry, was, therefore, not only a waste of time, but morally wrong. Gissing, for example, in *The Emancipated* (1893) entitled a chapter which described his painter hero falling in love as 'The Artist Astray'. Nineteenth century writers delighted in fraught, melodramatic situations where a vibrantly emotional artistic genius was polarized between the apparently opposite attractions of women and work.[9]

The rival claims of art and love were complicated by contemporary ideas about beauty. The cornerstone of the generalized mysticism surrounding the artist usually culminated in theories postulating the value of Beauty, traditionally manifest in the female form. A superlative beauty was depicted as a proof of divinity, the essential physical factor required to inspire the artist's representational work.[10] As the foundations of traditional religious creeds crumbled, people who still instinctively craved belief concentrated, like the eighteenth century philosopher David Hartley, on the value of natural beauty as an indirect means to grace, which was also manifest in the beauty of art. The importance of a superlative, inspiring beauty was shown in a poem by Christina Rossetti about an artist and the fair woman who 'fills his dreams':

> A queen in opal or in ruby dress,
> A nameless girl in freshest summer greens.
> A saint, an angel – every canvas means
> The same one meaning, neither more nor less.
> He feeds upon her face by day and night.[11]

Similarly, the idea of a painter worshipfully feeding on a face was clearly expressed by a romantic artist in Chapter XXXVII of George Eliot's *Daniel Deronda*. He argued that a man would happily honour a beautiful woman he found inspiring by painting her a thousand times, preferring such idealized repetition to the use of an ordinary model, however grand the subject: 'Every painter worth remembering has painted the face he admired most, as often as he could. It is a part of his soul that goes into his pictures. He diffuses its influence in that way. He puts what he hates into caricature, he puts what he adores into some sacred, heroic form.'

A curious kindergarten version of this theme – that of the artist's higher nature being spiritually inspired by an ideal beauty – occurred in Emma Marshall's *Castle Meadow* (1897). She described the effects of a little girl's tubercular beauty on a young urchin. The first stage in this metaphysical transformation occurred early in Book One, 'The Childhood of Genius', when Johnnie Crome heard Dulcibel call him a wicked, cruel boy for pulling hairs out of a cat's tail. He was deeply affected. It was the first time Dulcibel, known as Bell, had spoken – 'suddenly the boy's manner changed. He became aware of the beauty of the picture before him. . . . The eyes that took all this in were the eyes of an artist. . . .'[12]

Mrs Marshall staged a trite death-bed scene in order to impress her reader still further with the strong bond between Johnnie and Bell. The latter's godly appeal was such that on hearing she was ill Johnnie bravely hastened to visit her, unhesitatingly making a twenty-six mile journey to an unknown destination. The child genius's use of Bell's word 'pilgrimage' to describe this undertaking recalled the latter's obsession with the rigours of *Pilgrim's Progress* (1678). Arriving tired and weary, Johnnie was, according to Mrs Marshall, amply rewarded by what were, in effect, moralizing clichés derived from *Pilgrim's Progress,* and a glance of divine pity from Bell's gentian eyes.

Finally, Mrs Marshall emphasized the effect of Bell's personality on Johnnie's creativity in Book Two, entitled 'The Child is Father to the Man'. Crome's tough struggles – including life in the proverbial artist's garret – had been secretly nourished by the recollections of her beauty:

> Thoughts of her came to him sometimes, like an angel's visit, unawares, as they did now. He went to a pile of old drawings heaped in a corner, and after some searching drew out a rough bit of paper, on which was a rude attempt to represent boughs of roses, and beneath the figure of a sleeping child, . . . Her words came back to him, –
> 'Mind you come to the City, and keep in the straight narrow way.'[13]

A variation on the standard theme of ideal, inspiratory beauty occurred in *The Picture of Dorian Gray*: the slight figure, finely curved scarlet lips, beautiful blue eyes and crisp gold hair of the painter's muse belonged to a boy who stepped out on to the dais with the air of a young Greek martyr, and made 'a little *moue* of discontent to Lord Henry, to whom he had taken rather a fancy'. Lord Henry later learnt how important this attractive young Adonis was to the painter:

It is not merely that I paint from him, draw from him, sketch from him . . . he is much more to me than a model or a sitter. . . . 'A dream of form in days of thought' . . . is what Dorian Gray has been to me. The merely visible presence of this lad . . . ah! I wonder can you realize all that that means? Unconsciously he defines for me the lines of a fresh school, a school that is to have in it all the passion of the romantic spirit, all the perfection of the spirit that is Greek.[14]

A belief in the inspirational nature of ideal beauty provoked the crisis in *Mrs Bligh* (1892), a romantic novel by Rhoda Broughton (who also wrote *Cometh up as a flower, Doctor Cupid, Alas!* etc.). The artist hero, whose face could light up with feeling as he inflated his nostrils, parted his lips and dilated his eyes, was naturally attractive to women. One particular devotee, Mrs Bligh, on hearing that his work was in a decline, went as far as to persuade a well-bred and well-formed young friend to sit for him, for her beauty would automatically secure the sculptor's 'artistic salvation'.

The writer gave her heroine one especially rousing speech, as she tried to sublimate her jealousy – for art.

'Many women' – with a gallantly swallowed sigh – 'admired women . . . would think it no great hardship to have him talk to them for an hour, or a couple of hours at a time. . . . You think that you are doing a good work . . . when you allow these factory girls [visited for charity] to drag you about . . . you do not seem to see how very much greater an act of charity it would be to give essential help at a critical moment – with so little cost to yourself, too – to a man of real genius.'[15]

The young beauty was eventually convinced but Mrs Bligh was left jealously regretting the 'horrible irony' behind the situation she had created: Pamela, choking with 'maiden shame', explained that as the fascinating artist had such a caressing manner to women she had only been afraid of getting 'too much *sous le charme*. I was afraid that I might – I might – lose my head!' The irony was intensified when the sculptor, posing her as Aurora for his new statue, referred to himself as poor old Tithonus.

Although a superlative beauty could be considered a visual proof of divinity and the ideal physical factor required to inspire an artist's work, the claims and attractions of the lady's personality were frequently represented as the beguiling wiles of an evil temptress, the gravest threat to the artist's budding career. The artist, irresistibly drawn to a woman whose appearance personified his objective ideal, saw as much of her as he could, in every sense, because her presence provided such a stimulus to his all-important aesthetic creativity. In such conditions, given the relative intimacy of sittings and a general bohemian disregard for convention, it was impossible for the sensitive, impressionable artist not to begin to respond to such an attractive being with growing subjectivity. His own charm, the lady's, or a combination of the two, soon secured a dangerous degree of emotional involvement: an intense visual obsession rapidly developed into a serious psychological commitment. The tense *ménage à trois* existing between man, woman and art now became further entangled. Art became an integral part of the man's love-making because the artist not only wanted to celebrate his earthly mistress, but relied on his creative triumphs to secure her admiration and respect. However, the more a woman secured the artist's personal attention the quicker his work floundered. For, having sold himself to Mammon,[16] letting his high, spiritual ambitions become obscured and side-tracked by worldly infatuation, the artist could no longer expect to receive, let alone interpret and define, supernaturally inspired vision.

Browning displayed great finesse when exploring this theme in 'Andrea del Sarto (called the Faultless Painter)'. Throughout this apparently casual, conversational monologue suggestive understatement and seemingly flippant ironies enforced a strict lesson. The variance between fleeting transcendental vision and practical achievement depended on the artist's moral worth. Speaking to his adored wife, Lucrezia, coaxing her to sit for him, he heard a whistle below – her cousin calling for her. Disturbing insinuations hinged on this apparently trivial incident. Lucrezia, his model for the virgin, was unfaithful to him, and he, in order to please her, acquiesced in the exploitation of his art so that money could be provided for her so-called 'cousin'. The fact that Andrea's creativity was being harnessed to pay the 'cousin's' gambling debts (for Browning's Victorian contemporaries found the wilful squandering of money particularly deplorable), and also that the artist seemed to consider his fate as a punishment for another moral failure, his heartless rejection of his old parents, added to his unsavoury situation. The painter, who had earlier fulfilled Lucrezia's wishes by deserting the welcoming court of the French king, who was an ideal patron honouring his abilities and furthering his career, had irrevocably prostituted his talent. He had allowed his infatuation with his wife's temporary, physical beauty to supersede and contaminate the essential claims of his profession, which implied a continued unworldly devotion to the creation of timeless, spiritually inspired aesthetic perfection. While Andrea del Sarto's work might appear technically faultless, he had blighted his true creativity by forfeiting the right to metaphysical vision.[17] His acute consciousness of his own predicament, where true greatness had been sacrificed for present profit, provokes the reader's condemnation while securing his sympathy. This is particularly true when, with wistful envy, the tolerant but essentially weak painter spoke resignedly of other more hopeful artists:

> There burns a truer light of God in them,
> In their vexed beating stuffed and stopped-up brain,
> Heart, or whate'er else, than goes on to prompt
> This low-pulsed forthright craftsman's hand of mine.
> Their works drop groundward, but themselves, I know,
> Reach many a time a heaven that's shut to me,
> Enter and take their place there sure enough,
> Though they come back and cannot tell the world.
> My works are nearer heaven, but I sit here.[18]

In *The Worshipper of the Image* (1899) Richard Le Gallienne portrayed a similar tussle between the opposing claims of love and art by describing the bitter rivalry which existed between a charming woman and a fascinating image with a perculiarly lifelike presence.[19] The ambiguous connections existing between these two alien powers are astutely evoked by the fact that they belonged to an identical aesthetic type. Le Gallienne's hero originally bought the image which represented art, and was known as Silencieux because it looked astonishingly like his beautiful wife. She, at first enchanted by the modelled face, became increasingly suspicious of its magnetic presence as her husband grew increasingly obsessed by its 'cold music'. The image spoke to him, explaining that she had inspired artists, such as the young sculptor, and poets, such as himself, for hundreds of years. She tried to concentrate his attention wholly on herself, the Face of Eternal Beauty, by ruthlessly severing his closest earthly links: 'you have given your allegiance to the warm and pretty humanity of a day. . . . But it is all in vain.'[20]

Silencieux, who was closely associated with evil, isolated him from his family. Once, for example, when Antony took her into the country a venomous adder approached the carving, coiling itself round her white throat and moving restlessly under her chin until with a movement of infinite grace it clasped her neck and 'softly neared its lips to hers. Its black tongue darted to and fro along that strange smile.' Le Gallienne then made his decadent creation, the beautiful image with poison-kissed lips, tell Antony that she demanded a human sacrifice of her 'lovers'. Overcoming his initial repulsion, he brought his only daughter, forcing her to embrace the carving's icy mouth, and raving, after his daughter's subsequent fatal illness, that he had sacrificed her to the Moloch of Art. Similarly, after his wife's suicide he found a strange light emanating from the radiant wide-eyed image, from whose lips hung a 'dark moth with the face of death between his wings'.

This writer's theme hinged on the fact that, having drawn energy from the elimination of her closest rival, the image of art would ultimately destroy the hero himself – for he had been warned that he would die on seeing the open eyes of the death-mask. Links between destruction and impersonal sexuality – such as the sequence in this story opening with the traditional European symbol of cold-blooded, erotic evil, the snake, and connecting a series of unnatural deaths with the coldly sensual mouth of a sculpture – were generally reserved for temptresses symbolizing the tantalizing powers of immoral feminity.[21]

These depraved creatures resolved the artist hero's battle between the attractions of passion and art by revealing that they were not only beauties but fascinating *femmes fatales*. Such a woman, suddenly tiring of her prey, would cruelly forsake a besotted artist, thus breaking his will to create. The romantic cult of the *femme fatale* produced a being who, like a Hollywood version of Madame Bovary, was exaggeratedly glamourised and devoid of all realistic blemishes, banalities and absurdities. In dramatic terms she provided a perfect foil to the character of the divinely-inspired creator.[22] Threatening the talent and vision of the sensitive artist with her arrogantly hynotic personal power, she represented the essence of pagan destruction.

An excellent example of such a powerful temptress occurred in *Dionea,* a tale by Vernon Lee.[23] The narrator, who was studying 'The Exiled Gods' related how her sculptor hero became a devotee and victim of a latter-day pagan goddess. A convincing series of incidents paved the way for the sculptor's hopeless obsession and subsequent destruction. Dionea's heathen nature was indicated from the beginning – in a series of pointed contrasts between her behaviour and that of the nuns who brought her up. As well as being identified with traditional attributes of Venus such as myrtle and roses she was, like many other *femmes fatales,* closely associated with the sea and its uncontrollable power.[24] Her dangerous presence provoked a previously dedicated priest to commit suicide, while a persistent farmer was struck, at an opportune moment, by lightning. The sculptor – victim number three – was as irresistibly drawn to her as her other admirers had been. After using her as a model, he began not only to ignore his miserable wife, but to think more of Dionea's beauty than of his work, becoming curiously jealous and at the same time worshipful. She, swathed in her constant self-satisfaction, utterly uninterested in her vassal, did nothing to release him from his intolerable predicament. Vernon Lee, in describing her artist hero's last actions, left the reader with no doubt as to the pagan nature of his infatuation and destruction. He had not simply formed an unfortunate friendship but had, in some fatalistic fashion, allowed himself to be mesmerized by a superhuman presence: he was last seen alive worshipping Dionea, Venus like, on a rose-decked altar.

Charles Lee was one of the many writers who regurgitated similar material, as in *Cynthia in the West* (1900). Cynthia the heroine was closely associated with the mysterious properties of the moon. Lee tried to make her a symbol of the impersonal attractions traditionally associated with the moon, mysterious mistress of tides, growth and affections, uncomfortably recreating the goddess Diana in his priggish heroine, who was not so much naturally chaste as naturally frigid. Her utter disgust at a mild rustic courtship where two friendly bumpkins swayed along a dark road exchanging the odd kiss provides material for psychoanalysis.

But if Lee is unable to persuade his reader of Cynthia's charm, he is certainly constant in mentioning it. He began his second-rate melodrama by explaining Cynthia's mawkish effect on the male members of an artistic colony. By the time he has revealed that Forester, his painter hero, was himself besotted, the reader is in no doubt (as in the case of the hero in *Dionea*) about the danger of his predicament. One unhappy slave, his proposals recently rejected, told a vulnerable newcomer that Cynthia made one feel as though 'she's a goddess and you're a wriggling worm'. But how could the lamp help it, poor Cynthia asked on another occasion, if moths *would* burn themselves at its flame?

Lee contrasted this refined *femme fatale's* exclusive allure with the lowly, and neglected, charms of Forester's model. In the author's final skimpy ending Cynthia made friends with the despised and envious model and melted on seeing the hero rescued from drowning, but this momentary affirmation of possible happiness carried little weight, coming as it did after Lee had built his novel upon so many misunderstandings. The general impression given by the book is of yet another mediocre author who liked nothing better than to concoct endless situations designed to try, rather than challenge, the emotions of a 'sensitive' artist.

Ironically the vain, callous selfishness and amused indifference characterizing the *femme fatale* who could wreak such havoc in the artist's life often reflected many of his own attitudes and characteristics, for the happy bohemian was often, objectively speaking, rather a 'chauvinist pig' himself. This point was made by Ouida in *Two Little Wooden Shoes* (1874), where the handsome painter hero 'knew well' that when the hound hunted the faun, when the king coveted the vineyard, etc., etc., 'there is only one end possible'. . . . This sensual sadist – 'women are never grateful, my dear, except when they are very ill-treated' – had endless affairs based on the principle of here today and gone tomorrow, always making sure that the 'forgetfulness ever afterwards' was his own.

Later in *The Incomplete Amorist* (1911), Edith Nesbit, while still presenting the orthodox, romantic view of the artist, was not completely prejudiced in his favour; glimpsing and indeed criticizing the ruthlessness of his amorous activities. This painter hero's unhappy love affair was seen not so much as an unwarrantedly tragic blow from Fate, but as the working of poetic justice. The author quoted an effusive page from a young girl's diary revealing the virtuous attractions of Mr Vernon. He was kind, straightforward, and truthful. It was such a comfort, as she was meeting him secretly, to know he was as good as gold. 'I revere him', the touching entry concluded, adding: 'I believe he is really noble and unselfish, and so few men are, alas'. The noble Vernon was equally happy with their encounters: the fact that he occupied the thoughts of an innocent little girl with a face like a kitten filled him with unbounded delight: he was about to indulge in his 'favourite sport' feeling sure, like those who hunt with the fox, that Reynard 'enjoys, equally with the hounds and their masters, the pleasures of the chase'.

Vernon's thoughtless, condescending, incomplete concept of

love (suggested by the title, *The Incomplete Amorist*), his habitually hypocritical attitude to the 'pleasures of the chase', suffered an abrupt shock when, after making a career of playing with other people's affections, he fell deeply in love with the 'good little girl' he had already seduced at the beginning of the novel. As chapters provokingly entitled 'The Man' and 'The Other Man' suggested, she, too, was changeable: she abruptly abandoned the flirtatious artist. But, as a sad former mistress pointed out, his behaviour was merely being rewarded in kind.

The nineteenth century fictional artist's struggle to balance the claims of art and romance often ended when a *femme fatale* entangled his emotions to the extent that she annihilated his creative interest. His trials could also be resolved in another equally tragic but less dramatic fashion: he could marry. This proved equally unsatisfactory. Cohabitation swiftly transformed his ethereal Muse into a bourgeois tyrant. Consuming time, money and energy, she eroded his creative liberty with regular domesticity. In *The Newcomes* the artist hero went from the frying pan into the fire, for, having been long tormented by the tantalizing Ethel Newcome, he married a sweet, innocent sylph called Rosie, who, growing curiously like her mother, speedily developed into a nagging housewife. Unsympathetic towards his work, restrictive in her social attitudes, she soon lost all charm, becoming a source of boring interference. Clive grew increasingly bewildered, careworn and dismal, retiring sadly to his studio to escape her bleating demands for conventional jaunts and snobbish entertainments and her unfeeling criticism of his 'horrid' messy artist's ways. The practical, habitual, humdrum and institutional aspects of matrimony (as opposed to the symbolic union of souls suggested by last page proposals), and the romantic concept of the free, intuitive painterly life were incompatible. Man, born free, was everywhere enchained by marriage.

Novels in which the orthodoxly charming artist hero married comparatively early in the story, where his marriage, an important element in the plot, was discussed in positive terms, and which ended with him declaring his complete love and total commitment to his spouse were rare. Tom, the hero of *Limitations* by E. F. Benson, was warned of the dangers of matrimony and other matters when he first decided to sculpt: his father, who had heard of sculptors becoming involved with their models, warned that this was a profession in which a man had 'unlimited opportunities for making a fool of himself'. This parental agony seemed uncalled for when Tom became engaged to a sweet, respectable girl with a passion for parish visiting – but the writer, having pointedly entitled his story *Limitations,* proved that a 'perfect' marriage could be just as debilitating as a sleasy liaison. The artist's domestic union was – apart from minor problems – undeniably fruitful but his aesthetic and visionary ambitions remained unfulfilled. Tom spoke, at the end of the novel, of three crises in his life. While he was happy about one, which concerned his love for his wife, he was dejected about his other 'still-born' revelations, one of which had been religious and the other artistic. A well-intentioned friend, querying the scuptor's pessimistic evaluation of his own career, drew his attention to his largest, most ambitious work:

> 'Do you call that nothing?' said Manvers, pointing to the shrouded Demeter.
> 'Worse than nothing. It is a dead child. It had better never have been born.'

The idea that an artist's method of production was a begetting of children occurs elsewhere. In the preface to Scott's *The Bride of Lammermoor,* for example, a painter looked at his work just as a 'fond parent looks upon a hopeful child', and in *Roderick Hudson* an aesthetic failure was described as an abortion. However, in *Limitations* the comparison was more complex. The use of abortive imagery – that of the still-born, symbolically shrouded, dead child – was particularly forceful in the context of the sculptor's contentedly fertile marriage: domestic fecundity had curtailed artistic creativity. This implication, and its reverse, added to a general understanding of the artist hero's tendency, as a type, to find himself involved in unnaturally tragic relationships with women. Added to his flighty, rebellious bohemianism, his temperamental need to preserve a degree of personal detachment in order to preserve his spiritual vision, was the fact that the artist's ties with his work were not only practical but emotional, as intense and demanding as those of a mother with her offspring.[26] In this situation, when the romantic artist's primary emotional ties, as well as his idealistic ones, were best engrossed in his creative work, normally close, stable, mutually enriching human relationships became essentially superfluous, badly balanced, and unnatural.

Unhappy affairs led to tragic breakdowns. An emotionally or domestically destructive woman was often simply an agent provoking a far more interesting dramatic situation – that within the artist's mind. Under stress, the artist's particular temperament made him particularly vulnerable.

Joseph Hatton showed, in *The Tallants of Barton,* how an artist's creative powers were indisputably linked with his capacity for emotional reactions. Conclusive proof of his hero's 'genius' for painting was provided by the quality of a work which had been stimulated, originally, by the painter's deep feelings on parting from a dear friend. Hatton began, significantly, by recording with a fictional rather than objectively aesthetic metaphor that the 'story was wonderfully told: the picture was a poem on canvas – full of human nature, brimming over with sympathy', adding that: 'As a work of art – for conception, drawing, perspective colour, it was a truly grand picture.'[27] This exceptionally positive painter's achievements explain why romantic writers cultivated an artist's intensely emotional and subjective qualities. For, by reacting to influences and impressions with exceptional force, and by concentrating his energies upon his feelings, the artist could produce works of genius.[28]

George Gissing in *The Emancipated* (1893) demonstrated just such an obsessional bias, invariably selecting and praising the concept of the romantic artist as a sensitive egoist. He was a privileged being who could not be judged like other men. Art was undoubtedly the grandest thing in the world, the ultimate expression of strength and beauty. The creator of art, therefore, was a gifted superior. While it was unhesitatingly assumed that the common herd 'must' be bound by social rules and standards, the artist was, in this novel, encouraged to intensify any natural differences between himself and his fellow men by indulgently defending his freedom to use his time and sensibilities as he wished.

Gissing described, for example, how a civilized young lady, meeting a particularly vain and pompous young fop for the first time, curbed her normal critical judgement. For, although she suspected that his pretentions rested on 'impudent' work, she felt that if this painter was really a genius then he had 'the right to vary from the kindly race of men'. Gissing's puritanical heroine became 'emancipated' as she absorbed this truth. Where she had formerly been devoted to useful causes she now learnt to cherish art and to allow artists the right to a temperamental *carte blanche*. The painter hero, himself determined to brook no interference, summed up this philosophy when he said: 'I am right to persevere, I am right to go on pleasing myself.'[29]

The popular nineteenth century beliefs in the artist's need to defend his sensibilities, his 'right' to please himself, were stressed at the expense of other characteristics. The artist's impressionable imagination became a liability when it was revealed that he could not only be inspired, but dangerously swayed, by external experiences and sensations. In William Black's *A Princess of Thule* (1874) the charisma of the aesthetic Lavander masked a vulnerable lack of control. A modest, dependable, and rather reassuringly 'ordinary' friend recognized that the young hero was 'not commonplace – he fancied he could see in him the occasional flash of something like genius; and many and many a time, in regarding the brilliant and facile powers, the generous impulses, and the occasional ambitions of his companion, he wondered whether these would ever lead to anything in the way of production, or even of consolidation of character'. . . .[30] Fictional artists were incompetent and unreliable. They lacked self-discipline and self-sufficiency. Witness the description of Bertie, in *Barchester Towers,* seen by Trollope as a self-centred parasite:

> He had no principle, no regard for others, no self-respect, no desire to be other than a drone in the hive, if only he could as a drone get what honey was sufficient for him. Of honey, in his latter days, it may probably be presaged, that he will have but short allowance.[31]

In retrospect, apparently flattering visual descriptions of a charming artist hero had often indicated his inherent weaknesses: his exciting, dramatic appearance never suggested method or reliability – the antithesis, for example, of the sturdy physiques and clean, practical uniforms distinguishing an efficiently disciplined soldier or even a trusty boy scout. Again, as with these telling visual descriptions, apparently light-hearted early accounts of bohemian artists usually gave hints of incipient instability: one of the chief attractions of the artistic temperament was its energetic, versatile, escalating range, but ecstatic abandon, sultry sulks, extravagant impulses and savage furies did not add up to mental maturity. Even with a genteel artist, such as Du Maurier's Little Billee, intense emotions could easily curdle into hysteria. The fictional artist, whose frenzied nervous fits accelerated his decline, could easily develop into an anti-social manic-depressive. When he was at the mercy of an unproductive mood, the egoism which had previously served as a positive spur to his ambition, making him concentrate his attention on his own ideas, could become a restrictive force. Instead of being able to dismiss any particularly unsatisfactory episode from his memory, or write it off as experience gained, he was apt to magnify his own problems over-indulgently. Without a saving sense of divine comedy, undistracted by concern for others, he cocooned himself in his own woes, unhealthily and unhappily obsessed by the importance of his own self-inflicted isolation.

The most masterly exponent of the artist's psychology was Henry James, whose Roderick Hudson not only embodied virtually all the romantic traits found in the artist as a type, but was depicted with a literary skill unsurpassed by other authors.[32] This is particularly true in passages dealing with the sculptor's temperament, for James attained a rare degree of detachment which, coupled with his delicately constructed and cohesive imagery, allowed him to present Roderick's mental makeup with unusual refinement. Compare, for example, the very different, crudely sensational style used by Lucas Malet in *The Wages of Sin* (1891) to describe the precarious temperament of the painter hero before he died in falling from a cliff into the ocean below. This was a long-winded, ostensibly moral novel – 'art like religion lives by sacrifice' – which disguised a healthy appetite for sex and violence with a veneer of profound disapproval. James Colthurst slowly seduced a voluptuous country girl and proceeded with her to Paris, where he fell ill and his kind companion resorted to prostitution; thus, as the author put it with characteristic relish, keeping life in him 'at the sacrifice of what remained to her of good fame; thereby making his life here, in a sense, not his own. She had given his life back to him but had given it back polluted.' The ungrateful artist was deeply distressed by this melodramatic relationship and became increasingly neurotic, particularly when it began to hamper his subsequent courtship of a rich blonde prude. Although his 'electric' character, which made the prude consider their first embrace a 'baptism of fire', was compared with Judas, a whirlpool, a Beast and a Tartar, these simple if savage labels hardly elucidated the artist's peculiar, fluctuating emotionalism.

In James's art, however, seemingly innocent details had more implicit significance, and therefore added up to a much more plausible *dénouement* showing that the artist hero had always carried the seeds of his own destruction within him. James injected into a flattering early account of Roderick Hudson's ethereal grace the subtle comment: 'The fault of the young man's whole structure was an excessive want of breadth': his narrow forehead and shoulders gave an air of 'insufficient physical substance'. Unimportant at the time, these remarks about his structural vulnerability seemed, in retrospect, to have given apt physical clues to his mental weakness and unbalance: [33] 'He was brilliant, but was he, like many brilliant things, brittle?'

His light frame was powered by nervous energy. This emotional energy was his greatest attraction. Roderick, a 'colorist' in conversation as well as dress, was renowned for his 'entertaining temper'. In retrospect his volatile moods were suggestively immature, erratic and swamping. Hudson, who could sit by the hour 'watching the flies buzz', could, in response to some exterior stimulus, leap from flat disinterest to feverish excitement. Hearing, for example, that he was to have the chance of going to Europe, he smashed a bust. James used the unthinking exhibitionism underlying this lively act, when Hudson had impulsively destroyed not only his own labour and a work appreciated by his family but a commission, to betray how the sculptor's temperament was ruled by egotistical emotional instinct, not long-term logic or consideration for others. This anticipated a later incident when, regardless of the fact that he was already deep in debt, he refused to honour a contract, saying he was an artist, not a tailor.

The sculptor's temperamental displays had grown increasingly hysterical after he failed to come to terms with a personal crisis brought on when Christina Light, the beautiful, ambitious woman with whom he was in love, married a rich prince. Hudson, who had been swayed by her mysterious personality (in a way which James equated with Ulysses being tempted by the Sirens) became unsettled by the turn of events and had a severe breakdown. He spent hopeless introverted months when he sat dressed all in white, lethargic and withdrawn, his mind experiencing, as James put it, a 'dead calm' in the tropics, his imagination as motionless as the phantom ship in 'The Ancient Mariner' (a poem equating, some argue, the failure of creation with being in the doldrums).

Devoted friends then brought him to Switzerland where his deep depression was transformed into wild, manic enthusiasm. Having accidently seen Christina again, he became utterly obsessed, and in rashly following her fell to his death. The sculptor with 'radiant unscrupulous eagerness' demanded money to finance his journey both from his own fiancée and his best friend. When this exhausted friend finally rebuked him for his heartless use of his fiancée (poignantly adding that Hudson's thoughtless actions had wrecked his own chances), the artist responded with transcendental egoism, soulfully lamenting his own tarnished persona.

Genius, 'a two-edged blade', was frequently described in images of fire and light, traditional symbols of wild, anarchistic activity and pure spiritual vision. The close links between a divine gift and an emotional hazard made pure genius volatile, insecure. Gloriani, a rarely glimpsed mature, self-cultivated creator, put it succinctly – 'Passion burns out, inspiration runs to seed'.[34] The first long account of Hudson described him as having an eye 'in which there came and went a sort of kindling glow'. His temperament was reflected in his quick and mobile face 'over which expression flickered like a candle in the wind'. Neither of these latter images was specifically connected with light or fire: they were ambiguous. While the words glow and candle suggested steady light, kindling and flickering suggested the more uncertain action of flames.

The sculptor's talent could also be seen in terms of both fire and light. An early admirer said: 'The flame is smouldering, but it is never fanned by the breath of criticism.' But when Roderick went to Rome to become a 'rising star' in the art world, copious light was used to exalt his capacity. A friend coming in from a dark street saw, within the formal frame of a doorway, three artists, standing before Hudson's statue of Eve. The ardent young hero had lifted up a lamp whose light, suggesting a halo, covered his head and face with 'picturesque symbolism, Roderick, bearing the lamp and glowing in its radiant circle, seemed the beautiful image of genius which combined sincerity with power'.[35] Christina Light summed up her first admiring impression of this contemporary Apollo with the dramatic disclosure:

> 'When I first knew you I gave no sign, but you had struck me. I observed you as women observe, and I fancied you had the sacred fire.'
> 'Before Heaven I believe I have!' cried Roderick.

His swelling vanity was punctured like a chilled *soufflé* by her more rudely realistic digression on the present nature of his so-called sacred fire. It was minimal.

> 'It flickers and trembles and splutters; it goes out, you tell me, for whole weeks together. From your own account it's highly probable that you are a failure. . . . You have gone up like a rocket in your profession they tell me; are you going to come down like the stick?'[37]

Here James is making one of his favourite points that wild enthusiasm courts retributive disaster. Energy, he suggests with characteristic obliqueness, will inevitably be exhausted by superficially flashy display. James creates a telling compound image in forecasting the unnerving nature of the artist's catastrophic loss of creative power by equating him with the plummeting remains of a spent firework, for falling had already been equated with failure.

In a discussion of genius which took place long before Roderick became famous, his connoisseur friend said that he had read that it was a kind of somnambulism; the artist performed feats in a dream, but if he wakened he might well 'lose his balance'. This disturbing concept of the artist's precarious insecurity was later paraphrased in 'a vision of Roderick, graceful and beautiful as he passed, plunging like a diver into a misty gulf. The gulf was destruction, annihilation, death. . . .' This prophetic vision deftly anticipated the scene in which Hudson, recklessly advancing through the Alps, symbolically lost his balance – 'falling from a great height'.[38]

The element of danger associated with genius came not only because the artist could completely lose his exalted position, but because such a reversal was unannounced, swift and final. Roderick himself affirmed: 'Nothing is more common than for an artist who has set out on his journey on a high-stepping horse to find himself all of a sudden dismounted and invited to go on his way on foot. You can number them by the thousand – people of two or three successes; the poor fellows whose candle burnt out in a night.'[39] This passage, connecting loss of height with loss of light, stressed the impersonal efficiency of fate. Suddenly, in the duration of a night, ability could be undermined and vision extinguished. The artist's impulsive temperament could not direct its own destiny. Hudson could not control the disintegration of his daily and creative lives: 'The whole matter of genius is a mystery. It bloweth where it listeth and we know nothing of its mechanism.'

Without detracting from the biblical mystery romantically surrounding the nineteenth century conception of genius, James skilfully used practical as well as poetic metaphors to suggest the abstract laws governing its presence. His talent was similarly discussed as a practical asset. His patron told him his genius was a gift, adding – 'don't speculate on it'. The spendthrift sculptor, who worked in moments of joyous inspiration, not with sustained effort, wondered apprehensively who could assure him his 'credit was for an unlimited sum'. Realistic banking terms revealed that his divine gift was only an unspecified short-term loan.

Hudson overspent in every sense. As a youth he had lived 'too fast'. The artist whose first bronze was entitled 'Thirst', and who equated his talent with a cup of wine, continually sought new sensations, new stimulants. When working on his first large statue, he denied himself all breathing time because he was 'so gloriously in the mood'. This breathless exaggeration was an essential part of his character: 'We must live as our pulses are timed, and Roderick's struck the hour very often'. A timepiece which strikes the hour very often strikes it too often. James made a series of effective comparisons between the artist's temperament and clockwork. Roderick, for example, lacked the moderation of the modest little landscapist, Sam Singleton, whose consistent working method was like the regular 'tic, tic, tic' of a clock. Hudson's devoted patron, considering this 'insect'-like symbol of clockwork continuity, at first regretted that his wayward protégé lacked Singleton's 'vulgar' steadiness – 'But then, was Sam Singleton a man of genius?' Genius flourished in exotic temperaments, not tedious, safe, single-minded ones. The vulnerability of the heroic artist's ultra-sensitive, emotionally responsive personality to negative influences, as well as visionary ones, was an inevitable, almost necessary evil: Hudson said the best compliment you could pay a man of genius was to call him a beggar or a madman. Recognizing the element of calculated risk threatening his own sanity, he asked: 'what should you do if the watch should run down, and you should lose the key?'

A high proportion of potentially promising fictional artists gradually coming to think themselves unloved, persecuted and generally misunderstood, courted death with passive resistance to fatal illnesses, or with dramatic suicide bids. Such endings were often described in terms suggesting doomed martyrdom, sacrifice, or even crucifixion.[40]

In *The Atelier du Lys* Margaret Roberts described how an art student literally worked himself to death, expiring in a cheerless Parisian garret. Privation, loneliness, homesickness and disappointment had combined to sap his strength, taking away – in the writer's fatalistic phrase – all desire for 'further battle with fortune'. Walter Pater provided a subtler study of an artist ill-equipped for a prolonged battle with fortune in *A Prince of Court Painters*. This story, included in his *Imaginary Portraits* (1877), was neither art historical survey nor objective biography. It showed, instead, how Pater incorporated genuine aspects of

Watteau's personality – such as the subject matter used by the painter – into an imaginary interpretation which he developed, like an oyster enveloping grit, into one of the most polished and plaintive evocations of the doomed creator found in romantic literature.

Pater manages, in this tale, to describe an ultra-sensitive artist's premature death in such a way that the tragedy appears as the normal, almost the expected, outcome of his career. Pater's method was to insinuate, from the beginning, that there was something strangely sorrowful about his charming painter hero even as a child. He wove negative undercurrents through the story to such an extent that he effectively neutralized the shock and horror naturally provoked by such an untimely death. Thus he created a character ill at ease in the world, whose intense restlessness, viewed in retrospect, suggested that he was living on borrowed time.

There was irony in the fictional artist's choice of compositions: this fictional Watteau created and popularized 'Fêtes Galantes' whose frivolous hedonism had a light coquetry and gaiety strongly at variance with his own singular gravity and sombre mien. It is implied that his talented hero painted elegant, silk-clad ladies and gentlemen relaxing in noble parks and gardens not because he actually found satisfaction in such scenes, but because such sights recalled his lost hopes, his tarnished ideals: Watteau formed his exquisite compositions out of a perverse sense of compensatory nostalgia. His art evoked the 'magical exhilaration of his dream' rather than happy satisfaction in the world as he knew it. The brooding storm behind some of the artist's most gracious trees indicated a threat to the courtiers who played the 'garden comedy of life' beneath them. The vulnerability of these courtly masqueraders was combined with pointed references to the superficial gaiety of the clown – the first glimpse Pater gave his reader of the artist was as a youth tucked into a niche to draw the players at the local fair. Watteau's graceful touch, showing a fastidious omission of the more vulgar realities, made Harlequin, Clown and Columbine into figures from fairyland. It was surely significant that Watteau chose to depict these artificially frivolous figures like 'infinitely clever tragic actors, who, for the humour of the thing, have put on motley for once, and are able to throw a world of serious innuendo into their burlesque looks, with a sort of comedy which shall be but tragedy from the other side'.[41] The connection is clear: the unhappy artist, like the subject matter he favoured, had, throughout the course of his life, reflected something of the essential melancholy of the comedian.

The working methods of Pater's hero, as well as his material, were presented in a way which contributed, with muted emphasis, to the reader's fatalistic view of him: Watteau's painterly technique, often executed on objects such as fans which could themselves perish with the slightest change in fashion, conjured up short-lived power. It was characteristic that his colours changed and faded not long after his death, but from the very first, and also that he preferred to sketch and plan rather than paint and finish. He was temperamentally inclined to rush into impatient action, hardly making any preparations, or even cleaning his palette: the narrator mused that there was a kind of greed or of grasping in this humour – as if things were 'not to last very long, and one must snatch opportunity'.

The painter's appearance was also manipulated to suggest a lack of reliable strength, or stable energy (similar to that which James had created in *Roderick Hudson*); the young genius with the unquiet expression developed into a correspondingly fragile creature whose large eyes were disturbingly restless. He had a hectic quality. He was never in a state of grace. He seemed, to Pater's stolid female narrator, who sensibly equated dignified wisdom with a peaceful disposition, to be 'so brilliant, petulant, mobile'. The restlessness which she had considered natural in an ambitious young man grew, disconcertingly, as his talent developed. He was 'disquieting and meagre like a woman with some nervous malady'. Despite his success, this frail, highly strung creature seemed bored by daily life:

> Restless, he travelled to England that veritable home of the consumptive. . . . To have run into the native country of consumption! Strange caprice of that desire to travel, which he has really indulged in so little in his life – of the restlessness which, they tell me, is itself a symptom of this terrible disease! [42]

The painter was fêted, on his return, by fellow artists who recognized the value of his gift. The narrator's comment at this point was very telling: 'There is something in the payment of great honours to the living which fills me with apprehension, especially when the recipient of them looks so like a dying man'. Pater seemed to imply, in the old Promethean pattern, that it was the very quality of his hero's genius which made him most vulnerable: the artist was at risk because he had been honoured to such an unusual extent. Pater's qualifying clause, however, reminding the reader that the painter was unwell, draws his reader back to a more easily accepted and ostensibly logical cause for concern. One of this author's final comments was that the unhappy idealist he portrayed had been a sick man all his life.

By slowly and surely developing the idea of his hero's inner tension, a frantic state, with moments of profound boredom, Pater convincingly indicated a tubercular disposition. Having continuously included relevant symptoms, before officially identifying them as such, he led his reader to accept the artist's weakness as an integral part of his constitution. Thus the artist's consequent deterioration appeared as the natural outcome of what seemed to be an inherited medical condition. This unemotional and relatively objective handling was certainly effective. The reader subconsciously acquiesced in Watteau's untimely death because this author had presented the popular conception of the doomed artist with such smooth finesse.

Pater was rare in avoiding the sudden melodramatic jarring effect which so frequently accompanied the exit of romantic figures in nineteenth century literature – as, for example, when Lucas Malet, in *The Wages of Sin,* makes a malevolent drunk try to tip his painter hero into the ocean: a somewhat crude form of divine retribution. Pater's delicately moulded story, however, achieves an unusual degree of pathos because of its controlled restraint and his gently realistic means of exterminating his tubercular victim.

Physical sickness again, was employed by George Moore to finish off a young painter in 'Mildred Lawson', one of the stories in *Celibates* (1895), but in this case Moore placed emphasis not on a gradual constitutional decline but rather on an artist's chagrin which made him an easy victim to a fatal disease. Specific symptoms were largely irrelevant unless recognized as the physical symbols of a psychic malaise. The feeble artist explains what he ascribes to the 'fault of luck':

I have been in bad health for some time. I've been disappointed. My painting hasn't gone very well lately. That was a disappointment. Disappointment, I think, is as often the cause of a man's death as anything else. The doctors give it a name: Influenza, or paralysis of the brain, failure of the heart's action, but these are the superficial causes of death. There is often a deeper reason: one which medical science is unable to take into account.[43]

Another typical example of an artist romantically courting death and disaster rather than accepting difficulties or trying to work out any form of mundane compromise occurred in 'The North Coast and Eleanor', included in *Renunciations* (1893). Here Frederick Wedmore played on the fact that belief creates reality. George Norton, a painter hero who measured his love by its intensity rather than its resilience, told his sweetheart that the world was 'too strong' for them and would inevitably destroy their relationship. He projected his pessimism on to his surroundings to such an extent that lingering, foolishly, to discuss the possibilities of drowning on a remote and treacherous beach, fantasy rapidly became fact.

A more obvious suicide occurred in *The Light that Failed* when Kipling made his painter hero, similarly disheartened by an unhappy affair, deliberately risk his life under fire. Kipling killed him in battle. Before his death this artist had gone blind: the title, *The Light that Failed,* suggested the intense pain, suffering and humiliation occasioned by this incapacitating physical loss and also symbolized broken inner vision.

A short story entitled *Wladislaw's Advent* by M. M. Dowie provided an example of a painter being literally mistaken for Christ. The hero was poor, ardent and ultra-sensitive. Wladislaw's beautiful head, with the young light broad beard, the pure forehead, and the long sorrowful eyes, was 'an ideal presentation of the Nazarene'. Wladislaw was in such extreme poverty that he finally consented to sit, as the main figure, for a painting of 'The Temptation' by a superficial but successful master. The hero was bewildered when he caught sight of himself in the dressing-room mirror: 'he stood there naked in the cold, taking his mind back along the familiar lines of the story, entering into the feelings of that Jew-man who was persecuted. . . .'[44]

Trying to find the studio in the dark, he opened a door to find himself faced with a blaze of light, with noise and general chaos. The worldly painter host, having forgotten his work, was holding a wild orgy. The sudden appearance of the otherworldly hero shocked the lascivious, drunken gathering into silence. But when the philistines recovered themselves the extent of their temporary fear was demonstrated by their cruel taunting of the naked Christ-substitute. This unhinged the already precarious sanity of the artist who had so recently identified himself with the persecuted saviour.

This fatalistic religious imagery recalled Promethean mythology, for, by expiring in such unrelievedly tragic circumstances, the artist had gone full circle, fulfilling the archetypal part in which creative genius was persecuted in 'compensation' for the unique quality of his talent.[45] The novelty was the vital emphasis placed upon the artist's own highly 'sensitive' temperament. This temperament – more than any liver-hungry bird or other external tragic force, any nemesis – was the vital agent in his self-created destruction. His angst-ridden ego was typical of the absurder extremes of unproductive romantic introspection. Even when a fictional artist defended his almost caricatured sensibility with nauseating selfishness, overt criticism was restrained. Enthusiastic nineteenth century authors, with varying degrees of competence, for the most part stalwartly invested the artist with undeserved glamour and pathos.

Even authors generally capable of a more objective viewpoint such as Browning or James were affected by their age's emotional desire to cast the artist as a being apart. To recall a passage already quoted from *The Europeans,* Gertrude Wentworth naïvely placed a painter on a pedestal:

> Felix was invested with this sacred character. Gertrude had never seen an artist before; she had only read about such people. They seemed to her a romantic and mysterious class, whose life was made up of those agreeable incidents that never happened to other persons.[46]

At first glance the reader appreciates James's teasing tone. His heroine's passionate association of the artistic type with unrealistic and unnatural excitement and the artificial exaggerations of fiction does indeed seem a little foolish. Remembering, however, how many of these uncompromisingly extremist accounts came from his own pen his mockery seems doubly ironic.

In *The Madonna of the Future,* for example, James's sad account of an artist realizing that his visionary qualities had never been matched by practical application and dying in a violent fever, the last stages of the hero's death were compared with a 'stray page from a lost masterpiece of tragedy'. Stressing the dramatic and imaginative, rather than the prosaic or realistic aspects of this painter, James had helped to construct Theobald's character with references to other stories about fictional artists.

He made his own idealistic but ineffectual hero say: ' "At least no merchant traffics in my heart! " Do you remember the line from Browning?' Theobald himself reminded a more sceptical character of one of Balzac's fictional failures – if one were able to get into his studio one would probably find something very like 'the picture in that tale of Balzac's – a mere mass of incoherent scratches and daubs, a jumble of dead paint! '[47] And the narrator to whom both these comments had been addressed told Theobald that he reminded him of that 'charming speech of the Florentine painter in Alfred de Musset's Lorenzaccio'.[48]

James's reference to de Musset's innocent artist was a clever way of evoking the equally imaginary source of Theobald's happiness. When the latter realized that the woman whom he had long worshipped for her beauty, planning to use her as an inspiratory model for a madonna, had in fact grown old and coarse, he despaired and 'burned out in delirium'. This sad fate was quoted, in turn, in yet another account of the fictional artist. Blanche Willis Howard, in *Guenn,* generalizing about an impoverished artists' colony in which there was scarcely a man whose circumstances were 'quite propitious', evoked the pathos of James's earlier literary picture: 'Yet unrevealed, in the gay little painter-world, were half-finished romances, tragedies with the fifth act undetermined, unwritten poems, pathetic Madonnas of the future.'[49]

The suggestion that the hopes of an entire colony of artists could be doomed as they matured was typical of the obsessive fatalism dogging the fictional artist. Yet the writers who constructed these sombre situations tried to surround their artists with an aura of haunting pathos. Bored by life, disappointed in work, unhappy in love, isolated by madness, deprived in death, the artist still retained a certain grandeur because of belief in the uniquely glorified, prophetic aspect of his creative role. He encompassed a full range of imaginative experience. Spanning the emotional extremes of nineteenth century escapism – both of swashbuckling bohemian frivolity and also of intense, idealized subjective tragedy – the artist proved himself a romantic hero incarnate.

The Declining Myth of the Artist

Two Hours of Fun and Flagellation
Highly Recommended.[1]

Was there any connection between the romantic extremism of
the fictional artist and his actual counterparts? Chapter one has
already suggested the close links which existed between many
writers and their artist heroes, as the former – frequently failed
artists themselves – incorporated personally nostalgic and envious
subject matter into their works. This indication of blurred
barriers between fact and fiction becomes increasingly apparent
as the reader recalls other contexts providing close parallels for
the exaggerated themes already discussed. Art historical, bio-
graphical, autobiographical, written and visual categories merged
and overlapped to the extent that the reader is led to the general
conclusion that not only was there often genuine material underlying these fictional myths but that the image of the unorthodox
creator was often cultivated in life as much as in literature; a
theory which would place these literary effusions in the light of
welcome publicity.

The kind of romantic biography created by Lady Morgan when
she wrote about Salvator Rosa continued to be popular, and
recognizable art works were often included as the focal point of
a sentimental tale, as, for example, in *The Parson's Daughter*
(1899), subtitled 'Her Early Recollections and How Romney
Painted Her'. The work of contemporary art critics provided yet
another example of the close creative links between art and
literature in this period – particularly when these art critics were

131

skilled creative authors in their own right, such as Hazlitt, Thackeray, Moore, James and Wilde. Ruskin was the supreme example of an influential critic with the power to form public opinion about the artist's role. Writing with a high-powered romantic idealism, often surpassing that found in pure fiction, he directed much of his drive to eulogizing contemporary artists, as, for example, when he championed Turner in *Modern Painters* (1843-60). Discussing a painter's qualifications, he directed the reader to his mental and moral condition, stating that an artist's imagination implied 'sublime qualities of mind' and intense feeling, and detailing the esoteric qualities required for his 'sacred invention':

> Sacred, I call it deliberately: for it is thus, in the most accurate sense, humble as well as helpful; meek in its receiving, as manifest in its disposing . . . not because it forms, but because it finds. For you cannot find a lie; you must make it yourself. False things may be imagined, and false things composed; but only truth can be invented.[2]

This eloquent critic thus underlined, and contributed to, fictional attempts to cast the artistic creator in a visionary and prophetic role.

It was a sign of his impact as an advocate for the status of the artist that there were not only oblique references in fiction to his theories but many direct records of his dominating views, in novels such as *Harry Coverdale's Courtship* (1855) by Frank Smedley, or *Gerald Fitzgerald* (1858) by George Herbert, or *Ravenshoe* (1861) by Henry Kingsley.

Another connection between fact and fiction was stressed by authors who placed their characters in bohemian settings very like those inhabited by real artists: the sites inhabited by fictional artists were often recognized by contemporary readers with a knowledge of the picturesque parts of London, Rome or Paris. Clive Holland clearly indicated this in an introductory note at the beginning of *Marcelle of the Latin Quarter*:

> In the following romance of the Quartier Latin a few of the names of streets have been altered; either because, during the period of time covered by the story, they have been known by two or more designations or for other sufficient reasons. In like manner real persons who figure in the book have in some cases been disguised under names other than their own.

Those readers, however, who know the Quarter will probably have little difficulty in locating the various scenes of the story.

Where Clive Holland had been careful to disguise his real characters, others were less cautious. Du Maurier, including a realistic picture of Whistler in his first edition of *Trilby,* found himself up for libel.[3]

A more appreciative portrait occurs in *Aylwin* where Watts-Dunton not only made obvious references to Rossetti's tastes, such as that for wild animals, but stated that there were deeper affinities between Rossetti and his own zoo-keeping, gypsy-loving painter,[4] D'Arcy. The writer added an appendix to his novel acknowledging the parallels which readers had found between the two painters. Not only were D'Arcy's picturesque surroundings modelled on Kelmscott, but his behaviour was modelled on Rossetti's bohemian impulses. Watts-Dunton explained that the attractions of D'Arcy were based on Rossetti's 'personal fascination', which affected every member of society with whom he came in contact. But while Rossetti/D'Arcy might exercise a demonic attraction on others, he was very much at the mercy of his own temperament. The impression of a creature of varying moods – gay and frolicsome at one moment, profoundly meditative at another, and then deeply dejected – was 'true to life'. It is more than hinted, says Watts-Dunton, tactfully, that D'Arcy's tragic dejection was caused by the loss of someone he had loved deeply, adding that it was just such a loss that had produced Rossetti's melancholy moods. The face of the lovely girl who sat for D'Arcy's best work, and prompted him to say that a rare beauty could provide half the inspiration in a fine painting was modelled on Mrs Morris: Watts-Dunton's fiction showed, in his own words, 'documentary evidences . . . in every respect'.

Rossetti not only contributed to the fiction written about the artist but his paintings provided a parallel treatment. By painting Elizabeth Siddal as Beatrice and Jane Morris as Venus he was not merely communicating personal feelings but the kind of obsessions found throughout contemporary literature, where fictional artists were forever torn between fleshly and ethereal loves – as in *Thorniton's Model* (1872) by Margaret Hunt, or *Miss Brown* by Vernon Lee. In a painting such as his life-like portrait of Elizabeth Siddal (who had eventually become his wife after a long engagement), painted a year after her death, and entitled 'Beata Beatrix' (c. 1863), he recorded a belief (prevalent in both

'How They Met Themselves'

Rossetti produced this tense, neurotic image after his marriage to Elizabeth Siddal in 1860. It suggests the incompatibility
of his romantic ideals (suggested by anachronistic mediaeval garb)
and everyday life. The honeymoon couple, surrounded by claus-
trophobic foliage, appear to be in a state of shock gazing at
ghostly images of themelves.

literature and art) in a woman's beauty as an expression of a spiritual ideal.[5] In a painting such as 'Astarte Syriaca' (1877) and similar images of Jane Morris, he recorded a general fascination with the aloof sexuality of the *femme fatale*.[6]

Just as Rossetti's life and work provided an obvious example of a bohemian painter who bore out many of the suggestions about nineteenth century artists found in fiction, so his contemporary, Frederick Leighton, afforded an equally obvious example of a gentleman artist. As a young man studying in Rome, he had been singled out by Thackeray who, while spending the winter of 1853-4 there, may well have based some of Clive Newcome's obvious attractions on the success of this elegant young swell. Yet even though Lord Leighton, as he became, was a pillar of society, elements of his career still reflected the myth of the artist as the romantic outsider.

His house, conceived in the late eighteen-fifties, was a case in point – for it was not only designed to fulfil the practical needs of the painter's profession, but to publicize an element of exoticism seldom found in ordinary dwellings. The artist's studio, a room fifty-eight feet long by twenty-eight feet wide, was designed not only to catch appropriate light, but also, as its gilded apse and peacock blue screen indicated, to produce a picturesque setting confounding the norms of philistine furnishing. Val Prinsep, William Burges, G. F. Watts, Luke Fildes, Marcus Stone and Hamo Thornycroft subsequently followed Leighton's example and took up residence on the old Holland Park estate in houses indicating that real artists, like their fictional counterparts, considered themselves unusual citizens, and proved it by creating a distinctive and an unorthodox environment.

The most remarkable feature of Leighton's building was probably the Arab Hall (1877-9). This richly colourful chamber, inspired by a twelfth century moslem palace in Palermo, was described by Mary Eliza Haweis in *Beautiful Houses* (1882) as a 'Moorish dream', 'a vivid impression projected by a nineteenth century mind'. Vernon Lee, visiting it in 1883, considered that its cupola, central fountain, Persian tiles and mosaics by Walter Crane made it 'quite the 8th wonder of the world'. Frederick Leighton himself graced his surroundings as elegantly as had Moore's fictional artist, Lewis Seymour, in *A Modern Lover*. Vernon Lee described him 'surrounded by fashionable women, a blend of Olympian Jove and a head waiter, a superb decorator and a superb piece of decoration'.[7]

Leighton's own view of the kind of image which should be

'*Leighton House*'

This house, whose history and décor is described in detail by Richard and Leonée Ormond in *Lord Leighton* (1975), with its enormous high studio and eccentric features indicates how actual artists, like their fictional counterparts, sought special environments to suit their particular projected by an inspired artist was more serious, and had been expressed in an early painting – 'Cimabue's Celebrated Madonna is Carried in Procession through the Streets of Florence' (1853-5). This large and balanced work, bought by Queen Victoria, not only revealed a thorough knowledge of Renaissance painting, but an idealistic appreciation of the artist's role in and around this particular epoch – a recurrent theme in nineteenth century literature.[8] (It was indicative of the cross-currents existing between nineteenth century artists and writers that Leighton later illustrated *Romola,* the novel in which George Eliot discussed a fictional 'Piero di Cosimo' as part of a Renaissance panorama). Leighton, painting Cimabue, drew on his knowledge of Vasari to create a composite image, with figures dressed in subtly romanticized versions of fifteenth and sixteenth century costumes, designed to evoke artistic prestige.

Leighton placed a wreathed Cimabue (holding Giotto by the hand) in the very centre of his triumphal frieze. The artist preceded his painting, which was held shoulder high, with candles burning before it on a large trestle. The pale cloth on the trestle, combined with Cimabue's garments, formed dominant parts of the light central area, while the artist's 'celebrated' image provided an equally conspicuous upright – cutting the horizontally banded wall in the middle distance. Leighton's crowd, massed on either side of Cimabue, reflected significant sociological, as well as visual, variations. It was a representative procession. A bishop, with a group of aristocratic spectators at a window above him, was conspicuous on the left while the King of Naples was introduced to the right of this entourage. Pretty girls, motley citizens, elegant youths, city fathers, musicians, a dog, a baby and the poet Dante were all assembled in this symbolic tableau arranged by Leighton to show society paying harmonious homage to genius.

The youth whose first offering for an Academy Exhibition, whose first real bid for popular fame, had rested on this idealistic picture of the artist receiving public acclaim became remarkably successful in his own right, apparently defying the fictional myth of the persecuted creator. And yet the ascetic ambition which inspired this President of the Royal Academy, as he later became, also hurt him, feeling, as he did, that it deprived him of human affection. Before he had tasted fame he painted 'Cimabue's Madonna'; afterwards, revealing the other side of the coin, he painted 'Captive Andromache' (1888). Having adopted, as he grew more established, a more classical style, he employed a classical story to reveal a subjective sense of desolation.

Leighton believed that a dramatic design should suggest both what had preceded and what would follow it, and his painting 'Captive Andromache' recalled Hector's prophecy that, after his death, his wife would live in exile and it also emphasized her own potent forebodings of a lonely existence spent in mourning her husband and children.

Where Leighton had let Cimabue's luminously painted body link the two halves of his triumphal procession, which proceded across the relief-like surface in a general movement from left to right, Andromache's bowed figure was incongruously static – whereas the garments of Cimabue and the young disciple who clasped his hand were connected with the rest of the painted procession, Andromache's dark draperies produced a cocooning effect. Her particular stillness seemed all the more noticeable because of the deeper spatial area behind her, the rhythmic serpentine flow of figures she interrupted, and the self-contained units in which she had no part; her gaze fell significantly on a happy family group in the foreground, reminding the reader of her own lonely future. Isolated alike from all the young, old and gaily coloured people in this peaceful scene, she evoked a poignant sense of tragedy:

> Like his heroine he was perpetually cut off from those around him, and from the relationships and emotions which are the source of human happiness. . . . Leighton himself saw his exile as the inevitable result of his role as an artist. Art was his religion, and he its votary.[9]

If the President of the Academy felt that he was enacting the creative equation, expressed by so many nineteenth century authors, between artistic inspiration and priestly purity, James was willing to put forward a very different interpretation. For if Leighton in 'Captive Andromache' illustrated the idealism so often associated with the fictional artist, James in *The Private Life* (1892) supplied a measure of vitriol of the kind which so often counterbalanced such idealistic views. He created a fictional portrait of Leighton quite unlike that reflected by Adelaide Sartoris in *A Week in a French Country House* (1867), or even by Benjamin Disraeli in *Lothair* (1870). In the former Mrs Sartoris drew on her knowledge of the young Leighton she had come to know while he was still studying in Rome, describing, in 'Mr Kiowski', a charming linguist whose conversation rushed on like a mill stream, and whose drawings of mothers and children

revealed an extraordinary tenderness. This feeling youth metamorphosed, under Disraeli's pen, into a more worldly specimen.
'Gaston Phoebus' adored entertaining. He had a belief, not without foundation, that everything was done better under his roof
than under that of any person.'[10] The hint, in Disraeli's portrait,
that such an 'eminent' host might attract malice was born out
by Henry James's subsequent account of Leighton as 'Lord
Mellifont', who painted as he talked and talked while he painted
– 'and if the painting was as miscellaneous as the talk, the talk
would equally have graced an album'. Under the ironic title *The
Private Life,* James contrasted Lord Mellifont with Clare
Vawdrey; comparing Lord Leighton, the public performer, with
Robert Browning, the private poet. While Vawdrey's outward
personality lacked Mellifont's mellifluous charms, his creativity
was profound – unlike the artist who, for all his cultivated person, was demolished as an empty shell. Talking about him was
like speaking of the dead, and done 'with that peculiar accumula-
tion of relish. His reputation was a kind of gilded obelisk, as if
he had been buried beneath it; the body of legend and reminis-
cence of which he was to be the subject had crystallized in
advance.'[11] The relish with which James, who recorded his
intense 'envy' elsewhere,[12] seized this opportunity to attack
Leighton, through Mellifont, showed that there was no dividing
line between the emotions aroused by real or fictional artists.

What was surprising about the fictional artist was his conformity to, rather than his deviation from, a recognizable pattern. Whether rebellious outsider or punished outcast, he was
always depicted as a man apart; the romantic hero *par excellence*.
Variations within this stereotyped casting did not suggest development so much as decline. Although novels such as Somerset
Maugham's *The Moon and Sixpence* (1919), continued to re-
iterate the bohemian myth, there was a general watering down
process.[13] This, viewed simplistically, could be interpreted in
terms of contemporary history, charting or echoing a gradual loss
of hopeful vitality as the century moved from the aggressive
idealism inspiring the first stages of the French Revolution[14] to
the stultifying stages of *fin de siècle* decadence. The attraction of
the earlier romantic heroes often stemmed from their intense
emotional energy, but the enthusiasms they generated did not
necessarily exclude the possibility of practical enterprise. The
disillusioned appeal of later romantic heroes was, however, based
on a detached disdain for normal existence, which they did all
they could to ignore or to camouflage with mental smokescreens.

As the century wore on, literary reiterations of the theme of the romantic artist began to tarnish. This stereotyped image began to lose the emotional colour and moral structure it had originally possessed. A caricatured view of this deterioration was seen in comparisons between widely differing authors drawn from opposite ends of this romantic period, such as Blake and Le Gallienne. The fiery energy and heroic vision of the earlier writer showed up the simpering pretension of the latter. While Le Gallienne, as examples in chapter five have already illustrated, cultivated subtle eccentricities and a detached viewpoint, Blake believed in glorious madness and forceful originality: 'Active Evil is better than passive Good'. He also believed in stimulating dispute: 'Without contraries is no progression'. He both encouraged and provoked contrasts. The fact that Los, his creation in *Jerusalem,* was an artistic figure did not cut him off from the rest of existence but instead made him feel responsible for its welfare. Blake's artist managed to be a powerful mythological entity and at the same time an active participator in worldly events: 'All things acted on Earth are seen in the bright Sculptures of Los's Halls, & every Age renews its powers from these Works.'[15] In addition to the Wondrous Art in his halls, and the wondrous weaving produced by his womenfolk (the buildings of Los being compared with the woofs of Enitharmon, his wife) Los worked, Vulcan-like, at a great forge. Blake's fabulous but also practical creator was significantly defiant towards Albion, the poet's symbol of England.[16] His Los took it upon himself to rebuke Albion for the country's present ills:

> Thou wast the Image of God surrounded by the Four Zoas.
> Three thou hast slain. I am the Fourth; thou canst not
>   destroy me.
> Thou art in Error; trouble me not with thy righteousness.
> I have innocence to defend and ignorance to instruct:
> I have no time for seeming and little arts of compliment
> In morality and virtue. . . .[17]

This esoteric character, who was so directly involved with the nation's greater moral good, was also literally brought down to, or attached to, earth. For Blake showed how Los, after his courageous attack on current affairs, was unfairly threatened with divine retribution . . . 'here upon London stone, / Between Blackheath and Hounslow, between Norwood and Finchley.'[18] Blake's direct use of the word 'here' combined with the concrete image of stone and specific suburban districts, demonstrates how this stimulating writer effectively focused his most imaginative myths – such as that of Los, the last of the Four Zoas – on objective reality. Blake viewed contemporary life in the round. He made Los, for example, demand in a moment of raging fury, why he and his companions should call on God for help, 'and not ourselves, in whom God dwells'. Los decried their unhappy situation as one reflecting an ignoble 'pretence of Art to destroy Art; a pretence of Liberty / To destroy Liberty: a pretence of Religion to destroy Religion', a generalizing of 'Art & Science till Art & Science is lost'.[19] The fact that Los, part and parcel of the Hermetic tradition, recognized divinity within himself and readily connected art and religion, science and politics symbolized Blake's very positive, all-inclusive thinking.

In contrast with Blake's cosmic vision, the work of such *fin de siècle* authors as Le Gallienne seemed designed not so much to heighten reality as to mask it. Where Blake's creative fantasies had flourished in and consequently enriched ordinary existence, Le Gallienne's concept of the withdrawn creator (who significantly flees the material world of Blake's stone and suburbs for an isolated and hallucinatory death) reflected a complete lack of interest in and therefore neglect and negation of, the value of everyday actions and responsibilities. Le Gallienne's effete protagonist lacked all that courageous involvement in the major occurrences of his time which had so distinguished Blake's dramatic hero.

Such comparisons show how early romantic works, such as Blake's, were more concerned with provocatively idealistic escapism than later, and generally slighter, efforts which often recorded a pathetic desire for escapism at any price. Le Gallienne's spineless character lacked Los's peculiar wisdom and spiritual status. Art for him was not a moral force so much as a purely aesthetic one. Praise of beauty, once vigorously synonymous with divine worship, lost its religious overtones to the extent that it often came, by the turn of the century, to be associated with deliberate amorality; an almost passively experimental surrender to hedonistic impulses.

This philosophy was succinctly expressed by Walter Pater in the conclusion of his influential *Studies in the History of the Renaissance* (1873). At first Pater repressed his argument in favour of art for art's sake, passion for passion's sake, fearing legal reprisals. His influential views were, however, taken up and popularized, particularly at the turn of the century, by intellectual

'*Dante Gabriel Rossetti, in his back garden*'
This wicked caricature by Max Beerbohm (printed in *The Poet's Corner*, 1904) presents Rossetti and his bohemian entourage – which includes the poet Swinburne, a goitrous model and a selection of wild animals – with a teasing sense of absurdity. (Compare this late image of Rossetti with his own intense self-portrait in 'How They Met Themselves'.)

disciples such as Oscar Wilde. Wilde's ambiguous ideas were reflected in those of his aesthetic hero, Dorian Gray: 'There were moments when he looked on evil simply as a mode through which he could realize his conception of the beautiful.'[20]

The decadent quality of the later romantics was symbolized, in microcosm, by the personality of Walter Hamlin, around whom Vernon Lee constructed *Miss Brown, A Novel*. Hamlin's ennui was stressed from the very beginning of the novel. Many authors introduced the reader to fictional artists when they were enterprising youths and striplings, letting the reader gain sympathy for their heroes by accompanying them on the kind of adolescent escapades which would endow them with an exciting sense of *joie de vivre*. True, she included references to the picturesque joys of foreign travel, one of the commonest means of establishing a young artist as an adolescent hero, but significantly did so in the past tenses. She made Hamlin begin by describing these episodes in such a way that the reader was convinced that this man had nothing to do with the vigorous enthusiasms of youth:

> It was melancholy to admit that Italy also had ceased to interest him. . . . He tried to realise the time when all these things had given him a thrill, had gone to his head, nay, when the mere sense of being in Italy had done so; but now the words 'thrill' and 'intoxication' seemed false, disgusting, and vulgar.[21]

Where other authors frequently made use of idyllic scenery as a means of promoting and enhancing the romantic attractions of a fictional artist, Vernon Lee did the complete opposite.

The man whose aura she equated with a kind of shade, a faint penumbra, comes to be seen as the heir of a family of inbred slave-trading perverts, whose portraits betrayed telltale signs of what she archly referred to as 'emasculating vice'. Vernon Lee's suggestion that enfeebled genes were bound to have a debilitating effect on this hero or anti-hero whom she described as 'nervous, and wistful and dreamy, as if he were tired of his family having lived so long', provided an apt, if unconscious, symbol of the whole faltering romantic movement. Earlier romantic heroes generated active energy, even if short-lived, but their later and more decadent counterparts like Hamlin, the tired man who found intoxication vulgar, seemed to lose even this neurotic, fitful vitality as they became more cynically and passively detached.

Although Vernon Lee made Hamlin the last pre-exhausted

descendent of a flea-bitten family, in a moral sense, she was at pains to show that he had inherited considerable worldly assets and a *recherché* social position. She continually stressed Hamlin's aristocratic origins, not merely to add to the superficial attractions of his character, but to stress his selfishly isolated and snobbish attitude to life. This was unusual. Very different was the way that Thackeray, in *The Newcomes,* had shown how his painter hero Clive Newcome – although less revolutionary than many artists – tried to repudiate the claims of birth and opt for a bohemian life. Clive was glad, for example, to befriend the talented son of a butler. He himself actively rejected both prejudice and pretensions of social superiority. Thackeray demonstrated Clive's essentially classless outlook in the dialogues which he set up between the artist and his cousin Ethel, a snob and avid social climber. Ethel approved of a hierarchy based on power through possession, but Clive believed in a more flexible aristocracy of ability. They quarrelled bitterly when he rejected her worldly advice that he should use his family connections to secure a large income, and when he criticized her callous pursuit of men with titles.

The roles occupied by Clive Newcome and Ethel were reversed in discussions between Walter Hamlin and his beautiful friend, Anne Brown. Miss Brown, who had begun to ooze social conscience, discovered that her aesthetic companion was an intolerant reactionary. Unlike the majority of rebellious bohemians who showed a comradely sympathy for others also living from hand to mouth, Hamlin could show all the *blasé* lack of interest associated with unearned aristocratic opulence. See, for example, his attitude towards his estate at Cold Fremley. When Miss Brown pointed out that overcrowding had lead to incest, Hamlin, blind to the human problem, could only rhapsodize on the beauty of the place. He rejected all her practical suggestions for rebuilding his village, providing work, and starting drainage schemes. The novelist was surely being ironic when she made him say that he would sooner die than spoil that 'peaceful' bit of countryside. The decadent aesthete preferred unhealthy marshy expanses to the prospect of profitable farming land, stating blandly that there was 'something very grand and tragic in this sin flowering like evil grasses in that marsh'.

This was indeed a characteristic response. Vernon Lee always showed him meeting any serious moral appeal at a tangent. While many other nineteenth century authors gradually revealed that their romantic heroes were driven by a streak of unsympathetic egoism, Vernon Lee, herself disenchanted with the decaying type she portrayed, always made this selfishness blatantly obvious. Parodying the man of feeling popularized in romantic literature, she made his caricatured 'sensitivity' seem even less attractive than the utilitarianism he despised. Lacking the positive spiritual and intuitive qualities needed to complement materialism, his attitude suggested a pathetic irrelevancy.

It was highly revealing that before the confrontation over Cold Fremley, the artist asked Miss Brown to stand beside his painting of her as Beatrice. Their differences were exposed in their attitudes to this symbolic interpretation. Anne found the comparison distasteful, and then forgot it. Hamlin, on the other hand, was happy to view the living girl in terms of the 'mystic, wistful woman of unreality' he had invented. Where other fictional artists had been able to see into a sitter's very soul, elucidating their personality with visionary clarity, Hamlin achieved the reverse. His portrait was pure fantasy, a concoction of his own making which obscured Anne's essentially down-to-earth personality, masking it in 'unreality'.

Where other authors, such as Rossetti in *Chiaro dell' Erma*, had evoked Dante's legendary poem about Beatrice when describing how an ideal beauty could provide an inspiratory link with the divine powers, Vernon Lee showed that Hamlin's Beatrice-fixation was just another form of self-indulgence. His vanity was tickled by the cold-blooded thought that he could shape Anne's personality, just as Pygmalion had 'moulded the limbs of the image'. The final irony occurred, however, when they became engaged and Vernon Lee – reversing the usual pattern by which authors made a married artist a martyr – diverted the reader's pity towards the future Mrs Hamlin. Anne's increasing sense of nausea prevented the reader from feeling any amusement on discovering Hamlin's final delusion – that he had at last inspired a grand passion. Thus this author not only refrained from stressing the positive aspects of the Promethean creator, but also the obviously negative ones. Hamlin had none of the energy, wit or enterprise of the true villain, of the archetypal Promethean thief. He lacked the aggressive gusto of the rebellious satanist becoming, in the final analysis, the least interesting of all bores – a self-congratulatory narcissist.

Vernon Lee stressed that Hamlin's sly weaknesses were symptomatic of his era: he belonged to an artistic school which was literally 'running to seed . . . the great men have done all that could be done in the way of beautiful suggestiveness – the little ones can only do suggestiveness of all sorts of vague nastiness'.[22] Hamlin, self-confessed expert on the hashish of sinful desire, was in an 'aesthetic daydream with its enervating visions of impure beauty and forbidden things'[23] – a current delusion which, this author argued, rotted his art and personality alike because it was not based on any kind of spiritual optimism but on a belief in the 'fatal supremacy' of evil and ugliness.[24]

De La Pine, a painter whom Aubrey Beardsley included in *Under the Hill*,[25] a story which he wrote between 1894 and 1896, illustrated again how the amorality of the decadent movement could influence the stereotyped image of the fictional artist. Many authors had used artists to conjure up an aura of innocent bohemian revelry, as Thackeray did with young Clive Newcome, but Beardsley used his painter to help to project a coy love of the pornographic.

Beardsley's short phantasy was based on the adventures of the Chevalier Tannhäuser with Venus. These central characters visited De La Pine's studio, where Beardsley at once established the artist's credentials with characteristic sexual imagery:

> De La Pine's glory as a painter was hugely increased by his reputation as a fouteur, for ladies that had pleasant memories of him looked with a biased eye upon his fêtes galantes merveilleuses.
>
> Yes, he was a bawdy creature, and his workshop a regular brothel. However, his great talent stood in no need of such meretricious and phallic support, he was every whit as strong and facile with his brush as with his tool.[26]

Beardsley went on to describe one of De La Pine's brushworks, but he devoted as much space to an account of the painter's butler – 'a work of art in himself; his great, scarlet, pimply face strangled in a lawn stock'. . . . Another intimation that this artist's creativity was not of supreme importance came from the way Beardsley spoke of Venus's coiffeur, Cosmé. De La Pine was painting his portrait of this admired personage who was loved by everybody: 'To begin with he was pastmaster in his art, that fine, relevant art of coiffing'. . . . Beardsley, who could thus easily elevate hairdressing to an art, indulged a similar passion for fashionable superficialities in his treatment of the painter.

Beardsley gave the artist's usual picturesque appearance, colourful habitat and eccentric *joie de vivre* a new flavour: 'The painter was in purple and full dress, all tassels and grand folds.

His hair magnificently curled, his heavy eye-lids painted, his gestures large and romantic, he reminded one a little of Maurel playing Wolfram in the second act of the Opera of Wagner.'[27] Other fictional artists, such as James's Roderick Hudson, had often looked fanciful. But Beardsley, by painting De La Pine's eyes and comparing him with someone in a theatrical part, emphasized this desire for fancy dress. Where Moore's Lewis Seymour had seemed precious in his choice of décor, De La Pine's taste was decidedly *bijou*.

His delicately appointed salon was the scene of a delightful little *partie carrée* which De La Pine gave for Venus, Tannhäuser and Cosmé, paying intimate deference to Tannhäuser's masquerade of wearing female costume. The artist flirted with him outrageously, whispering to him behind his hand and even pressing his foot beneath the table. The decadent naughtiness of the painted painter continued as he provided a tour of the pleasures of the town, which included a voyeuristic visit to an operetta promising:

Two Hours of Fun & Flagellation
Highly Recommended
PINK CHEEKS

There were a dozen or so tempting box openers: they were beautiful young creatures in plum-coloured jackets with tapering yellow trousers that strapped under the instep and fitted 'smoothly across their behinds'. Their build, their delicate features, and the short ringlets that played around their shoulders left their sex a matter of doubt; but this ambiguity, De La Pine explained happily, was matched by their readiness to sustain the role of either.[28] Rejoining his friends, after an interval, he appeared in a gorgeously flowered dressing-gown,

> explaining that he had been detained with two of the box-openers. His make-up had suffered terribly, but his spirits not at all, and he gave a droll account of his affair with the two little creatures, in one of whom he had discovered a fellatrice of surpassing artistry. . . . High praise, this, from a connoisseur like the painter![29]

The calculated crudity of some of Beardsley's innuendoes had rarely been associated with the fictional artist in nineteenth century fiction. The sexual encounters which Moore included, for example, in *Lewis Seymour and Some Women* were discreetly suggestive, sometimes almost atmospheric, in comparison with some

147

'A Footnote'
    This telling image, from the eighteen nineties, is passive when
compared, say, with Haydon's dramatic image of himself as
'Curtius', and detached rather than mystical when compared with
Dyce's painting of Titian as a boy. Beardsley, who has elongated
his ears to make them fawn-like, has literally tethered himself to
Pan, pagan god of earthly sensuality. (Brian Reade discusses this
image, and the subsequent one in his finely produced *catalogue
raisonée, Beardsley,* 1967.)

of Beardsley's more explicit eroticism. When an author such as Moore mentioned Lewis Seymour's sensual adventures, or Kipling those of his painter hero, Dick Haldar, they used this kind of *risqué* material to add spice to the escapist image of the fictional artist. But the latter's appeal was primarily based on his unorthodox personality and overall romantic aura. It was typical that 'Ouida', an author who concentrated on the sentimental aspects of characterisation, showed in *Two Little Wooden Shoes* (1874) that it was the intense charisma of her artist which had also been responsible for making him a successful seducer. Beardsley, on the other hand, put saucy nuances well before any hint of serious character-building. He seems, with decadent logic, to have based the attraction of the figures in *Under the Hill* on their capacity for licentious experiences. This was in no way to be confused with experience pursued as a source of wisdom. Indeed, this author's simplistic attitude was symbolized by his presentation of De La Pine's sexual, rather than emotional, manoeuvrability.

Beardsley, on first introducing this painter, had unequivocally equated his creative talent with his sexual prowess. The one was as good as the other. Yet it was obvious that both the author and his characters preferred sexual pursuits to aesthetic ones. The widespread pattern, established throughout the century, which showed that an artist at the mercy of his physical desires forfeited spiritual inspiration did not apply in this case. De La Pine's guilt-less sexual abandonment could be read as a sound victory for the forces of Mammon.[30]

The 'art for art's sake' movement tended to popularize things artistic as much, or more than, art itself – reflecting a change from a direct focus on the personality of the creative artist to a more widespread focus on the art world at large.[31] Attention became diffused and shared between the practising artist and that most sensitive of artistic phenomena, the astute collector of *objets d'art,* the connoisseur. Early in the century the difference between the connoisseur and the artist had seemed simpler: the former, usually considered a gentleman, bought works of art while the latter, usually considered a craftsman, sold them. A connoisseur had been a man of taste in the eighteenth century sense, a man whose knowledge of art was but a single facet of his carefully cultivated and generally detached and erudite mind. Henry Tilney's knowledge of the picturesque in Jane Austen's *Northanger Abbey* (1818) affords a good example of the way in which a gentleman could discuss artistic topics without implying any close relationship with professional artists as such. He and his sister, while out walking discussed the countryside and 'decided upon its capability for being formed into pictures'.

Later nineteenth century literature recorded increasingly emotional aesthetic appreciation, in the persons of various fictional connoisseurs, whose more eager regard for the arts led to a correspondingly intense appreciation of its creators. Many authors used considerate connoisseurs of this kind to demonstrate the extent of the artist's influence, rather as Elizabethan writers had exploited the deeds of devoted courtiers to underline regal prestige. Just as, in the Renaissance, wise courtiers had been shown humbling themselves before a king in respect for the divine authority he bore, so, in this later period, tolerant connoisseurs were similarly seen to neglect their own interests in favour of an artist's – in tribute to genius.

This zealously dedicated attitude was clearly shown in *Roderick Hudson,* which provided a particularly revealing study of the psychological relation between patron and protégé. The former, Rowland Mallet, was originally introduced as a rich but disappointed bachelor who gently regretted his amiable but unproductive existence. James showed how his superficially bland and uncomplaining nature harboured secret fancies. Mallet fondly believed that happiness resulted from spectacular work on behalf of an idea, or the production of an artistic masterpiece: his most recurrent day-dream was of himself as a 'vigorous young man of genius without a penny'. James thus cleverly prepared the reader for Mallet's all-absorbing interest in just such a man.

Mallet's appreciation of Hudson was not, therefore, based on an objective desire to buy a collection of works of art but on a subjective kind of wish-fulfilment; this was securely based, in keeping with contemporary thought, on the premise that the artist was the ideal heroic type:

> When it first occurred to me that I might start our young friend on the path of glory, I felt as if I had an unimpeachable inspiration. Then I remembered there were dangers and difficulties, and asked myself whether I had a right to drag him out of his obscurity. . . . When I see a young man of genius standing helpless and hopeless for want of capital, I feel – and it's no affectation of humanity I assure you – as if it would give at least a reflected usefulness to my own life to offer him his opportunity.[33]

Mallet's unpretentious hope of a 'reflected usefulness' captured the overall tenor of his patronage. James made him see his own inspiration and worth simply as a means to an end, that of self-lessly serving the artist and furthering his career. Unconcerned about his own expectations after speculating on this unknown prodigy, Mallet, with typical chivalry, wondered whether the artist would face new problems – an obliging attitude the author crystallized over his attitude to money. Far from feeling it enabled him to give specific orders and instructions, or even to expect a modicum of gratitude, this kind connoisseur felt enriched by being able to 'offer' his resources as though they were alms.

Henry James showed that Mallet stood by the sculptor, ulti-mately to satisfy his own innate sense of responsibility. However, Mrs Bentham, another rich, lonely, frustrated character in George Moore's *A Modern Lover,* went still further in portraying a patron who systematically shied away from any disinterested appraisal of either her protégé or the nature of their relationship. Where Mallet had moments of complete disillusionment and resentfully criticized Hudson's insensitive behaviour, Mrs Bent-ham allowed nothing to cloud her vocational commitment. After Mrs Bentham's first glimpse of the attractive painter Lewis Seymour, Moore described her getting into a carriage and vanish-ing 'like a good fairy'. This frivolous phrase contained an unpleasant germ of truth, for Lewis parasitically absorbed her time, money, and energy with as little thought of repayment as the heroes of fairy-tales would have expended their supernatural aides.

Moore described her altruistic position in terms of falsely maternal feelings. The fastidious Mrs Bentham metamorphosed into an 'animal robbed of her young', as she saw the 'lamb' that she had found starving on the hillside was about to be stolen from her. Moore's choice of this evocative image – an animal robbed of its young – had a twofold effect. It captured the primi-tive force of her feeling, while at the same time specific refer-ences to a lamb rescued, in a biblically defenceless state from the wilds, produced an embryonic concept of spiritual guardianship. More cause for jealousy later prompted Mrs Bentham to expand on this idealistic suggestion and say that her suffering was not purely selfish, for she had determined that her young lover would be a 'great artist, that she would be his protector and that this would be her glory, her consolation'. This concept of the con-noisseur/patron gaining triumph at second-hand by acting as a passive protector, rather than an intellectual spur or scourge, led Mrs Bentham to say that her very life, if necessary, must be sacrificed if she could succeed in presenting a genius to the world. Lewis Seymour, the pampered fraud in question, benefited from his patroness's sense of having a protective 'mission' as her actions became increasingly masochistic.

Towards the end of the century, however, the prestige accorded to the artist was frequently transferred to the connoisseur who could become active to the point of sadism. His care for the arts and those associated with them was often unpleasantly manipulatory. Where the artist had been praised for creating superlatively life-like works, the often equally astute connoisseur began to devote his energies to forming living people into abstract moulds. This was indicated by the sinister machinations of someone like, say, Osmond in James's *The Portrait of a Lady* (1881), an amateur watercolourist who showed more taste than achievement, but used an artistic vocabulary to describe his psychological manoeuvres, such as his mental 'placing' of people, and his desire to impose mental 'finish' on their actions.[34]

Another example of the way in which the artist's powers were taken over by essentially uncreative aesthetes was seen in the relative positions of Basil Hallward, Dorian Gray and Lord Henry in *The Picture of Dorian Gray*. Basil Hallward, the artist, was a relatively minor figure, whose lack of true bohemianism was illustrated by his conservative wearing of formal evening dress, and the respectable manner in which he was served by his own impeccable butler. Gray himself, a far more picturesque character, whose physical beauty was described as a 'form of genius', was indulgently described as dabbling in tasteful whims such as the selection of orchids. But the real artistry in the novel was reserved by Wilde for his witty connoisseur, Lord Henry, who occupied the place of an *eminence grise* deftly shaping and moulding Gray's personality as it took his fancy. Wilde showed him doing this by offering his young puppet a book, or a concert trip, or a piece of advice at opportune moments with a curiously proprietorial air:

> . . . To a large extent the lad was his own creation. He had made him premature. That was something. Ordinary people waited till life disclosed to them its secrets, but to the few, to the elect, the mysteries of life were revealed before the veil was drawn away. Sometimes this was the effect of art, and chiefly of the art of literature, which dealt immediately with the passions and the intellect. But now and then a complex personality took the place and assumed the office of art.[35]

Female artists also began to assume the 'office of art' and absorb the artist's prerogatives. Some of the examples given earlier in chapters three and five of artists struggling to keep sane while facing numerous difficulties in their personal affairs showed that the women they encountered, instead of being professional equals, often belonged to two different categories – ladies and models. The former, who had little connection with this technical life[36] were considered socially superior to the artist while the latter were frequently dismissed as the lowest of the low. Models, although considered a passive necessity in the art world, absorbed little of its creative prestige. They were, by definition, ill-educated and impoverished.[37] Their physical beauty, the quality which won them the most admiration, also brought them infamy. The fact that models removed their clothes, even for the purest aesthetic reasons, was treated with caution. No lady would do it. It was disgusting, degrading and obviously the first step to a life of vulgar exhibitionism and sordid prostitution.[38]

Trilby, Du Maurier's generously amoral heroine, provided a classic symbol of the model's doubtful respectability in this period. Brought up in the Latin Quarter, she had posed 'for the altogether' since she was a child and had no qualms about it. Prudish Du Maurier, obviously unhappy with her natural and unprejudiced attitude, swiftly altered it. Little Billee, his English painter hero, came into a studio to see his constant companion debasing herself by wantonly displaying her body to a group of strangers. It was too much for him. He stood with his shoulders up and his eyes staring and then, lifting his arms, fled in horror. Trilby, horrified in her turn to see how she had upset her sensitive friend, began intuitively to follow his reasoning, and to feel like an untouchable. Du Maurier made this traumatic incident the last in her modelling career, for it gave the girl such a sense of shame that it provided the first healthy step in a new, 'British' outlook on life:

> Hitherto, for Trilby, self-respect had meant little more than the mere cleanliness of her body, in which she had always revelled; alas! it was one of the conditions of her humble calling. It now meant another kind of cleanliness, and she would luxuriate in it for evermore; and the dreadful past – never to be forgotten by her – should be so lived down as in time, perhaps, to be forgotten by others. . . .[39]

The fictional artist's problems frequently arose from his becoming physically attracted to a social inferior, such as a model, while romantically enamoured of an aloof and refined social superior. Nineteenth century authors often made the most of such class differences which provided a useful framework for the tense situations in which they played off the bohemian artist's unique social and creative position against all the contrasts they could muster. Writers who wished to emphasize an artist hero's unique spiritual and constructive gifts automatically concentrated on the sensual and emotional characteristics of the women whom they provided as foils to his genius. This traditional drama – where male creativity glowed against an enhancing background of female irrelevance – obviously lost impact as women began to trickle into masculine preserves and develop their own creative talents. The old cliché of the sensitive artist, whose powers were demonstrated by the wondering female hangers-on who surrounded him, lost its usefulness once women had begun to abandon their natural occupations as housewives and temptresses and started to experiment with the arts. Thus a mounting influx of female artists began to threaten the male creator's rarity value.

It was, at first, a novelty to find a genuine, practising female artist in nineteenth century fiction. Delicate painting and drawing were lady-like accomplishments of the same calibre as pressing flowers or embroidering fire screens:[40] the practice of art by young ladies such as Jane Austen's Emma or George Eliot's Lucy[41] had the character of a harmless hobby. Louisa Costello in *Clara Fane* (1848), for example, described Lady Seymour as:

> one of those amateur painters who pass a good deal of their time sitting opposite a piece of canvas spread out on an easel, surrounded with colours in cakes and in bottles, with as many brushes, and as much oil and varnish and turpentine as would serve half-a-dozen artists . . . [she made] copies, more or less correct, of the *chef d'oeuvres* of first masters: and staring Sybils, squinting Cencis, woebegone Giacondas, and crooked Venuses looked from the walls in self-contented complacency, amidst confused rocky masses of Salvator, pink and blue misty Claudes, or black and green Poussins, generally pronounced by those judges she consulted, better than the originals.[42]

The fact that judges told her that her 'more or less' correct copies of the old masters were better than the originals, shows that women were not expected to excel in the arts.

An occasional female artist, however modest her efforts, began to echo the effects generated by her male counterparts. She gained new prestige. Authors who produced two of the first characters of this kind were themselves women. Charlotte Brontë used femine creativity as an effective means of adding to her heroine's appeal in *Jane Eyre* (1847). When Jane first went to Thornfield Hall to teach a little girl she discovered in the schoolroom a new cabinet piano of superior tone and also an 'easel for painting and a pair of globes'. The easel appeared as part of a governess's standard equipment. Her painting, on the other hand, was so far above the usual standard of work likely to come from a governess that her grisly employer, Mr Rochester, at first rudely assumed that she had copied it. But once he was convinced that her work was genuine, his attitude to her changed remarkably, so that he no longer condescendingly regarded her merely as a dependent menial. She had displayed the original, imaginative mind of the artist and thus began to stimulate his increasingly passionate curiosity.[43] Similarly, Anne Brontë made Helen Graham, the heroine of *The Tenant of Wildfell Hall* (1848), attract male admiration for her artistic skill. She supported herself in her flight from a drunken husband by executing some rather smart sketches from nature, which were sold through a London dealer. In Chapter VI the hero discovered her drawing some trees with a 'spirited though delicate touch'. As she was not talkative he stood passively watching her ply her pencil: 'it was a pleasure to behold, so dexterously guided by those fair and graceful fingers'.[44]

'Graceful' was a characteristic word to describe a female artist's work. Lady Cecilia, a character in *Magdalen Wynard, or The Provocations of a Pre-Raphaelite,* let her daughter study water colours but forbade oils as they were 'so very masculine'. Nineteenth century writers generally considered that women found it easier to grasp the intuitive rather than the constructive aspects of art.

Mrs Oliphant, in *The Three Brothers,* showed how Mrs Severn personified this dictum. Although she won much praise for daringly attempting to paint in this way, such praise was always qualified. Her knowledge of anatomy, for example, was thought 'feeble' even though 'bits of life' stole on to her canvases, and mention of her feeling for sentiment or eye for colours was matched by remarks on her tentative drawing ability. 'It was never very firm, we are bound to admit; and we are also obliged to confess, against our will, that the padrona catered a great deal for the British public in the way of pretty little babies, and tender little nursery scenes. Her pictures were domestic, in the fullest sense of the word.'[45]

Other authors were more caustic. Moore made an erudite artist in *A Modern Lover* voice the opinion that the new race of nauseatingly-idealistic women artists, who had 'not yet had time to thoroughly digest what they have learnt, much less to create anything new',[46] were a plague of locusts. They were going through nineteenth century Europe as the Vandals had before them, devouring everything in their path. And Henry James, with his usual understatement, inserted into *Roderick Hudson* a gentle caricature of the new species in a dithering lady-artist called Augusta Blanchard who painted people with their backs turned because, as he gently remarked, she was a little weak in faces.

Most nineteenth century authors establishing a painter hero had been at pains to suggest at least the possibility of latent greatness – if only to add drama to his ultimate failure. But Mrs Ritchie began the first chapter of *Miss Angel* (1875) – a romantic and pseudo-historical biography of Angelica Kauffman – by deliberately belittling the abilities of her heroine. The fact that she modelled this character on Angelica Kauffman, one of the first women artists to gain widespread recognition in Britain, reflects a dawning interest in the general phenomenon of women artists. But her scathing criticism of the aesthetic merits of her character recorded the comparative value accorded to female creators of this kind.

It is ironic that when the novelist belaboured Angelica's creative shortcomings she could equally well have been pinpointing her own weaknesses, for Angelica's often sentimental subject matter echoed this lady authoress's own flowery style and love of romantic clichés. Mrs Ritchie was obviously dominated by the convention that sexuality should determine creativity, feeling, subconsciously, that if she had made Angelica as adept at such a practical art as town planning as she was at projecting a pretty mood of 'innocent enthusiasm' she would destroy her heroine's appeal. Certainly, in a final passage where Mrs Ritchie compares Angelica's reactions with those of her husband, Antonio, the couple's attitudes suggest obvious sexual-stereotypes. Antonio's monopoly of logical enterprise detracts, as one might expect, from his little woman's sweeter sensibilities. They were:

. . . united and yet unchanged, and true to their different natures. 'If you watch them before a picture . . . you see

Antonio, gifted with eloquence, speaking with energy, judging, dissecting, criticizing; Angelica, silent, with animated eyes, listens to her husband and gazes attentively at the canvas. You may read in her face and see her true opinion there. She speaks at last, but it is to dwell on the beauty and charm of the works before her. Hers is the nature of the bee', continues her old biographer: 'she only sucks honey from the flowers.'[47]

Thus although a few authors (such as Ouida in *Ariadne* (1877), were able to produce women artists who could compete with their masculine brethren in terms of creative skill and personal intensity, Mrs Ritchie was more typical in providing her readers with an altogether more tentative version of the established male artist, for Angelica lacked the wilder bohemian urges and more destructive fatalism of many of her male counterparts. Mildred Lawson, a fascinatingly cold-blooded study in Moore's *Celibates* (1895), provided another example of an unresolved interim type. The factors governing her choice of career, her attitude towards learning art as a discipline, and her actual achievements, all pointed to a lack of inner belief in her own talents and resources – a restriction which she, and those around her, appeared to accept as normal.

Her aesthetic ambitions, seen as a means of escape from Surrey, were eminently understandable but decidedly uninspiring. Moore made it clear that Mildred saw art as a means to an end. The scale of that end was defined by terms in which she first pictured her career. She had met 'ladies who had studios' and admired their independence: they had spoken of studying in Paris and going to a nearby village to paint. 'Each had a room at the inn, where they met at meal-times, and spent the day in the woods and fields.' Her concept of art was blissfully free of any pedantic technical or idealistic credos, unperturbed by the aims of either Old Masters or contemporary pioneers. Moore's slight images led the reader to affiliate her imaginatively with the 'ladies who had studios', a genteel phrase suggesting a purely decorous degree of involvement, and a charming picture of artistic life which conjured up not so much a determinedly conscientious and volcanic commitment as a lazy, relaxed life on an unchaperoned health farm. Instead of dramatically drawing a contrast between Mildred's ambitions and abilities – as did many male artists whose potential was disastrously eroded by latent vices – Moore began by dwarfing the very scale of Mildred's ambitions. Depriving her thus of all inspiratory hopes he made her failure a certainty, but one lacking all the tragic possibilities of her masculine counterparts.

Although Mildred studied amongst the 'cleverer' male students she achieved little. Replying to a friendly suggestion that she should try to work in the forest of Barbizon, Mildred was pessimistic:

> 'I'm afraid it would make no difference. Elsie and Cissie have spent years here, and what they do does not amount to much. They wander from method to method, abandoning each in turn. I am utterly discouraged, and made up my mind to give up painting.'[48]

It was particularly significant that she automatically associated her own personal lack of faith and direction, and her own feeble abilities, with those of two other equally futile, female artists. In her mind her failure was obviously associated with her sex.

To emphasize this supposition, Moore described two men, who, despite being obsessed by Mildred, were unwilling, or unable, to offer her the slightest real encouragement about her work. Ironically they were both rising painters and therefore were, in theory, well aware of the professional challenge she faced, but their subjective view of her blinded them to her objective ambitions which were symbolized by her attempts to develop her artistic interests. Moore emphasized the impression of an overtly masculine attitude by making the two men react according to exactly the same pattern, although their personalities were poles apart. The first, Ralph Hoskin, was weak and melancholy. He proposed and then, having been rejected, died clutching a bunch of Mildred's violets. This adoring lover surely went the whole hog in proving the sincerity of his affection, and yet had been capable of surprising insensitivity over Mildred's working future. When she refused marriage, giving the reason that she had the opportunity of learning to draw in Paris, he, while remaining perfectly serious about his own professional needs, had considered her careerist argument perfectly ridiculous; for, as he blandly explained, 'Women never succeed in painting'.

This tactless remark was characteristic of the negative effects of romantic idealization, where women were worshipfully etherealized to the point of imbecility. Morton Mitchell, a more aggressive artist, made the same mistake:

> 'These hands, how white they are in the moonlight.' He took

her hands, 'Why do you trouble and rack your soul about painting? A woman's hands are too beautiful for a palette and brushes.'[49]

His talk of moonlight and soul-racking, his chivalrous gesture and poetic praise suggested that rampant romanticism was an enemy to sexual equality. The abstract words 'a woman's hands' made the sentence a general statement: Moore's passage shows that it was irrelevant to consider decorative, ivory-handed femininity and genuine, practical creativity in the same breath.

Moore thought primarily in terms of personality and showed far more awareness of caricatured sexual taboos than Mrs Ritchie. He made his heroine consciously recognize, and reject, the egoism permeating this kind of romantic devotion. Mildred felt that Hoskin didn't think she would succeed simply 'because he wanted her to marry him'. Such a marriage would, in Mildred's eyes, have been a trap, as she would be expected to 'give up her whole life' to her husband; a dismal outlook.

However, Moore indicated that she was no more attuned to real female independence than the men around her, and was undisturbed by the equally tortuous motives underlying her own actions. Perhaps from a deep-rooted resentment, this woman was perfectly happy to use her powerful sexual charm with cynical detachment in order to promote her interests through the men she attracted. She was, for example, particularly callous with Ralph Hoskin and calculating with Morton Mitchell. Observers agreed that Mildred had never had a deep commitment to painting but had taken it up because it would help her socially, adding acidly that she had 'taken up' Morton Mitchell for the same reason. Not content to project her desires on to a successful man, she hesitantly attempted to form and fulfill her own ambitions as a female artist but, becoming increasingly frustrated, seemed to vent her unharnessed energies on the opposite sex. In Mildred Lawson, Moore produced a curiously unresolved hybrid combining the uncultivated talents of an amateur with the vengeful mentality of a *femme fatale*.[50] Just as more novels towards the end of the century included female artists, and those at the turn of the century often granted them increasing independence and achievement, so even the publication of a mediocre work such as *Women Painters of the World* (1905) by Walter Shaw Sparrow shows that female artists were beginning to be taken more seriously. A contributor began by explaining, for example, that as a type they had earlier suffered from both prejudice and lack of opportunity, and had achieved little in the adverse conditions produced by the early years of Victoria's reign. By the time he wrote, however, the absurd, unnatural and revolutionary aspects of women indulging in this profession had been well eroded by a succession of women painters (such as Kate Greenaway) who, he said, had been 'conscious at first of their leading-strings, but who have shown a development more than corresponding to that of the conditions under which they worked'.[51] Such comments mirror an altering social climate in which female artists were viewed as a fast-developing band whose ability was increasing. After having been unfairly slighted for their sex, they were now beginning to be in the happy position of being unnecessarily praised for it. Egalitarianism was all the rage.

Just as female egalitarianism contributed to ousting the fictional artist from his supreme position as a romantic hero, so the general growth of democratic principles also helped to whittle away his prestige. People at last began to tire of self-centred, temperamental heroes in both fact and fiction. The artist's emotional individualism proved outdated when there was a compensatory swing towards increasingly factual and mass-orientated ideologies. It was significant that in chapter fourteen of *New Worlds for Old* (1908), a work in which H. G. Wells described the advantages of a new socialist society, the artist was accorded no special privileges. And later, in *Men Without Art* (1934), Wyndham Lewis rejected artistic pretension on utilitarian grounds, remarking sternly that the 'vocation of Art has indeed been the excuse of this array of persons who are amongst the most worthless specimens'. As exclusively political doctrines absorbed the interest previously channelled into religious fervour, the artist lost his primary source of imaginative ascendancy and influence. Where earlier writers had instinctively blended creativity and subjectivity – discussing genius, as in 'Adonais', in terms of personality – a more impersonal and cynical attitude began to develop as the artist, as in Joyce's *A Portrait of the Artist as a Young Man* (1914), became an invisible god of creation, 'refined out of existence, indifferent, paring his finger-nails'.[52]

As hunger for an unsectarian visionary hero evaporated, there was no longer the same urge, among either authors or their public, to see the artist as a glamorized prophetic figure. And, as the artist's metaphysical importance waned, so too did his traditional methods of indicating it. In the nineteenth century it had been possible for authors to ignore aesthetic developments towards abstraction – such as Whistler's decision to call a portrait of his mother an 'Arrangement in Grey and Black' – and concentrate on the concept of an artist proving his spiritual worth with the kind of inspired realism which let him capture elements of soul in portraiture. But as the twentieth century progressed, so did the vogue for increasingly abstract art, which was reflected in works such as Virginia Woolf's *To The Lighthouse* (1927), where Lily Briscoe's method of painting was closely bound up with the recent theories, elaborated by Roger Fry and Clive Bell, about 'significant form'.

Indeed the fashion for abstraction was so strong that representation provoked wondering pity. When Gombauld, for example, the moody artist in Aldous Huxley's novel *Crome Yellow* (1921), produced strikingly realistic works his viewers showed polite dismay. A fashionable young lady made her way, on a flimsy pretext, to the disused granary where the artist slaved away with a 'kind of concentrated ferocity' at his 'terrific' new idea. Prepared to praise, she was stunned into bewildered silence when she actually saw his *chef d'oeuvre*. Instead of the cubist masterpiece she eagerly anticipated, she saw . . . a picture of a man and a horse, 'not only recognizable', but, to make matters worse, showing undeniable signs of *trompe l'oeil*. What could she think? What could she say? Representation went out with the Old Masters. Shocked, disgusted and disorientated, she turned the conversation with a gasping outburst which unmistakably indicated her knowledge of genuine aesthetic values:

> When I was in Paris this spring I saw a lot of Tachuplitski. I admire his work so tremendously. Of course, its frightfully abstract and frightfully intellectual. He just throws a few oblongs on to his canvas – quite flat, you know. . . .[53]

This new, intellectual approach (combined with new technical expertise in photographic realism) undermined the basic feasibility of the old nineteenth century means of illustrating creative genius with accounts of ultra realistic, 'spiritual' renderings.[54] Although these suggested reasons for the fictional artist's fading *raison d'être* are negative in themselves, their net effect was clearly demonstrated in a new emotional attitude to the artist. He became a joke.

A sure sign that the artist's semi-divine status was being systematically eroded was that increasingly detached authors came to treat him with a refreshing new frivolity. Nineteenth century literature had recorded the amusing pranks of groups of young art students, teased minor artistic figures, and described specific comic incidents in the lives of their serious artist heroes which were obviously designed to show their capacity for *bonhomie*. Nonetheless it had also determinedly treated the most banal major figures with a degree of intensity and respect bordering on the obsequious. Although George Moore's ironic treatment of his artist hero Lewis Seymour had seemed relatively daring in the context of similar contemporary themes, its irreverent tone was placid compared with later, increasingly unguarded twentieth century works. Priam Farll, the principal but decidedly unheroic character in Arnold Bennett's novel *Buried Alive* (1908), was, for example, a cowardly, portly, middle-aged bumbler whose prosaic retirement symbolized the steady dilution of the myth of the romantic idealist which had been so closely woven into the fabric of the fictional artist. Farll produced works which sold for phenomenal sums, and received England's greatest tribute when his 'body' was buried with full pomp in Westminster Abbey. Tiring of what Bennett convincingly portrayed as the artificial and worthless prestige attached to the person of a famous artist, he masqueraded as his dead valet and settled down, with a comfortable builder's widow, to an apparently Utopian existence in Putney, which

> seemed to breathe romance – the romance of common sense and kindliness and simplicity. It made his own existence to that day appear a futile and unhappy striving after the impossible. Art? What was it? What did it lead to? He was sick of art, and sick of all the forms of activity to which he had hitherto been accustomed and had mistaken for life itself.[55]

Later novels went further than querying the claims of art, and treated art and artists in such a way as to give the impression of their being utterly ludicrous – something nineteenth century authors had always tried to hide.[56] P. G. Wodehouse, for example, wrote a splendid parody of the idealistic artist fighting to preserve his spiritual integrity in a philistine world, in a short story entitled 'Rough-Hew Them How We Will', published in 1914. The hero was a part-time waiter whose prosaic idea of the 'earthly paradise' was to marry the waitress with whom he worked and buy a cigar shop in Brixton. But, instead of finding the appreciative connoisseur he longed for, Wodehouse's sensitive hero met snubs and rejections: the author described, for example, how his already suffering artist became destitute, after hitting his employer with a French roll. This dramatically tragic situation was relieved, in the nick of time, by an opportune American who foiled his suicide bid and went on to provide greater success. Immediately impressed by the artist's great work, he questioned its inconographical theme. Wodehouse, like so many before him, had already evoked this artist's romantic sensitivity in terms of his intuitive response to the beauties of nature – 'The Awakening' depicted a cool woodland scene in which a shepherd seemed about to waken a beautiful girl:

> 'He's stooping,' said Paul [the artist], fervently, 'to bestow upon his loved one a kiss. And she, sleeping, all unconscious, dreaming of him – '
>
> 'Never mind about her. Fix your mind on him. Willie is the "star" in this show. You have summed him up accurately. He is stooping. Stooping good. Now, if that fellow was wearing braces and stooped like that, you'd say he'd burst those braces, wouldn't you?' . . . 'No!' said the young man, solemnly, tapping him earnestly on the chest. 'That's where you're wrong. Not if they were Galloway's Tried and Proven. Galloway's Tried and Proven will stand any strain you care to put on them . . . wear Galloway's Tried and Proven, and fate cannot touch you.'[57]

Fate, in the expansive person of the general manager of Galloway's Tried and Proven, had intervened to save the creative arts. Wodehouse thus deflated any remaining remnants of his hero's mystic aura by interpreting his creativity not as a source of visionary inspiration but, on the contrary, an aid to material enterprise. Wodehouse's intoxicated artist, on the verge of a brilliant career, learnt gratefully of the ease with which he could secure fame and fortune. 'Cut out that mossy bank,' advised his new friend, 'put Willie in shirt-sleeves instead of a bath-robe, and fix him up with a pair of Tried and Proven and win three thousand dollars plus an indefinite retaining fee: You've got the goods.'

It was no coincidence that an American should have been the one to achieve this change, using brash advertising terminology to bring the artist to a realistic use of his talents. For, just as elements of French culture had, in the previous century, been evoked by writers who wanted to romanticize the artist, so, in the twentieth century, hearty American attitudes helped to deflate artistic pretentions. In *The Third Violet* (1897), for example,

Stephen Crane lets an American, while describing his own race as hideously modern, provide a cynical account of traditional studio behaviour:

> 'Jinks! Don't I wish I had a big studio and a little reputation! Wouldn't I have my swell friends come to see me, and wouldn't I entertain 'em!' He adopted a descriptive manner, and with his forefinger indicated various spaces of the wall. 'Here is a little thing I did in Brittany. Peasant woman in sabots. This brown spot here is the peasant woman, and those two white things are the sabots. . . .'

This honest approach, which helped to make romantic art anachronistic, and mysticism irrelevant, later resulted in novels such as William Golding's *Free Fall* (1959), where a painter seduces and deserts his 'Beatrice' without maiming his creativity – painting some very 'good pictures', which are hung in the Tate.[59] This novelist has gone a long way from the nineteenth century idea that the artist was a tortured priest who, on sinning, lost his talents.

A passage from *The Horse's Mouth* (1944) had earlier hinted at this decline in esoteric feeling. Joyce Cary's artist was busily painting a she-whale on a chapel wall when he noticed her smile:

> I had a shock. I was touched, of course, to see this affection in a favourite child, but I thought I must be dreaming again. 'My dear girl,' I said, 'my petsie – do be careful – remember your delicate constitution.' And all at once the smile broke in half, the eyes crumpled, and the whole wall fell slowly away from my brush; when the dust began to clear I saw through the cloud about ten thousand angels in caps, helmets, bowlers and even one top-hat, sitting on walls, dustbins, gutters, roofs, window-sills and other people's cabbages, laughing. That's funny, I thought, they've all seen the same joke. God bless them. It must be a work of eternity, a chestnut, a horse-laugh.
>
> Then I perceived that they were laughing at me. And I should have got up and bowed if my swing had been steady enough. But it was waggling more than ever. 'Hi,' I said, 'don't do that. I'll come down quietly.' For I didn't want to cause any trouble. I wanted a new studio quickly. I wanted to get that whale straight down again before I lost the feeling of her.
>
> But of course they couldn't hear me because of the amuse-

ment. And all at once the swing turned right over and I fell off into a blanket held by six art enthusiasts or friends of democracy.[60]

The artist was then removed in an ambulance, and there the novel ended. Cary's achievement illustrates the value of considering literature in a comparative context. Pleasant in itself, this passage becomes more witty as the reader recalls its nineteenth century predecessors. Cary parodied the stereotyped romantic artist whose spirituality had been indicated both by references to living works and to his sources of metaphysical inspiration. A fictional character like James's Roderick Hudson agonizingly referred to an unsuccessful work as an abortion: Cary's painter Gully Jimson took the implicit idealism out of this equation between an artist's aesthetic oeuvre and human offspring by informally nicknaming his favourite child, this painting of the whale, his 'petsie'.

Where a nineteenth century artist such as Rossetti's Chiaro dell' Erma proved his divine status by his visionary episodes, Cary's painter saw 'angels' with the opposite effect. It was significant that the ethereal raiment of Chiaro's spirits contrasted forcibly with the more prosaic bowlers Cary described. Similarly, while Rossetti's supernatural figures conscientiously encouraged his hero, Cary's 'angels' found the artist a good excuse for a belly laugh. And where Chiaro had been humbled and overawed by the presence of his visitors, Cary's hero was inclined to jest: he had a passing thought – rather in the Marx Brothers' style – of making a bow in mid-air. Finally, where Chiaro rose to new personal and creative heights after his experience, capturing the image of his mystic lady, Cary's painter literally tumbled to the ground, his mind still occupied by the crumbling image of his female fish. Cary thus showed how this twentieth century artist, instead of towering over the materialistic mob with his divine revelations, literally fell off his perch into the comforting support of a democratic blanket. Instead of exploiting the symbolism of the fall – in the way of such writers as Henry James when he manipulated it with dramatic force to make Roderick Hudson an undeniably tragic figure – Cary used it simply to suggest that his painter was, in the classic sense of the word, a fool.

As the importance of the fictional artist dwindled, authors naturally evolved new escapist formulae to satisfy, and also to define, changing cultural needs. One of particular interest in the context of this thesis was the hero of science fiction. For where-

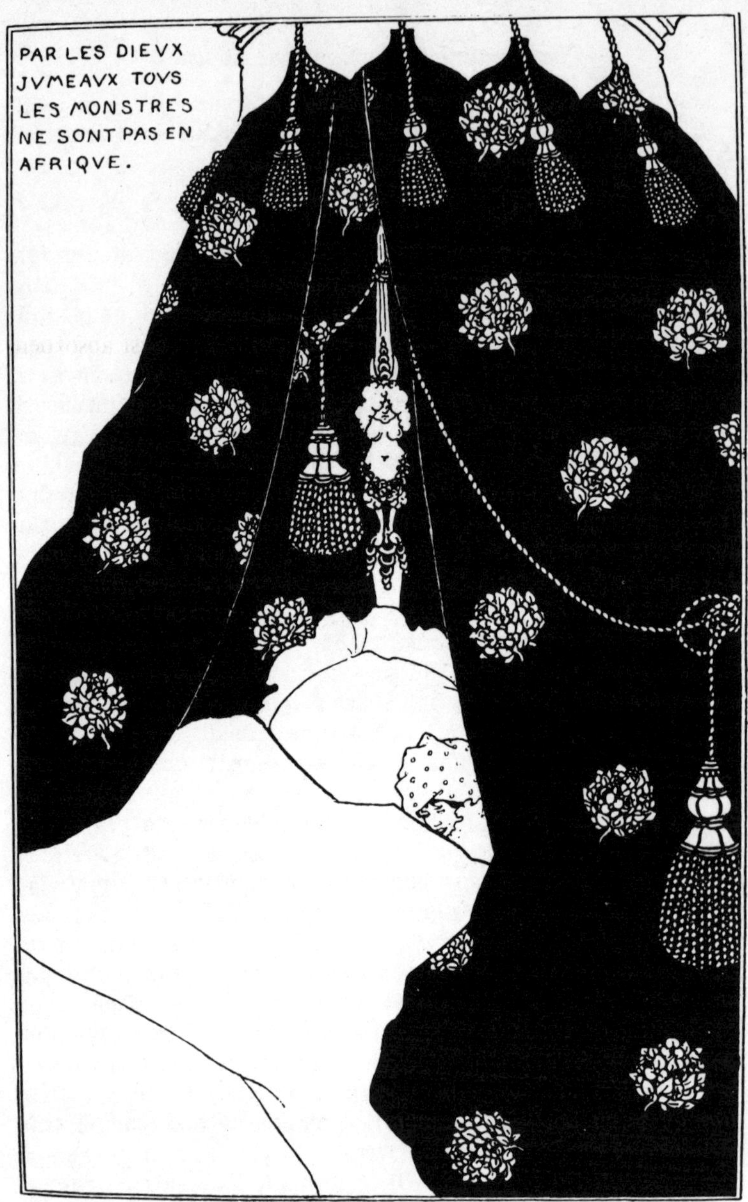

'Self-portrait in Bed'
The caption on this drawing implies that the artist is making a joke of his own peculiarity. The enormous tassels and decorative hangings on this lavish bed dwarf the face of this tubercular artist who shows himself cocooned away from reality. This tiny face, in its nightcap, reflects the dwindling powers of the artist hero.

as, at the beginning of the nineteenth century, society's escapist needs were easily fulfilled by the unorthodox bohemian life of the artist, by the beginning of the twentieth century social restrictions and hierarchies were already starting to dissolve, and so the artist's formerly attractive freedoms paled. People, as always, sought wider horizons. Who wanted yet another titilating peep at the artist and his model in their scruffy Parisian studio when they could explore the secrets of the unknown?[61]

In an age of relatively easy earthly travel, the scientist absorbed increasing attention as an adventurer of unlimited scope in time and space and all the wonders of the universe. One of the earliest signs – and an isolated one – of this development was Mary Shelley's novel *Frankenstein* (1818), a peculiar synthesis of the old Prometheus myth and what is now called science fiction.[62] This novel centred around a talented scientist (some of whose characteristics, such as his abnormal preoccupation with his work, were reminiscent of those associated with artists), and his monstrous creation. The almost human character of this object testified to the power of its creator in the same way that magic connections and paintings testified to the ability of an artistic creator. This new scientific addition to – or interpretation of – the old theme was to define this magic, archetypal force, which was used to vitalize the monster: it was called electricity.

Although the persona of the creative hero underwent great changes, and the scientific hero tended to stress his isolation from society by reticence (as when H. G. Wells produced an invisible scientific hero) rather than temperamental displays, the difference between the 'mad scientist' and the 'sensitive artist' was not always so marked. The fact that the nineteenth century's supreme symbol of creative genius, the romantic artist (with his peculiar fusion of God-like powers and personal eccentricities) evolved, in the twentieth century, into that of the scientific hero amounted to a revitalization of one of the oldest creative myths, that of Daedalus or his northern counterpart Illarien, who, as an artist, created life-like human forms and, as a scientist, sought to control the skies.

Notes

Chapter One
The Evolution of the Fictional Artist

1 Averil Beaumont, *Magdalen Wynard; or, The Provocations of a Pre-Raphaelite* (1871), Vol. I, p. 66.

2 Philip Gilbert Hamerton, *Thoughts About Art* (1889 edition), p. 108.

3 He included this embryonic discussion, mentioning English and French authors, in his *Thoughts About Art* (1873). It is rare to find fictional artists considered in their own right, instead of simply being lumped together under an umbrella heading dealing with creative and sensitive figures.

4 Oliver Goldsmith, *The Vicar of Wakefield* (1944 edition), p. 66.

5 William Makepeace Thackeray, *The Newcomes* (1962 edition), Vol. I, p. 198.

6 William Makepeace Thackeray, *The Adventures of Philip* (1862), p. 148.

7 Henry James, *Roderick Hudson* (1969 edition), p. 96. See also p. 106. Drawing on a different kind of notoriety Trollope, in *Can You Forgive Her?* (1864), based a romantic day dream on Raphael's much publicized relationship with Fornarina.

8 As an admirer tells Longley, the painter hero of *Magdalen Wynard; or, The Provocations of a Pre-Raphaelite:* 'You can do a thousand times more good as a painter, and inspire more high and noble thoughts by one of your thoughts than by any sermon.' Vol. I, p. 62.

9 In the early Victorian period when pictorial artists began to become popular their visionary qualities made them exceptions at a generally unheroic time. See Mario Praz, *The hero in eclipse in Victorian fiction* (1956).

10 P. B. Shelley, 'A Defence of Poetry', *Shelley's Essays and Letters* (Ed. Ernest Rhys, 1886), p. 35. To a certain extent he here contradicted an earlier view (p. 6), where he exalted poetry over the other arts, arguing that their methods and media interposed 'between conception and expression.' The essay, first written in 1821, was first published in *Essays, Letters from abroad etc.* (2 Vols. ed. Mrs. Shelley, 1840).

11 Strong beliefs in the poet's idealized role could also provoke scorching criticism, such as Byron's or Browning's attacks on Wordsworth for his suspected apostasy.

12 See William Hayley's *Essay on Epic Poetry* (1782) where Chatterton's disastrous end illustrated the belief in the fatal vulnerability of natural talent.

13 *Works* ed. H. Buxton Forman (1880) III, pp. 20-21. See Harold Bloom, *Shelley's Mythmaking* (1959) *passim.*

14 S. T. Coleridge, *The Complete Poetical Works* (1912), p. 298.

15 Lord Byron, 'Childe Harold's Pilgrimage', St. CXIII, *Poetical Works* (1896), p. 218.

16 Lady Morgan, *The Life of Salvator Rosa* (1824), p. iii.

17 She also referred to Salvator to conjure up picturesque intensity in *The Wild Irish Girl* (1806), where the aristocratic hero pretends to live by sketching in order to try and capture the affection of the romantic heroine.

18 He was fascinated by Goethe's early tale of a sentimental artist who committed suicide in *The Sorrows of Young Werther* (1774) and by Sir Herbert Croft's long apology for Chatterton in *Love and Madness* (1780).

19 The idea of the escapist bohemian was also popularised by being adapted for the stage in melodramas and operas, such as Puccini's 'La Bohème'.

20 William Hazlitt, 'On the Pleasure of Painting', *London Magazine*, December, 1820. Text from *The Best of Hazlitt* (compiled by P. P. Howe, 1952), p. 25.

21 The theory that music was, as Pater put it, the 'source of all inspiration' may have led to a greater interest in musical heroes towards the turn of the century. *Maurice Guest* (1908) by Henry Handel Richardson presents a musical hero in the romantic tradition.

22 William Wordsworth, *Poetical Works* Ed. Thomas Hutchinson rev. edn. E. de Selincourt (1946), p. 489.

23 The dramatic impact of the painter's work, and its spontaneous appeal were also quoted in popular novels:

'What a grand thing it is, too, the painter's art; of all the arts the most satisfying! . . . The effect of the artist's work on the beholder is instantaneous, the reward of his genius is immediate; to say nothing of his own personal delight and satisfaction.'
Joseph Hatton, *The Tallants of Barton* (1867), Vol. I., p. 67.

24 Charles Lever, *The Martins of Cro' Martin*, Harry Lorrequer edition (1876-78), Vol. I, p. 55.

25 Although colourful painters and sculptors were popular romantic figures in nineteenth century literature it was significant that architects, such as Dickens's character Martin Chuzzlewit, were not. They were the most respectable group in the artistic hierarchy, and also the most orthodox of the fraternity in the sense that they were generally educated in logic and mathematics and more likely to work in the more clinical atmosphere of a drawing office. The brief appearance of the sentimental Bosinney in *The Forsyte Saga* (1922) was exceptional.

26 Morley Roberts, *Immortal Youth* (1902 edition), p. 73.

27 Ibid., p. 49.

28 George Saintsbury, discussing *The Newcomes*, remarked that Clive, the artist hero, appeared to resemble Thackeray in his love of drawing, and in his limited success therein, and perhaps in some of his later hardships and misfortunes.

In *Roderick Hudson* (1876) James drew on his own visual sensitivity and on his first hand experience of the American artists he met in Rome in 1873, such as the sculptor William Wetmore Story (who had earlier intrigued Hawthorne). While the aloof personality of James's fictional connoisseur, Rowland Mallet, might be seen as a reflection of James's cautious side, Hudson himself – with his desire to shine in Europe – shared many of his creator's own ambitions. Again, the sculptor's fascination with Christina Light echoes James's own curiosity about Elena Lowe, a mysterious beauty whom he met when travelling.

Similarly Rudyard Kipling founded the elusive, egocentric heroine of *The Light that Failed* (1891) on his childhood sweetheart, Florence Garrard, a beautiful dark Pre-Raphaelite girl who broke off their engagement while he was in India, provoking these lines.

> One brought Her Fire from a distant place,
> And She – what would She know of it? . . .
> Sudden She crushed the embers 'neath Her heel, –
> And all light went with Her.

See Charles Carrington, *Rudyard Kipling His Life and Work* (1955), pp. 41-55.

Walter Pater was another writer with close psychological links with art. Writing of his *Imaginary Portraits* (1887), for example, he said: 'I call a manuscript a portrait, and I mean readers, as they might on seeing a portrait, to begin speculating – what came of him?'

29 George Moore, *Flowers of Passion* (1878), p. 107.

Chapter Two
The Artist's Appearance as Romantic Hero

1 William Makepeace Thackeray, *The Newcomes* (1962 edition), Vol. I, p. 176.

2 George Moore, *A Modern Lover* (1883), Vol. I, p. 59.

3 Entitled *Lewis Seymour and Some Women* (1917).

4 George Du Maurier, *Trilby* (1947 edition), p. 8.

5 Blanche Willis Howard, *Guenn, A Wave on the Breton Coast* (1884 edition), p. 245.

6 William Makepeace Thackeray, *The Newcomes* (1962), Vol. I, p. 251.

7 Charles Clark, *Lord Falconberg's Heir* (1868), Vol. 2, p. 174.

8 Anthony Trollope, *Barchester Towers* (1925 edition), p. 84.

9 Rare glimpses of elderly artists often showed very similar instincts, as, for example, in the case of an old man with refined features and expressively mobile brows whom Margaret Oliphant described in *The Three Brothers* (1870). His hair and beard were almost white, he sported a black velvet bonnet, such as Dutch painters wear in their pictures, and a velvet coat. Even at his age he was 'not above adding' a deft touch to the picturesqueness of his appearance 'by means of dress'.

10 Henry James, *Roderick Hudson* (1969), p. 37.

11 George Moore, *A Modern Lover* (1883), Vol. II, p. 80.

12 Mary Anne Hardy, *The Artist's Family* (1857), Vol. I, p. 5.

13 In Watts-Dunton's *Aylwin* the painter D'Arcy (modelled on Rossetti) kept wombats, kangaroes and other animals in his wild garden.

14 Mary Anne Hardy, *Paul Wynter's Sacrifice* (1869), Vol. 2, p. 191.

15 George Moore, *The Confessions of a Young Man* (1904 edition), p. 60.

16 Theodore Watts-Dunton, *Aylwin* (1901 edition), p. 234.

17 George Du Maurier, *Trilby* (1947 edition), p. 9.

18 George Moore, *A Modern Lover* (1883), Vol. II, p. 9.

19 Ibid., Vol. II, p. 22.

20 Ibid., Vol. II, p. 23.

21 George Eliot, *Middlemarch* (1962 edition), p. 189.

22 A later suggestion added to the heroic quality of his plight: he had perhaps found a 'defiant entertainment' watching the storm and challenging the elements. *cf* parallel use of storms in desolate areas in

other romantic works, such as the series of wild storms in *Wuthering Heights* (1847).

23 Henry James, *Roderick Hudson* (1969 edition), p. 346.
24 Du Maurier made the same negative point in *Trilby* where he provided an illustration of a painter working in the Barbizon forest which he entitled 'The good Life'. This was a romantic vignette of an artist in a broad brimmed hat sitting under a leafy tree, with the back of his easel to the fore, so that his actual work was a complete mystery.
25 Joseph Hatton, *The Tallants of Barton* (1867), Vol. I, p. 66.
26 An open window, as in Wallis's famous painting of 'The Death of Chatterton', was a favourite romantic symbol of the desire to escape, or of the flown soul.
27 Joseph Hatton, *The Tallants of Barton*, Vol. I. p. 157.

Chapter Three
The Artist Versus Society

1 Wilkie Collins, *Hide and Seek* (1889 edition), p. 31.
2 George Du Maurier, *Trilby* (1947 edition), p. 86.
3 Wilkie Collins, *Hide and Seek* (1889 edition), p. 147.
4 Ibid., p. 150.
5 Quoted in *The Oxford Companion to English Literature* (4th edition 1969), p. 100.
6 Henry James, *The Europeans* (1973 edition), p. 31.
7 Ibid., p. 24.
8 Ibid., p. 69.
9 Ibid., p. 61.
10 Ibid., p. 71.
11 Ibid., p. 54.
12 Robert Browning, 'Fra Lippo Lippi', *Poetical Works* (2 Vols., 1902), p. 518.
13 Ibid., 518.
14 Margaret Vere Farrington, *Fra Lippo Lippi* (1890), p. 31.
15 Theodore Watts-Dunton, *Aylwin* (1901 edition), p. 207.
    Many bohemians' own lack of restrictive self-consciousness made them not only more amusing than most people, but also more interesting for:
        intellect, as they called it, clearness and brightness and talk, and the absence of ceremony, were sweeter than any other conditions of society . . . they filled the rooms wtih discussion of everything on earth and heaven – art news, political news, society news, a little of everything; they held hot discussions on social questions with the zeal of people immediately concerned, not with the languor of good society. Margaret Oliphant, *The Three Brothers* (1870) I, p. 264.
16 George Moore, *A Modern Lover* (1883), Vol. I, p. 199.
17 Ibid., p. 108.
18 George Moore, *A Modern Lover* (1883), Vol. I, p. 45.
19 See, for example, how Dickens tactfully glossed over the practical aspects of prostitution in *Oliver Twist* (1837-8).
20 Rudyard Kipling, *The Light that Failed* (1891), p. 122.
21 Ibid., p. 131.

22 Thomas Hardy, *The Well-Beloved, A Sketch of a Temperament* (1958 edition), p. 15.

23 See his Introduction to the 1832 edition of *St Ronan's Well*.

24 Sir Walter Scott, *St Ronan's Well*, Vol. XVII, Holyrood Edition, (n.d.), p. 67.

25 William Makepeace Thackeray, *Vanity Fair* (1913 edition), p. 55.

26 Anthony Trollope, *Barchester Towers* (1925 edition), p. 163.

27 Ibid., p. 80.

28 Ibid., p. 93.

29 Mary Jackson, *Maud Skillicorne's Penance* (1858), Vol. I, p. 89.

30 Anthony Trollope, *Barchester Towers* (1925 edition), p. 87.

31 Ibid., p. 88.

32 Charles Lee, *Cynthia in the West* (1900), p. 6.

33 In this novel, Breton sailors dismissed artists as lunatics: 'The unconscious artist goes his way. . . . The sailors' thoughts are free. They exercise their sovereign right of ridiculing what they do not understand.' (p. 70). The author builds on this lack of understanding when several ignorant villagers unite in attempts to murder the painter hero.

34 Charles Lee, *Cynthia in the West* (1900), p. 163.

35 William Makepeace Thackeray, *The Newcomes* (1962 edition), p. 284.

36 Ibid., p. 294.

37 Ibid., p. 280.

38 Ibid., p. 296. She felt – significantly – that art would, however, be suitable for Clive's protégé who was only a butler's son. J. J. Ridley's butler father was overcome with pride when he saw his painter son received by his own august employer, Lord Todmorde : 'my Lord have ordered a pictur of John James in the most lib'r manner, and have asked my son to dinner, sir, at his Lordship's own table, which I have faithfully served him five-and-thirty years.' (Ibid., p. 278).

39 Clive himself complained bitterly of the 'difference between a poor painter and a young lady of the world'. Ethel publicly ignored him on one occasion, being embarrassed to own him because of his profession, when she came on him copying a picture in the Louvre as she strolled round with her fine friends. Similarly, when Clive was about to make a journey, Lord Kew was astounded to be told that the painter had bought a carriage: He would no more have thought of a young artist leaving Baden in a carriage of his own than of 'his riding on a dragon'.

40 Henry James, *The Tragic Muse* (New York edition, 1908), Vol. II, pp. 72-3.

41 George Du Maurier, *Trilby* (1947), p. 115.

42 Ibid., p. 150.

43 Ibid., p. 115.

Chapter Four
The Vulnerable Artist and His Supernatural Attributes

1 George Moore, *A Modern Lover* (1883), Vol. II, p. 14.

2 Robert Barnabus Brough, *Marston Lynch* (1860), p. 318.

3 Margaret Roberts, *The Atelier du Lys* (1877 edition), p. 240.

4 E. F. Benson, *Limitations* (1896), p. 27.

5 Charles Lever, *The Martins of Cro' Martin* (1876-8 edition), Vol. I, p. 51.

6 References to artists exhibiting in private galleries – as when Vernon Lee mentioned in *Miss Brown* (1884) that her hero was preparing work for a private gallery – were rare.

7 George Gissing, *The Emancipated* (1893 edition), p. 26.

8 George Moore, *A Modern Lover* (1883), Vol. III, p. 119.

9 Joseph Hatton, *The Tallants of Barton* (1867), Vol. I, p. 158.

10 Margaret Oliphant, *The Three Brothers* (1870), Vol. I, p. 290.

11 Rudyard Kipling, *The Light that Failed* (1891), p. 40.

12 John Galsworthy, *Villa Rubein and other stories* (1909 edition), p. 21.

13 G. H. Luquet, in an introduction to prehistoric mythology, described the significance of such representative image – especially in Palaeolithic times, when food depended mainly on hunting and the

> . . . essential role of magic was to ensure its success. Mimetic magic with animal disguises must have contributed. But Magdalenian man certainly had recourse to sympathetic or homeopathic magic, which relies on the theory that an operation performed on an image of a real being will produce the same effect on the being itself. *Larousse Encyclopedia of Mythology* (1959), p. 2. See also Ernst Gombrich, *The Story of Art* (1950), Chapter I.

14 'A popular and persistent miracle tells of the human responses of paintings, images or icons . . . statues of the Virgin, when injured, bled. The figure of Cyrus also yielded blood. . . . Weeping images also appear, as well as portraits which exude oil.

> Motions of various kinds are also attributed to images. Herman Joseph offered an apple to a statue of the Virgin and her child. The infant reached out and took the fruit. . . .'

> Examples taken from C. Grant Loomis, *White Magic, An Introduction to the Folklore of the Christian Legend*. The Mediaeval Academy of America, Cambridge, Mass. (1948), Publication no. 52, Chapter XII on Miraculous Images.

15 H. C. Agrippa, *De Occulta Philosophia* (1533), Vol. I, 38, p. 53, quoted by Frances A. Yates in *Giordano Bruno and the Hermetic Tradition* (1964), p. 132.

16 'Portraiture in its broadest sense is the representation of an individual, living or dead, real or imagined.' . . . *The Encyclopedia of World Art* (1966), Vol. XI, p. 476.

17 Horace Walpole, *The Castle of Otranto* (1765), p. 43.

18 Ibid., pp. 14 and 15.

19 The title (from which Lewis gained the soubriquet 'Monk') was altered in the three volume edition of 1798 to *Ambrosio, or The Monk*.

20 M. G. Lewis, *Ambrosio, or The Monk* (1798), Vol. I, pp. 64-65.

21 C. R. Maturin, *Melmoth the Wanderer* (1961 edition), p. 13.

22 Sheridan Le Fanu reiterated Maturin's interest in sinister portraits connected with the supernatural as, for example, in the 'Strange Event in the Life of Schalken the Painter' included in *The Watcher and other weird stories* (1895).

23 Though the novel was published in 1818 it was begun in 1797 and finished in 1803.

24 W. S. Gilbert and A. Sullivan, *Ruddigore* (Chappell and Co.'s edition of Gilbert's Eight Comic Operas, n.d.), p. 34.

25 Thomas Hardy, *Tess of the d'Urbervilles*, The Wessex Novels, Vol. VIII (1909), p. 282.

26 Published in *The Graphic*, Christmas Number, 1890.

27 Another of Hardy's characters, Susan Nunsuch, in *The Return of the Native* (1878) melted a curiously elaborate image of Eustacia Vye and stuck pins in it to reduce her to 'powerlessness, atrophy and annihilation'.

28 Wilde also was influenced by Balzac's *Peau de Chagrin* (1831) where a 'fatal skin' talisman measured the expenditure of its possessor's life. For other sources see Aatos Ojala, *Aestheticism and Oscar Wilde: Part I, 'Life and Letters'* (1954), pp. 209-211.
    Wilde's interest in the supernatural, and the possibility that spirit and matter might be interchangeable, was not altogether abstract speculation: the quest for an elixir of youth was actually demonstrated in his time by some of his magician friends. See Maurice Beebe, *Ivory Towers and Sacred Founts* (New York, 1964), p. 153.

29 Oscar Wilde, *The Picture of Dorian Gray* (1962 edition), p. 104.

30 Wilde supplied yet another example of Gothic material in the introduction and treatment of Gray's family portraits, for many writers of tales of terror used a series of paintings to suggest that their evil hero was a contemporary representative of an endless chain of evil incarnate.

31 Several other works such as Browning's poem 'Beatrice Signorini', where a jealous wife viciously knifes the image her painter husband has created of her rival, follow the same pattern of thought as that found in *The Picture of Dorian Gray*.
    Ibid, p. 234.

32 There are also reversals of Wilde's theme in which an image indicates uncanny powers by committing a murder itself. An example is found in William Morris's tale *The Writing on the Image*, in *The Earthly Paradise* (1868-70), Vol. IV. Morris described how someone robbing a mysterious underground chamber was killed by a knight made of brass and wood; the image fired a deadly arrow into an intruder's back.

33 Max Beerbohm, in *The Happy Hypocrite* (1897), the story of a man whose personality changes as he wears a mask, records a similar preoccupation.

34 Henry James, *The Sacred Fount* (1901), p. 54.

35 Ibid., p. 54.

36 See, for example, Vernon Lee's use of such sittings to provide her amorous artist hero with unchaperoned meetings: 'The latest excuse for seeing her was to paint her portrait. . . .' *Miss Brown* (1884), Vol. III, p. 107.

37 As Thackeray did, castigating the hypocritical hacks Gandish and Smee, in *The Newcomes,* who were guaranteed to have someone's 'head off their shoulders' as soon as look at them, and exposing the suspicious methods and motives of the royal portraitist in *The Rose and the Ring* (1855):
    Tomaso Lorenzo painted all the court, who were delighted with his works; for even the Countess Gruffanuff looked young and Glumboso good-humoured in his pictures. 'He flatters very much' some people said, 'Nay' says Princess Angelica, 'I am above flattery, and I think he did not make my picture handsome enough. I can't bear to hear a man of genius unjustly cried down, and I hope my dear Papa will make Lorenzo a Knight of the Order of the Cucumber.' *The Rose and the Ring* (1923 edition), p. 32.

38 Just as Moore's Parisian nightscape, discussed in chapter two, might well be taken as a paraphrase rather than a translation of a similar

subject by an artist such as Pissarro, so many other English writers created descriptions which could well be seen in terms of independent visual works. See, for example, the way in which Edmund Blunden in *Thomas Hardy* (1941) equates this writer's achievements with those of Turner and Wright of Derby.

39 Margaret Oliphant, *The Three Brothers*, Vol. I, p. 240.

40 Henry James, *The Madonna of the Future and other early stories* (1962 edition), p. 110.

41 The respectful praise such truthfulness usually earned the artist was amusingly reversed in *The Liar,* another short story by James. Its painter hero was more surprised by the reception of his astute portrait of a blustering cad.

42 George Gissing, *Thyrza,* a tale (1927 edition), p. 486.

43 It was common to describe symbolic portraits with a literary inspiration. One of the funniest examples occurs in *Aylwin* when the heroine, who had been painted as Coleridge's Geraldine, was shocked to see her future mother-in-law in the same canvas in the role of the Lady Christabel.

44 George Eliot, *Romola* (1927 edition), p. 198.

45 Ibid., p. 198.

46 A rare reversal of the usual situation occurred in *The Light that Failed,* when the artist hero, Dick Haldar, was trapped into sitting for his own portrait. Kipling first stressed the vulnerability of his position by letting him mediate on all the people he himself had 'laid open' for the purposes of his craft.

47 Vernon Lee, *Oke of Okehurst, Hauntings: fantastic stories* (1890), p. 187.

48 Charles Lee, *Cynthia in the West* (1900), p. 227.

49 Dante Gabriel Rossetti, Sonnet X 'The Portrait', *The Poetical Works of Dante Gabriel Rosetti* (1893), p. 181.

50 William Wordsworth, 'Lines, suggested by a portrait from the pencil of F. Stone', *Poetical Works* (1946 edition), p. 508.

51 Morley Roberts, *Immortal Youth* (1902 edition), p. 107.

52 'Painters and sculptors are descendants of cultural heroes. Experts in many skills, masters of many secrets of nature, these heroes competed with the Gods: Prometheus, who created man, Hephaestus or Daedalus, who created automatons of man . . . were punished for their transgression of the divine prerogative . . . which condemns emulation.'

   Ernst Kris, *Psychoanalytic Explorations in Art* (1953), p. 48. See also C. Kerényi, *Prometheus: Archetypal Image of Human Existence*, tr. Ralph Manheim (1963), and Denis Donoghue, *Thieves of Fire* (1973).

53 A bas-relief from a sarcophagus in the National Museum, Naples, shows 'The Creation of man': in the presence of Zeus, Poseidon, Hermes, Apollo and Hera, Prometheus prominently prepares to animate the body of the first man.

Chapter Five
The Artist's Tragic Temperament

1 Henry James, *Roderick Hudson* (1969 edition), p. 158.

2 Robert Browning, 'Youth and Art', *Poetical Works* (1902), Vol. I, p. 599.

3   This fitted in with the image of the artist as an individualistic bohemian who despised and avoided the establishment and formally organised and regulated groups, as when Little Billee acted so rebelliously against the doctrines and teaching of the Church of England.

4   As with the emotive pantheism expressed in works such as *The Prelude* and *Wuthering Heights*.

5   D. G. Rossetti, *Hand and Soul* (1895 edition), p. 15.

6   Wilderspin, aligning himself with Carlyle and Ruskin, attacked his age's interest in technical excellence rather than spiritual inspiration.

7   Watts-Dunton, *Aylwin* (1901 edition), p. 191.

8   Wilderspin declared, in his usual categorical fashion, that 'No man whose soul is stained by fleshly desire shall render in art all that there is in a truly beautiful woman's face'. . . . Ibid., p. 200.

9   This kind of sentiment, which added greatly to the artist's prestige as his creations were considered not only perfect but immortal, was popularised by Keats in his 'Ode on a Grecian Urn'.

10 The difficulty of striking a balance between art and life inspired much romantic literature, as, for instance, in the problems of Tennyson's house-proud soul in its symbolic Palace of Art. This kind of conflict between isolationism, which could be purifying or stultifying, and participation, which could be nourishing or nauseating, is discussed with great thoroughness by Maurice Beebe in *Ivory Towers and Sacred Founts*. He explains in his Introduction that the implication of the Sacred Fount myth is that life and art are so closely related that: 'one can exhaust or destroy the other. Because there is only so much life to be lived, that which is turned into art is made unavailable for living: the more kite-string in the air, the less in the hand, and one cannot have it in both places at once. Hence the continued struggle.'

    Ibsen was one of the few who managed to get round the problem. *In When We Dead Awaken* (1899) his sculptor hero at first ignores a woman's love, devoting all his energies to art, and studying her body to create a masterpiece. Later, meeting her again, he decides that life should include love, and the two go off together and are killed in an avalanche – the title and part of the text implying that, as life is eternal, this artist has literally been given a fresh start, a second chance.

11 Christina Georgina Rossetti, 'In An Artist's Studio', 24 Dec., 1856, *The Poetical Works of Christian Georgina Rossetti* (with memoir and notes etc., by William Michael Rossetti) (New York edition, 1970), p. 330.

12 Emma Marshall, *Castle Meadow* (1897), p. 10.

13 Ibid., p. 229.

14 Oscar Wilde, *The Picture of Dorian Gray* (1962 edition), p. 27.

15 Rhoda Broughton, *Mrs Bligh: a Novel* (1892), p. 279.

16 The artist's underlying priest-like role was responsible for many instances where material wealth as such was shunned or abused, as in *The Light that Failed* where Kipling equated his hero's interest in money with a threat to his talent.

17 In the prologue to 'Pacchiarotto and how he worked in distemper' Browning indicated that the artist should find his freedom by serving his metaphysical vision, should 'hope hard in the subtle thing / That's spirit: though cloistered fast, soar free'.

18 Robert Browning, 'Andrea del Sarto', *Poetical Works* (1902), Vol. I, p. 524.

19 The Pygmalion legend, describing how a sculptor fell in love with a beautiful female statue he had made which was subsequently brought to life by Aphrodite, was extremely popular in this century. It inspired such varied works as a section of William Morris's *Earthly Paradise* (1868-70) and a comedy by W. S. Gilbert, entitled, *Pygmalion and Galatea* (1891).

20 Richard Le Gallienne, *The Worshipper of The Image* (1900), p. 130.

21 Their evil was an integral part of their charm. Keats showed this in the ambiguous serpentine imagery of 'Lamia'. Browning echoed this imagery, when Andrea del Sarto referred to his wife as
> My serpentining beauty, rounds on rounds
> My face, my moon, my everybody's moon.

Vernon Lee was yet another who described a *femme fatale* as a serpent. Sacha, in *Miss Brown,* was twice referred to as a Lamia. The embrace of this amoral temptress who seduced her painter cousin, Hamlin, was described as 'caress of a lamia's clammy scales'.

22 There was a homosexual version of this hypnotic sensual image in *The Picture of Dorian Gray* where the artist thought his portrait of Gray showed a 'curious artistic idolatory'.

23 Included in *Hauntings: fantastic stories* (1861).

24 There was a decided tendency for such *femmes fatales* to be dark in colouring: black (such as the black-tongued snake and black moth mentioned in *The Worshipper of the Image*) was traditionally associated with the powerful, dramatic forces of evil. Compare, for example, descriptions of ebony-haired Ethel Newcome in *The Newcomes,* dusky Christian Light in *Roderick Hudson* and raven-haired Maisie, Kipling's *belle dame sans merci* in *The Light that Failed.* Such dark temptresses were often compared with paler, blonder women whose fragile, fair beauty seemed the epitome of innocence. Dionea, for example, was crudely juxtaposed with Waldermar's frail, domesticated wife, who was pathetically destroyed at the altar of Venue which her husband set up for her rival. Where Dionea was the dark destroyer, Gertrude was the pale victim. Dionea was earthy, southern and sensual but Gertrude was etherial, northern and spiritual. Her modest, delicate-lipped fair face was like that of a Flemish madonna. This 'snow-white saint' provided a striking contrast with Dionea, the Mediterranean siren who lacked all 'natural' piety.

25 When Tom lost a lavish income on his father's death, his lady-like wife found it hard to adapt, or rather to lower, her standards. Lacking the cheerful flexibility of a bohemian grisette, she suffered in these hard times when they had to empty their own slops and tell cook to prepare 'hash'.

26 The artist's exclusive emotional links with his work were often suggested by descriptions of art as his wife or mistress. Hazlitt, for example, said the painter invested his all in his career – fame, time, future, peace of mind, his hopes in youth, and his consolation in old age: 'The painter is wedded to his art – the mistress, queen and idol of his soul.' Similar images have already been quoted in *Chiaro dell Erma* by Dante Gabriel Rossetti, who wrote in 'To Art': 'I LOVED thee ere I loved a woman, Love'.

27 Joseph Hatton, *The Tallants of Barton* (1867), Vol. II, p. 62.

28 Similarly in Rhoda Broughton's *Mrs Bligh* the heroine equated genius with feeling: 'What he needs is an inspiration. If he could get hold of

an emotion of some kind he might do something big.' (p. 42).

29 George Gissing, *The Emancipated* (1893 edition), p. 96.
30 William Black, *A Princess of Thule* (1874), p. 82.
31 Anthony Trollope, *Barchester Towers* (1925 edition), p. 74.
32 James described this sculptor as one of a long series of talented artists who tested their genius in Rome. His preface stated: 'The very claim of the fable is naturally that he *is* special, that his great gift makes and keeps him highly exceptional; but that is not for a moment supposed to preclude his appearing typical (of the general type) as well.'
33 Similarly, Moore made equations between Lewis Seymour's vacillating character and structural weakness: his hermaphroditic physical tendencies were equated with 'effeminate' moral turpitude as, for example, at the close of the novel when the author described Seymour as the same 'beautiful, soft creature, bad only because he had not the strength to be good'. *A Modern Lover* (1883), Vol. III, p. 204.
34 On the other hand Gloriani (who also lends his studio for the setting of 'The Velvet Glove' and gives Strether a deep 'intellectual' sounding in *The Ambassadors*) was not at the mercy of his moods, but obviously had achieved a degree of objective organisation. He had a 'definite, practical scheme of art' unlike the vast majority of fictional artists for, as Rhoda Broughton pointed out more crudely in *Mrs. Bligh: a Novel,* in most of their lives 'there comes a moment when the fire seems to burn low'.
35 Rossetti provided another example of this kind of imagery when he said that the face of Chiaro dell' Erma had a 'glory upon it, as upon the face of one who feels a light around his hair'. And Margaret Oliphant also describes a similar incident in *The Three Brothers* where the talented painter, Suffolk, held up a lamp to display a painting, and was himself bathed in its light. (Vol. I, p. 291.)

This kind of imagery where a glorifying light was always directly associated with a fictional artist rather than his work, where a lamp held aloft had the curious habit of casting its brightness on the face and figure of the creator rather than on the work he was obviously exhibiting, corresponded with contemporary theories about the role of the artist. By the nineteenth century, purely mimetic theories of art grew into more idealised concepts popularising art as a means of revealing a superior kind of reality. This tendency has already been suggested in the previous chapter where fictional artists, when painting portraits, didn't merely echo a character's superficial physiognomy but went on to reveal elements of their spiritual nature. The romantic artist, in both fact and fiction, no longer considered himself as a mirror simply reflecting reality but as a glorified lamp, whose imaginative vision illuminated the world around him. Thackeray, in *The Newcomes,* equated the idea of genius with that of a light-house in a storm. (See Meyer C. Abrams, *The Mirror and the Lamp: Romantic Theory and the Classical Tradition* (1953) *passim.*) Failing creative powers were correspondingly equated with a loss of light, as when Hudson, losing his talent, compared himself with Dante, saying, 'But when his genius is in eclipse Dante is a dreadfully smoky lamp'.

36 The use of 'Light' for Christina's surname may, in itself, have been ironic.
37 Henry James, *Roderick Hudson* (1969 edition), p. 182.

38 Connections between writers and descriptions of fictional maimed birds provided parallel images to those used to describe the torments of painters and sculptors – see for example, Coleridge's awkward albatross, Lamartine's dying swan, or the comparison Flaubert made in the first version of *L'Education Sentimentale* between the poet and the goose nailed to a board and overfed to make its liver delicate: 'The animal had to be eaten, the poet had to speak; so much the better that they suffered in their very innards, if the flesh of the former is exquisite, and the latter's phrases are savory.' Despite the fact that imaginative flights seemed inevitably hampered or temporary, people took to the arts like flying lemmings. 'The fate of Icarus frightened no one. Wings! wings! wings! they cried from all sides, even if we should fall into the sea. To fall from the sky, one must climb there, even for but a moment, and that is more beautiful than to spend one's whole life crawling on the earth.' Maurice Z. Shroder, discussing the general creative trends of French Romanticism, uses this quotation from Gautier to open his final chapter, 'The Fate of Icarus' (*Icarus. The Image of the Artist in French Romanticism* (1961), p. 217. He emphasises that 'this myth includes the hero's fall as well as his flight, that it is ultimately a myth of ambition and failure. That other Icarian age, the Renaissance, tended to glorify the flight and to minimise the fall, to see in the fate of Icarus the fulfilment of a glorious destiny', but the Romantic era was dominated by his tragic drop. He argues convincingly that the nineteenth century Icarus-figure was a natural exhibitionist (agreeing with W. H. Auden that the irony of Breughel's picture of the flyer is that no one has seen him fall) who would rather proclaim weakness and inadequacy than nothing, celebrating descent, as in 'Plaintes d'un Icare' by Baudelaire.

39 Henry James, *Roderick Hudson* (1969), p. 164.

40 The idea of Christ as a friend of man who acted as a scapegoat for his sake has parallels with the Promethean myth first emphasised by Tertullian.

41 Walter Pater, *Imaginary Portraits* (1887), p. 2.

42 Ibid., p. 43.

43 George Moore, 'Mildred Lawson', *Celibates* (1895), p. 43.

44 M. M. Dowie, 'Wladislaw's Advent', *The Yellow Book: A Selection*, compiled by Norman Denny (London, n.d.), p. 304.

45 And, in any case, commonplace happy endings were a bore. Nineteenth century fictional artists fulfilled the old adage that classicism is health, romanticism illness, with their almost perverted capacity for doom and destruction. Henry James, having failed in *The Tragic Muse* to make Nick Dormer a sufficiently interesting character, later regretted he had not made the painter more of a failure, prefacing his novel with the explanation that 'Any presentation of the artist *in triumph* must be flat in proportion as it really sticks to its subject. . . . For, to put the matter in an image, all we then see – in his triumph – of the charm-compeller is the back he turns to us as he bends over his work. "His" triumph, decently, is but the triumph of what he produces, and that is another affair.' Recalling Promethean imagery he continued, 'His romance is the romance he himself projects; he eats the cake of the very rarest privilege, the most luscious baked in the oven of the gods – therefore he mayn't "have" it, in the form of the privilege of the hero, at the same time. The privilege of the hero – that is of the martyr of the interesting and appealing and comparatively floundering person – places

him in a quite different category, belongs to him only as to the artist deluded, diverted, frustrated or vanquished.' This point was neatly summed up by Lord Henry Wotton in *The Portrait of Dorian Gray:* 'Good artists exist simply in what they make, and consequently are perfectly uninteresting in what they are.'

46 Henry James, *The Europeans* (1973 edition), p. 61.

47 Similarly in James's short story *The Liar,* his painter hero felt that the woman he loved was like 'Thackeray's Ethel Newcome', an equation which helped to stress the hopeless nature of his passion. Literary cross-references of this kind were often practised by other writers as, for example, when Mrs Oliphant gave the young painter hero of *The Three Brothers* a moment when he felt like 'poor Andrea' in Browning's poem.

48 Henry James, *The Madonna of the Future and Other Early Stories* (1962 edition), p. 202.

49 Blanche Willis Howard, *Guenn* (1884), p. 71.

Chapter Six
The Declining Myth of the Artist

1 Aubrey Beardsley, *Under the Hill* (1959 edition), p. 77.

2 See John Ruskin, *Modern Painters* (1843-60), V (1860), part VIII, ch 4, 20-23 *passim.*

3 Du Maurier who, like Thackeray, illustrated his own works included a recognisable sketch of Whistler in a drawing entitled 'All as it used to be' which captured a jovial studio interior. See Leonée Ormond, *George du Maurier* (1969), p. 55. She compares this illustration and others from *Trilby* with Du Maurier's still more autobiographical images of bohemian life. Where Du Maurier had, in *Trilby,* captured the lively imbecilities of art students and shown Trilby herself wearing old slippers and an army jacket, Whistler had himself expressed the more *recherché* side of bohemian life in 'The Artist in his Studio' (1864) – where, rather than concentrating on the artist's intellectual or social merits, he tried to surround the willowy painter on the canvas with an atmosphere of picturesque elegance. The self portraits, and studio portraits of French artists such as Delacroix or Courbet are of interest since English writers showed such a fascination for Paris and the glamour and vitality of its community.

4 Augustus John was particularly interested in gypsies, as were many of his friends in Liverpool. Michael Holroyd has dealt with this interest in detail in *Augustus John, A Biography* (2 vols., 1974).

5 In *The Pre-Raphaelite Tragedy* (1942; 1965) William Gaunt recounted that Rossetti later thought he saw the soul of his wife in the form of a dead chaffinch (p. 123), and afterwards decided to reclaim the poems he had buried in her grave – as egotistical and melodramatic an act as any in nineteenth century fiction.

6 Vernon Lee, in *Miss Brown,* described how her hero produced a descriptive sonnet for a painting, recalling Rossetti's poems for paintings, and then, despite the fact that he had entitled it 'Venus Victrix', created an image of gloomy sensuality again recalling some of Rossetti's own achievements. Among many details, the author mentioned the model's 'wrought iron' hair, tower-like neck and prominent lips.

7 Vernon Lee, *Letters,* ed. I. Cooper-Willis (printed privately in 1937), p. 123.

8 A work such as William Dyce's 'Titian's First Essay in Colour' (1856-7) where the famous artist was depicted with flowers before a statue of the Virgin and child, implied the artist's importance came from a divinely inspired ability.

9 Leonée and Richard Ormond, *Lord Leighton* (1975), p. 127. This well-written study provides both valuable references and comments, such as those on Leighton's relationship with Mrs. Sartonis – whose relative inaccessability through marriage probably added, as these authors explain, to Leighton's reasons for admiring her.

10 Benjamin Disraeli, *Lothair* (1870), Vol. II, p. 40.

11 Henry James, *The Private Life, The Complete Tales of Henry James,* ed. L. Edel (1962-4), Vol. VIII, p. 196.

12 His envy made him contrast Leighton's appearance, attainments and glory with 'the so much more modest emoluments of the men of letters . . .'see Leon Edel, *Henry James: The Middle Years* (1963), p. 47.

13 Although more books about artists were published round the turn of the century than had been earlier on, most of these works tended to cover ground already mapped out in earlier fiction. Clichés about romantic artists, testifying to the original impact of the theme, abound in novels such as *Genevra* (1904) where Charles Marriott created an ultra moody painter hero, or *Fenwick's Career* (1906) where Mrs Humphry Ward described an artist whose unhappiness drove him to the verge of suicide, or *Daphne in Fitzroy Street* (1909) where E. Nesbit enlarged, with great sentimentality, on the attractions of Mr Henry, a dark genius with 'smoked topaz eyes', or *Comfortless Memory* (1928) where Maurice Baring produced an unhappy love story proving the incompatibility of passion and art, or 'The Death of Peter Waydelin', a short story included in Arthur Symons's *Spiritual Adventures* (1905), which described the fatal illness of a talented young artist as an 'obscure martyrdom', or *Sons and Lovers* (1913) where Lawrence used Paul Morel as a means of indirectly divulging autobiographical material, although he once slipped up, saying the fictional artist found it hard to get on with his work as the 'pen stopped writing'. The popularisation of bohemian life earlier achieved by works such as Puccini's opera 'La Bohème' was, in the twentieth century, sometimes felt in films, such as the sensational account of the artist Gaudier-Brezeska entitled 'Savage Messiah'.

14 As in Wordsworth's famous lines commemorating the beginning of the revolution.

15 William Blake, Jerusalem, II, *Poetry and Prose of William Blake* (Ed. Geoffrey Keynes, 1939), p. 451.

16 Just as Blake himself risked arrest for his revolutionary views.

17 Ibid., p. 485.

18 Ibid., p. 486.

19 Ibid., p. 488.

'Renew the Arts on Britain's shore / And War shall sink beneath thy feet'. See the chapter entitled 'Republican Art' in Morton D. Paley's *Energy and Imagination, The Development of Blake's thought* (1970). It was symbolic of the aggression of the earlier romantic heroes that Scott felt able in *Guy Mannering* (1815) to confuse an artist with a soldier when, for example, Harry Bertram, after taking the name of

Vanbeest Brown, is described sketching. Scott says that his 'manner indicated the profession which had been his choice'. William Black in *Love or Marriage?* (1868) showed his romantic hero abandoning art for a career in the army, but later authors were inclined to cast their romantic heroes in more foppish roles.
Oscar Wilde, *The Picture of Dorian Gray* (1962 edition), p. 19.

20   Oscar Wilde, *The Picture of Dorian Gray* (1962), p. 218. Gray, like Pater, was intrigued by Renaissance poisoners and the sophisticated and indeed artistic methods they had used. This aspect of romanticism may be traced back to De Quincey's series of lectures entitled 'On Murder Considered as One of the Fine Arts'. See also Wilde's 'Pen, Pencil and Poison'.

21   Vernon Lee, *Miss Brown – A Novel* (1884), Vol. 1, p. 3.

22   Vernon Lee, *Miss Brown – A Novel* (1884), Vol. II, p. 142.

23   Ibid., Vol. II, p. 149. The connections between drug taking and romanticism are explored by Alethea Hayter in *Opium and the Romantic Imagination* (1968).

24   This disreputable state of affairs was summed up by Max Nordau, the second edition of whose work *Degeneration*, was translated into English in 1895. Nordau defined the egoism, the excitable impulsiveness and inactive reverie of *fin de siècle* artists as 'Guérinsen: genius is a disease of the nerves.'

25   An example of the kind of literary work probably only known amongst a limited circle, this manuscript was left incomplete at Beardsley's death in 1898. Two vigorously expurgated instalments (Chapters, I, II and III) which had appeared in *The Savoy* in January 1896, were reprinted, with the same illustrations, in a volume entitled *Under the Hill, and Other Essays in Prose and Verse, including Table Talk, by Aubrey Beardsley* (1904) a posthumous collection of his literary work published in London by John Lane 'the whole being deemed unprintable by the editors'. John Glassco includes details of the history of the text, and varying views of Beardsley's achievement in his introduction to the Olympia Press edition of 1959, which he compiled by collating three texts and completing the manuscript (after page 69) to fit the drawings Beardsley had originally designed for it. Glassco praises what he calls this 'most finished, articulate' eroticism.

26   Aubrey Beardsley, *Under the Hill* (1959), p. 67.

27   Ibid., p. 68.

28   Ibid., p. 82.

29   Ibid., p. 89.

30   Particularly as Glassco interpreted the story – concentrating not on De La Pine's painting, but on his role as a perverted host, and on the personal recreation he found in sex.

31   See, for example, how in *The New Republic* (1878) W. H. Mallock sententiously describes how the guests visiting a country house have a mental 'menu' which provokes much pretentious conversation, especially when they discuss art, literature, taste, etc.

32   The connoisseur often played a very objective role in the ordering of a work as, for example, when the Earl of Shaftesbury gave such detailed and specific directions to clarify the kind of Hercules he wished to commission from the Italian painter Paolo de Matteis. The distinction between the two categories later became blurred when characters

such as Sir George Beaumont and Sir Charles Eastlake became known as both painters and patrons.

33 Henry James, *Roderick Hudson* (1969 edition), p. 53.

34 See also, how the American connoisseur in *The Golden Bowl* (1904) looks on the Italian prince his daughter marries as a 'representative piece'.

35 Oscar Wilde, *The Picture of Dorian Gray* (1962 edition), p. 84.

36 George Gissing made the painter hero of *The Emancipated* tell his two female admirers that they could not be creative: their function was only 'to be'.

37 Oscar Wilde put this clearly: 'As a rule the model, nowadays, is a pretty girl, from about twelve to twenty-five years of age, who knows nothing about art, careless, and merely anxious to earn seven or eight shillings a day without much trouble.' (Quoted from *Art and Decoration* (1920), p. 95.) That models had no notion of art or art theory could be a positive aid, for it made them more pliant to the artist's wishes, within the limitations dictated by their age and sex. In that classic bohemian manual, *The Newcomes*, Thackeray described a male model whose heredity profitably adapted him to make the most of each stage of growth, having seen similar metamorphoses in his own parents, such as his mother's practical evolution from a Venus to a Witch of Endor. Educated and refined people of decided character were useless, as James showed in *The Real Thing* (1892), the pathetic attempt of a 'real' though threadbare lady and gentleman to become models.

38 In *The Light that Failed* the hero warned a friend against becoming involved with a mere model as her status implied 'She's not a woman'.

39 George Du Maurier, *Trilby* (1947 edition), p. 75.

40 Singing and acting provided a more popular creative outlet, if only an interpretative and Svengali'd kind, in an age unaccustomed to career women. It was significant that James, when he equated the creative struggle of a man and woman in *The Tragic Muse,* compared his painter hero's endeavours with those of an actress. Bianca Piazzi, the actress in Geraldine Jewsbury's novel *The Half Sisters,* romantically equated her own devotion to a 'sacred calling' with demon-possession. The attractions of Sibyl Vane, the actress of *The Picture of Dorian Gray,* were closely bound up with her skill: Gray's imagination had been stirred by the way she realised the dreams of the great poets and thus 'gave substance' to art.

41 In *The Mill on the Floss* (1860).

42 Louisa Costello, *Clara Fane* (1848), Vol. II, p. 146.

43 The nature of her surprising work is conveyed by a description of one of the paintings which

> showed the pinacle of an iceberg piercing a polar winter sky: a muster of northern lights reared their dim lances, close serried, along the horizon. Throwing these into distance, rose, in the foreground, a head, inclined towards the iceberg, and resting against it. Two thin hands, joined under the forehead, and supporting it, drew up before the lower features a sable veil, a brow quite bloodless, white as a bone, and an eye hollow and fixed, blank of meaning but for the glassiness of despair. . . .

44 Anne Brontë, *The Tenant of Wildfell Hall* (1949 edition), p. 23.

45 Margaret Oliphant, *The Three Brothers,* Vol. I, p. 254.

46 George Moore, *A Modern Lover* (1883), Vol. I, p. 72.

47   Anne Isabella Ritchie, *Miss Angel* (1875), p. 321.

48   George Moore, *Celibates* (1895), p. 169.

49   Ibid., p. 171.

50   This hypothesis, if true, might well account for some of the emotional savagery shown by Gudrun, the young art mistress battling for Lawrentian fulfilment in *Women in Love* (New York, 1920; London, 1921). As female artists gained a degree of power, models, too, began to speak up for themselves – as, for example, in *The Common Law* (1911) by R. W. Chambers. This was a democratic American novel in which a model proved that she was far more independent than the artist she loved.

51   Walter Shaw Sparrow, *Women Painters of the World* (1905), p. 6.

52   A cynical and apparently amoral approach to the fictional artist can be seen in later twentieth century works, such as Anthony Burgess's *MF* (1971).

53   Aldous Huxley, *Crome Yellow* (1928), p. 116.

54   The folkloric idea of an image having a magical connection with the object it represented continued to be popular, even if showing no connection with artist heroes. Hawthorne, whose interest in symbolic and supernatural images had doubtless intrigued James, adapted the old theme in *The House of the Seven Gables* (1851) where Holgrave, the romantic daguerrotypist, produced an early photograph revealing the 'secret character' of the villain. Hardy also demonstrated this modern magic in 'The Photograph' where the narrator burned a woman's photograph in the fire watching the flames efface the woman whom he felt he had 'put to death that night'.

55   Arnold Bennett, *Buried Alive* (1908), p. 125.

56   Except perhaps Thomas Love Peacock who poked fun at everything.

57   P. G. Wodehouse, 'Rough-Hew Them How We Will', *The Man Upstairs* (1914), p. 88.

58   Stephen Crane, *The Third Violet* (1897), p. 200.

59   See Gerald Jay Goldberg, 'The Search for the Artist in Some Recent British Fiction', *South Atlantic Quarterly*, Vol. LXII (1963).

   Parallels may be found in real life as twentieth century artists, often Americans, lost interest in the romantic concept found in nineteenth century fiction of the artist as an idealised mystical hero whose work revealed his visionary powers. Robert Indiana, for example, by adopting the name of his native state as a surname minimised, rather than stressed, the importance of his own personality.

60   Joyce Cary, *The Horse's Mouth* (1968), p. 295.

61   After writing *Trilby* which became one of the most popular manuals of colourful artistic life, Du Maurier later produced a work entitled *The Martian* (1896).

62   Samuel Johnson had earlier, in *Rasselas, The Prince of Abyssinia* (1759), described an 'artist' whose knowledge of the 'mechanick sciences' enabled him to build many engines and who, feeling that the 'fields of air are open to knowledge', anticipated man flying through them.

Bibliography

Place of publication, unless otherwise stated, is London.

Abrams, Meyer H. *The Mirror and The Lamp: Romantic Theory and the Critical Tradition* (Oxford, 1971).

Arnold, Matthew. *Poems* (Ed. Kenneth Allott) (1965).

Austen, Jane. *Northanger Abbey and Persuasion* (1818; 1913).

Baldick, Robert. *The First Bohemian. The Life of Henry Mürger* (1961).

Balzac, Honoré, de. *Peau de Chagrin* (Paris, 1831).

Baring, Maurice. *Comfortless Memory* (1928).

Beardsley, Aubrey. *Under the Hill* (two vigorously expurgated instalments published in 1896: for details of its history see the introduction to the Olympia Press Edition, Paris, 1958).

Beaumont, Averil (pseudonym of Mrs Margaret Hunt. See also item under this name). *Magdalen Wynard: or, The Provocations of a Pre-Raphaelite* (2 vols., 1872).

Beebe, Maurice. *Ivory Towers and Sacred Founts. The artist hero in fiction from Goethe to Joyce* (New York, 1964).

Beerbohm, Max. *The Happy Hypocrite* (1897).

Bennett, Arnold. *Buried Alive* (1908).

Benson, E. F. *Limitations. A Novel* (1896).

Black, William. *Love or Marriage. A Novel* (3 vols., 1868). *A Princess of Thule* (2 vols., 1874).

Blunden, Edmund. *Thomas Hardy* (English Men of Letters, 1941).

Bowie, Theodore Robert. *The Painter in French Fiction: A Critical Essay* (Chapel Hill, 1950).

Brightfield, Myron Franklin. *Victorian England in its novels (1840-1870)* (Los Angeles, 1968).

Brontë, Anne. *The Tenant of Wildfell Hall* (1848; 1949).

Brontë, Charlotte. *Jane Eyre* (1847).

Brough, Robert Barnabus. *Marston Lynch; his life and times, his friends and enemies, his victories and defeats, his kicks and halfpence. A personal biography* (1860).

Broughton, Rhoda. *Mrs Bligh, A Novel* (1892).

Browning, Robert. *Poetical Works* (2 vols., 1902).

Burgess, Anthony. *MF* (1971).

Byron, Lord George Gordon. *Poetical Works* (1896).

Carrington, Charles. *Rudyard Kipling. His Life and Work* (1955).

Cary, Joyce. *The Horse's Mouth* (1944; Carfax edition, 1958).

Carlyle, Thomas. *Heroes and Hero Worship* (1897).

Chambers, Robert W. *The Common Law* (New York and London, 1911).

Clark, Charles. *Lord Falconberg's Heir* (1868).

Coleridge, Samuel Taylor. *The Complete Poetical Works* (Ed. E. H. Coleridge, 1912).

Collins, Wilkie. *Hide and Seek* (1854; 1889).

Costello, Louisa. *Clara Fane* (1848).

Crane, Stephen. *The Third Violet* (1897).

Croft, Sir Herbert. *Love and Madness. A story too true: in a series of letters between parties whose names would perhaps be mentioned were they less known or less lamented* (1780).

Dickens, Charles. *Oliver Twist* (1837-8). *Nicholas Nickleby* (1854). *Hard Times* (1855-7).

Disraeli, Benjamin (Earl of Beaconsfield). *Lothair* (1870).

Donoghue, Denis. *Thieves of Fire* (1973).

Dowie, M. M. *Wladislaw's Advent,* reprinted in *The Yellow Book: a Selection* (Ed. Norman Denny, n.d.).

Du Maurier, George. *Trilby* (1894; 1947).

Edel, Leon. *Henry James: The Middle Years* (1963).

Eliot, George. *The Mill on the Floss* (1860). *Romola* (1862-3; 1927). *Middlemarch* (1871-2; 1962). *Daniel Deronda* (1874-6).

Encyclopedia of World Art. Vol. XI (1966).

Faber, Richard. *Proper Stations, Class in Victorian Fiction* (1971).

Farrington, Margaret Vere. *Fra Lippo Lippi* (1890).

Galsworthy, John. *Villa Rubein and Other Stories* (1900; 1909). *The Forsyte Saga* (1922).

Gilbert, William Schwenck. *Pygmalion and Galatea* (1891). *Ruddigore, or The Witch's Curse*. Written in collaboration with Arthur Sullivan (1887; and edition by Chappell and Co., of Gilbert's eight comic operas, n.d.).

Gissing, George. *Thyrza* (1878; 1927). *The Emancipated* (1890; 1893).

Goethe, Johann Wolfgang von. *Die Lieden des jungen Werthers* (1774; Leipzig, 1787).

Goldberg, Gerald Jay. 'The Search for the Artist in some recent British fiction', *South Atlantic Quarterly* (LXII, 1963).

Golding, William. *Free Fall* (1959).

Goldsmith, Oliver. *The Vicar of Wakefield* (1776; Harmondsworth, Middlesex, 1944).

Gombrich, Ernst. *The Story of Art* (1950).

Goncourt, Edmond de and Jules de. *Manette Salomon* (Paris, 1867).

Hamerton, Philip Gilbert. *A Painter's Camp in the Highlands, and Thoughts about Art* (2 vols., 1862; Revised Ed., 1886). *Thoughts About Art* (1873; 1889).

Hardy, Thomas. *The Return of the Native* (1878). *Barbara of the House of Grebe* (*The Graphic,* 1890). *Tess of the d'Urbervilles* 1891; Wessex Novels, VIII, 1909). *The Well-Beloved. A Sketch of a Temperament* (1892; 1958).

Hatton, Joseph. *The Tallants of Barton. A Tale of Fortune and Finance* (3 vols., 1867).

Haweis, Mary Eliza. *Beautiful Houses* (1882).

Hayley, William. *Essay on Epic Poetry* (1782).

Hawthorne, Nathaniel. *The House of the Seven Gables* (1851).

Hayter, Alethea. *Opium and the Romantic Imagination* (1968).

Hazlitt, William. 'The Pleasures of Painting', included in *The Best of Hazlitt* (compiled by P. P. Howe, 1924; 1952). Originally included in *The London Magazine,* Dec., 1820.

Herbert, George. *Gerald Fitzgerald* (1858).

Holland, Clive [Pseudonym of Charles J. Hankinson]. *Marcelle of the Latin Quarter* (1900).

Holroyd, Michael. *Augustus John: A Biography* (2 vols., 1974).

Howard, Blanche Willis. *Guenn: A Wave on the Breton Coast* (1883; 1884).

Hunt, Margaret [see entry for Averil Beaumont]. *Thorniton's Model* (1873).

Huxley, Aldous. *Crome Yellow* (1928).

Huysmans, Joris-Karl. *À rebours* (Paris, 1884).

Ibsen, Henrik. *When We Dead Awaken* (1899).

Jackson, Mary. *Maud Skillicorne's Penance* (1858).

James, Henry. *The Madonna of the Future* (1873; New York, 1962). *Roderick Hudson* (1876; Harmondsworth: Middlesex, 1969). *The Europeans* (1878; Harmondsworth: Middlesex, 1973). *The Portrait of a Lady* (1880-81). *The Story of a Masterpiece* (1886; included in *The Madonna of the Future and other early Stories:* 1962). *The Liar* (1888). *The Tragic Muse* (1890; New York, 1908). *The Real Thing* (1892). *The Sacred Fount* (1901). *The Golden Bowl* (1904).

Jewsbury, Geraldine. *The Half Sisters. A Tale* (2 Vols., 1848).

Johnson, Samuel. *The Prince of Abissinia.* A Tale (2 vols., 1959). Title altered in US edition to *The History of Rasselas, Prince of Abissinia, an Asiatic Tale* (1768); and, in 1787 edition, to *The History of Rasselas, Prince of Abissinia. A Tale.*

Joyce, James. *A Portrait of the Artist as a Young Man* (1914).

Kerényi, C. *Prometheus: Archetypal Image of Human Existence.* (Tr. Ralph Manheim, 1963.)

Kingsley, Henry. *Ravenshoe* (1861).

Kipling, Rudyard. *The Light that Failed* (1891).

Keats, John. *Poetry and Prose, with Essays by Charles Lamb, Leigh Hunt, Robert Bridges and Others* (Oxford, 1922).

Kris, Ernst. *Psychoanalytic Explorations in Art* (1953).

Lawrence, D. H. *Sons and Lovers* (1913). *Women in Love* (1920).

Larousse Encyclopedia of Mythology. Tr. Richard Aldington and Delano Ames (1959).

Le Fanu, Sheridan. *The Watcher and other Weird Stories* (1895).

Lee, Charles. *Cynthia in the West* (1900).

Lee, Vernon [Violet Paget]. *Dionea. Hauntings: Fantastic Stories* (1861; 1890). *Oke of Okehurst. Hauntings: Fantastic Stories* (1861; 1890). *Miss Brown. A Novel* (3 vols., 1884). *Letters* (Ed. I. Cooper-Willis. Privately printed 1937).

Le Gallienne, Richard. *The Worshipper of the Image* (1899; 1900).

Lever, Charles. *The Martins of Cro' Martin* (1847; The Harry Lorrequer edition, 1876-8).

Lewis, Matthew Gregory. *Ambrosio, or The Monk* (3 vols., 1798).

Lippincott's Monthly Magazine (Philadelphia, Pennsylvania).

Loomis, C. Grant. *White Magic: An Introduction to the Folklore of the Christian Legend* [A publication of] The Medieval Academy of America (Cambridge, Mass., 1948).

Malet, Lucas [Mary St. Leger Morrison]. *The Wages of Sin.* (3 vols., 1891).

Mallock, W. H. *The New Republic* (1878).

Marriott, Charles. *Genevra* (1904).

Marshall, Emma. *Castle Meadow: a Story of Norwich a Hundred Years Ago* (1897). *The Parson's Daughter: Her Early Recollections and how Romney painted her* (1899).

Maturin, Charles Robert. *Melmoth the Wanderer* (1812; Lincoln, Nebraska, 1961).

Maugham, W. Somerset. *The Moon and Sixpence* (1919).

Moore, George. *Flowers of Passion* (1878). *A Modern Lover* (3 vols., 1883). *The Confessions of a Young Man* (1888; 1904). *Celibates* (1895). *Lewis Seymour and Some Women* (1917).

Morgan, Lady [Sydney Owenson]. *The Wild Irish Girl* (1806). *The Life of Salvator Rosa* (2 vols., 1824).

Morris, William. *The Earthly Paradise* (1868-70).

Mürger, Henry. *Scènes de la vie de Bohème* (Bruxelles, 1850; Paris, 1851). *The Bohemians of the Latin Quarter* (Trans. Henry Vizetelly, 1887). *The Latin Quarter* (Trans. Ellen Marriage and John Selwyn, 1901, 1905, 1908, 1920). (Also translated by Elizabeth Ward Hughes, 1931, and by Norman Cameron, 1949, 1960).

Nesbit, E. *The Incomplete Amorist* (1906). *Daphne in Fitzroy Street* (1909).

Nodier, Charles. *Le Peintre de Saltzbourg, journal des émotions d'un coeur souffrant, par Charles Nodier . . .* (Paris, 1803).

Nordeau, Max. *Degeneration* (In translation, 1895).

Ojala, Aatos. *Aestheticism and Oscar Wilde: Part I. 'Life and Letters'* in *Annals of the Finnish Academy of Science and Letters* (Helsinki, 1954).

Oliphant, Margaret. *The Three Brothers* (3 vols., 1870).

Ormond, Leonée. *George du Maurier* (1969).

Ormond, Leonée and Richard. *Lord Leighton* (1975).

Ouida, [Marie Louise de la Ramée]. *Two Little Wooden Shoes A Sketch* (1874). *Ariadne: The Story of a Dream* (3 vols., 1877; 1912).

Paley, Morton D. *Energy and Imagination, The Development of Blake's Thoughts* (Oxford, 1970).

Pater, Walter. *Studies in the History of the Renaissance* (1873; Fontana edition, 1967). *Marius the Epicurean* (1885). *Imaginary Portraits* (1887).

Praz, Mario. *The Hero in Eclipse in Victorian Fiction* (1956).

Radcliffe, Mrs Ann. *The Mysteries of Udolpho* (1764).

Railo, Eino. *The Haunted Castle, a Study of the Elements of English Romanticism* (1927).

Richardson, Henry Handel. *Maurice Guest* (1908).

Ritchie, Anne Isabella. *Miss Angel* (1875).

Ritchie, Leitch. *Wearyfoot Common* (1854).

Roberts, Margaret. *The Atelier du Lys: or, An Art Student in the Reign of Terror, by the author of Mademoiselle Mori* (1876; 1877).

Roberts, Morley. *Immortal Youth* (1896; 1902).

Rossetti, Dante Gabriel. *Hand and Soul* (The Germ, Jan., 1850; Hammersmith, 1895). *The Poetical Works* (1893).

Ruskin, John. *Modern Painters* (1843-60).

Sartoris, Adelaide. *A Week in a French Country House* (1867).

Schroder, Maurice. *Icarus, the Image of the Artist in French Romanticism* (Harvard Studies in Romance Languages XXVII) (Cambridge, Mass., 1961).

Scott, Sir Walter. *Guy Mannering* (1815). *The Bride of Lammermoor* (1819). *St. Ronan's Well* (1823; Vol. XVII, Holyrood edition, n.d.). See also 1832 edition.

Shaw, George Bernard. *Love Among the Artists* (1881).

Shelley, Mary. *Frankenstein* (1818).

Shelley, Percy Bysshe. *Shelley's Essays and Letters* (Ed. Ernest Rhys, 1886).

Smedley, Frank. *Harry Coverdale's Courtship* (1885).

Sparrow, Walter Shaw. *Women Painters of the World* (1905).

Symons, Arthur. *Spiritual Adventures* (1905).

Thackeray, William Makepeace. *Vanity Fair* (1847-8; 1913). *The Newcomes* (1853-5; Everyman edition, 1962). *The Rose and the Ring* (1855; 1923). *Philip* (1862).

Thorslev, Peter L., Jnr. *The Byronic Hero, Types and Prototypes* (Minneapolis, 1962).

Trollope, Anthony. *Barchester Towers* (1857; 1925). *Can You Forgive Her?* (1864).

Trollope, Thomas Adolphus. *Lindisfarn Chase* (1864).

Walpole, Horace. *The Castle of Otranto* (1765).

Ward, Mrs Humphrey. *Fenwick's Career* (1906).

Watts-Dunton, Theodore. *Aylwin* (1898; Snowdon edition, 1901).

Wedmore, Frederick. *Renunciations. A Chemist in the Suburbs, A Confidence at the Savile, The North Coast, and Eleanor* (1893).

Wells, Herbert George. *New Worlds for Old* (1908).

Wilde, Oscar. *The Picture of Dorian Gray* (1891; New York, 1962).

Wodehouse, P. G. *Rough-Hew Them How We Will,* in *The Man Upstairs* (1914).

Woolf, Virginia. *To the Lighthouse* (1927).

Wordsworth, William. *Poetical Works* (Ed. Thomas Hutchinson, revised Ernest de Selincourt, Oxford, 1946).

Wraxall, Sir Frederick Charles Lascelles. *Wild Oats* (1858).

Wyndham, Lewis, D. B. *Men Without Art* (1934).

Yates, Edmund Hodgson. *Land at Last. A Novel in Three Books* (3 vols., 1866).

Yates, Frances A. *Giordano Bruno and the Hermetic Tradition* (1964).

Index

Arnold, Matthew,
  'Epilogue to Lessing's
    Laocoön', 24
Austen, Jane,
  Northanger Abbey, 87, 149

Beardsley, Aubrey,
  Under the Hill, 146, 149
Beaumont, Averil,
  *Magdalen Wynard or The
    Provocations of a Pre-
    Raphaelite*, 75, 76, 155
Bennett, Arnold,
  Buried Alive, 162
Benson, E. F.,
  Limitations, 41, 78, 116-7
Black, William,
  Love or Marriage, 36
  A Princess of Thule, 119
Blake, William,
  Jerusalem, 140
Bridges, Robert,
  'Prometheus the Firegiver', 101
Brontë, Anne,
  The Tenant of Wildfell Hall,
    155
Brontë, Charlotte,
  Jane Eyre, 155
Brough, Robert Barnabus,
  Marston Lynch, 76
Broughton, Rhoda,
  Mrs Bligh, 110
Browning, Elizabeth,
  'Prometheus Bound', 101
Browning, Robert,
  'Abt Vogler', 23
  'Andrea del Sarto', 17, 111
  'Fra Lippo Lippi', 60
  'Youth and Art', 103

Byron, Lord, 16
  'Childe Harold', 19

Carlyle, Thomas,
  'The Hero and the Poet', 18
Cary, Joyce,
  The Horse's Mouth, 164
Clark, Charles,
  Lord Falconberg's Heir, 32
Coleridge, S. T.,
  'Kubla Khan', 18
Collins, Wilkie,
  Hide and Seek, 55
Costello, Louisa,
  Clara Fane, 154
Crane, Stephen,
  The Third Violet, 163

Dickens, Charles,
  Little Dorrit, 65
Disraeli, Benjamin,
  Lothair, 138
Dowie, M. M.,
  Wladislaw's Advent, 128
Du Maurier, George, 27
  Trilby, 16, 21, 30, 40, 51-2,
    54, 73-4, 153

Eliot, George,
  Daniel Deronda, 23, 108
  Middlemarch, 44
  Romola, 36, 96, 137
  The Mill on the Floss, 101

Farrington, Margaret Vere,
  *Fra Lippo Lippi,
    A Romance*, 60

Galsworthy, John,
  Villa Rubein, 82

Gilbert, Sir William,
   Ruddigore, 87
Gissing, George,
   The Emancipated, 76, 80,
     108, 118
   Thyrza, 95
Golding, William,
   Free Fall, 164
Goldsmith, Oliver,
   The Vicar of Wakefield, 15
Goncourt Brothers,
   Manette Salomon, 94

Hamerton, Philip Gilbert,
   Thoughts about Art, 14
Hardy, Mary Anne,
   The Artist's Family, 35, 37
   Paul Wynter's Sacrifice, 37
Hardy, Thomas,
   Tess of the d'Urbervilles, 88
   The Well-Beloved, 63
Hatton, Joseph,
   The Tallants of Barton, 47,
     49, 50, 80, 118
Haweis, Mary Eliza,
   Beautiful Houses, 135
Hazlitt, William, 27,
   'On the Pleasure of
     Painting', 23
Herbert, George,
   Gerald Fitzgerald, 132
Holland, Clive,
   *Marcelle of the Latin
     Quarter*, 56, 132
Howard, Blanche Willis,
   Guenn, 32, 69, 130
Hunt, Margaret,
   Thorniton's Model, 133
Huxley, Aldous,
   Chrome Yellow, 161

Jackson, Mary,
   Maud Skillocorne's Penance, 67
James, Henry, 9, 27,
   Roderick Hudson, 17, 33-4,
     45-6, 117, 120-4, 150, 156
   The Europeans, 57-9, 129
   The Madonna of the Future,
     20, 31, 44-5, 129
   The Portrait of a Lady, 152
   The Private Life, 138-9
   The Sacred Fount, 92
   The Story of a Masterpiece, 95
   The Tragic Muse, 68, 71
Jewsbury, Geraldine,
   The Half Sisters, 13-4
Joyce, James,
   *A Portrait of the Artist as a
     Young Man*, 160

Keats, John, 16
   'Adonais', 18
   "Negative Capability", 78
Kingsley, Henry,
   Ravenshoe, 132
Kipling, Rudyard, 27
   The Light that Failed, 16, 63,
     78, 81, 128

Lee, Charles,
   Cynthia in the West, 68, 99, 114
Lee, Vernon,
   Dionea, 113
   Miss Brown, A Novel, 75, 133,
     143
   Oke of Okehurst, 98
Le Gallienne, Richard,
   The Worshipper of the Image,
     112
Leighton, Frederick, 135, 137-8
Lever, Charles,
   The Martins of Cro'Martin, 25,
     79
Lewis, M. G.,
   The Monk, A Romance, 85
Lewis, Wyndham,
   Men Without Art, 160
Lippincott's Monthly Magazine,
   16

Malet, Lucas,
   The Wages of Sin, 120, 127

Marshall, Emma,
  Castle Meadow, 108
  The Parson's Daughter, 131
Maturin, Charles,
  Melmoth the Wanderer, 86
Maugham, Somerset,
  The Moon and Sixpence, 139
Moore, George,
  A Modern Lover, 29, 37, 40,
    61, 80, 94, 151, 156
  Celibates ('Mildred Lawson'),
    127, 157
  Lewis Seymour, 34, 41-3, 62-3,
    147
  *The Confessions of a Young
    Man*, 38
  'To a Lost Art', 27
Morgan, Lady,
  The Life of Salvator Rosa, 19
Mürger, Henri,
  Scènes de la vie de Bohème,
    20-1

Nesbit, Edith,
  The Incomplete Amorist, 115
Nodier, Charles,
  Le Peintre de Saltzbourg, 20

Oliphant, Mrs,
  The Three Brothers, 44, 75,
    79-80, 155
Ouida, 9
  Ariadne, 157
  Two Little Wooden Shoes, 31,
    115, 149

Pater, Walter,
  Imaginary Portraits ('A Prince
    of Court Painters'), 124-7
  *Studies in the History of the
    Renaissance*, 141

Radcliffe, Mrs Ann,
  The Mysteries of Udolpho, 85,
    87
Railo, Eino,
  The Haunted Castle, 84

Ritchie, Leitch,
  Weary-foot Common, 82, 95
Ritchie, Anne Isabella,
  Miss Angel, 25, 156
Roberts, Margaret,
  *The Atelier du Lys or An Art
    Student in the Reign of
    Terror*, 77, 124
Roberts, Morley,
  Immortal Youth, 25, 100
Rossetti, Christina,
  'In An Artist's Studio', 108
Rossetti, Dante Gabriel, 133
  Chiaro dell' Erma, 145
  'Hand and Soul', 105-6
  'The Portrait', 99
Ruskin, John,
  Modern Painters, 132

Sartoris, Adelaide,
  *A Week in a French Country
    House*, 138
Scott, Sir Walter, 16
  St. Ronan's Well, 64-5
  The Bride of Lammermoor, 88,
    117
Shakespeare, William, 17,
  A Winter's Tale, 83
Shaw, G. B.,
  Love Among the Artists, 24
Shelley, Mary,
  Frankenstein, 167
Shelley, P. B.,
  'Adonais', 18
  A Defence of Poetry, 18
  'Prometheus Unbound', 100-1
Smedley, Frank,
  Harry Coverdale's Courtship,
    132
Sparrow, Walter Shaw,
  Women Painters of the World,
    159

Tennyson, Lord Alfred,
  'The Lotos Eaters', 16

Thackeray, W. M.,
  'Bohemian', 57
  The Adventures of Philip, 16
  The Newcomes, 15, 24, 32, 58,
    70-1, 79, 101, 116, 144
  Vanity Fair, 65-6
Trollope, Anthony,
  Barchester Towers, 33, 66-8, 119
Trollope, T. A.,
  Lindisfarn Chase, 13

Walpole, Horace,
  The Castle of Otranto, 84
Watts-Dunton, Theodore,
  Aylwin, 30, 39, 47, 57-8, 61, 65,
    101, 106, 133
Webster John,
  The Duchess of Malfi, 83
Wedmore, Frederick,
  Renunciations ('The North
    Coast and Eleanor'), 128
Wells, H. G.
  New Worlds for Old, 160

Whistler, James McNeill, 21
Wilde, Oscar,
  The Picture of Dorian Gray, 16,
    89, 109, 143, 152
Wodehouse, P. G.,
  The Man Upstairs, ('Rough-
    Hew Them How We Will'),
    162
Woolf, Virginia,
  To the Lighthouse, 161
Wordsworth, William,
  Poetical Works ('Illustrated
    Books and Newspapers',
    'Lines',) 24, 100
Wraxall, Frederick Charles,
  Wild Oats, 52

Yates, Edmund Hodgson,
  Land at Last, 33, 36

Zola, Émile,
  L'Oeuvre, 94